Is International Law
Even Law?

Is International Law Even Law?

International Law from an International Relations Perspective

Leah L. Carmichael

LEXINGTON BOOKS

Lanham • Boulder • New York • London

Published by Lexington Books
An imprint of The Rowman & Littlefield Publishing Group, Inc.
4501 Forbes Boulevard, Suite 200, Lanham, Maryland 20706
www.rowman.com

6 Tinworth Street, London SE11 5AL, United Kingdom

British Library Cataloguing in Publication Information Available

Library of Congress Cataloging-in-Publication Data

Names: Carmichael, Leah L., 1981- author.
Title: Is international law even law? : international law from an international relations
  perspective / Leah L. Carmichael.
Description: Lanham : Lexington Books, [2021] | Includes bibliographical references
  and index.
Identifiers: LCCN 2021010022 (print) | LCCN 2021010023 (ebook) |
  ISBN 9781793628718 (Cloth)| ISBN 9781793628725 (ePub)
  ISBN 9781793628732 (Pbk)
Subjects: LCSH: International law. | Treaties.
Classification: LCC KZ3410 .C367 2021 (print) | LCC KZ3410 (ebook) |
  DDC 341–dc23
LC record available at https://lccn.loc.gov/2021010022
LC ebook record available at https://lccn.loc.gov/2021010023

Contents

List of Figures

List of Text Boxes

Acknowledgments

Special thanks to my family, to Maryann Gallagher—my colleague and friend who saw this material as textbook potential, and to all the International Law students who delved into these cases and presented these moot courts year after year (especially Delaney Burke, who really helped me in the editing process).

Introduction

Though there is no higher authority than states in the international system, states tend to comply with international law most of the time. Most confoundingly, even when states violate international law, they will often defend their actions as compliant with the law, either in a judicial organ or the court of public opinion. Why do states comply with international law when there is no higher authority enforcing it, and when in breach, why do states go to great lengths to defend their actions as being within these laws, even as it is clear they are not?

This chapter will offer an overview of international law, including how it is so fundamentally distinct from domestic law that some even question whether it is the law at all. Next, this chapter will explore two different fields of study that examine international law from either a legal or political perspective before presenting an integrated approach that considers the reasons why states choose to comply with international law, even as there is no higher authority, and why states defend their actions as complying with international law even as it is clear that they are violating it.

INTERNATIONAL LAW

Laws are rules established between actors that formally codify actors' rights and obligations and the conditions under which actors may enjoy these rights and meet these obligations. Domestic law establishes a legal relationship between the state and its citizenry. In this relationship, each actor has rights and responsibilities. Article I, Section 8 of the U.S. Constitution grants Congress both the right to tax its citizens and the obligation to use these taxes to provide for the common defense and the general welfare. From the citizens' perspective, the responsibility would be to pay taxes. The rights would be the enjoyment of a federal government that provides common defense and the general welfare in return. States establish, enforce, and adjudicate domestic law.

At first glance, international public law seems to function as domestic law.[1] There are legislative organs, such as the General Assembly of the United Nations, in which votes are cast in favor or against new rights and obligations for actors. Moreover, there are judicial organs, such as the International Court of Justice, the Permanent Court of Arbitration, and the International Criminal Court, that interpret whether actors comply with or violate their obligations under international law. And finally, there are enforcement mechanisms, such as military interventions ordered by the UN Security Council and warrants issued to arrest those alleged of egregious crimes.

And yet, the legal relationship established between actors in international law works differently than in domestic law. Domestic law establishes a hierarchical relationship between a state and its citizenry in which both may have rights and obligations. Still, the state has the power to create, enforce, and interpret laws and its citizens do not. Instead, international laws are foundationally rules created by states, implemented by states, and analyzed by states in a system with no higher authority above states.

There are vital roles for international organizations, such as the United Nations, to create, enforce, and adjudicate international law. However, effective these international organizations provide these roles; most do not have legal authority over their member-states. The one exception is the European Union, which does have legal jurisdiction over its member-states. As such, the European Union (which we will focus on in chapter 5) is considered the world's only supranational organization.

The rules within two different families may help highlight the differences between international and domestic law. I was the youngest in a large family with engaged, ever-present, perhaps even overbearing parents. My parents passed strict rules (often even taping these rules to the fridge as a reminder) and set stiff penalties when my siblings and I did not obey. As a result, though we each had rights and obligations, the relationship between parent and child was hierarchical like in domestic law.

As just one example, when I was a teenager, my parents were old and tired (their description, not mine). As only one example, they insisted on setting my curfew comically earlier than my peers. It was nine o'clock for most of my high school and ten o'clock when I was a senior (when most of my peers had no curfew or to be home by midnight). Specifically, the rule was I had the right to be gone with the car and be with my friends, so long as I met the obligation of returning home by ten at night.

One night, during my senior year, I decided to respect the letter of the law but not its spirit. When it came close to ten one night, I had the idea of inviting my friends home with me to hang out in our basement bonus room. Around 11:30 pm, my parents came down to the basement, and they were livid. Once everyone left (quickly), I attempted to explain my position. However, after only a few sentences, they made their judgment and imposed their punishment: two weeks, no car, and no fun.

In contrast, my partner had a much more anarchical childhood, growing up as one of three boys with a single mom. Though she was a doting and loving mom, she had to work full-time to keep everyone housed and fed as the primary provider in the family. As a result, many of my partner's childhood rules were decided by the three boys while unattended, roaming the pine forests, and swimming in northern Florida lakes.

Though extremely busy, their mom offered wise guidance and essential information for the boys quite often. Soon after they moved to Florida, she explained that alligators filled the lakes in their area, and thus she explicitly forbade them swimming in them unsupervised. Though this rule was for their safety, they often would jump in the lake on hot summer days, ignoring her request. Further, noting that there were snakes of all kinds in the woods, she gave the boys a pocket encyclopedia to identify which ones were venomous so they could successfully avoid them.

The very next day, when she went off to work, the three boys set off armed with the snake encyclopedia to learn all they could learn about snakes. They quickly decided the best way to do so was by collecting as many snakes as possible into an old plastic paint bucket with a lid. They planned to spend the day collecting snakes and then show their mom all they had learned when she returned home by expertly pointing out which of the snakes in the bucket were venomous and which were not. To do so, they determined they would need a pronged stick to be used to pin the snake to the ground. Once they did, they would then grab the snake by the tail and whirl it headfirst into the bucket before quickly returning the lid to keep the others from slithering out.

After their three brothers made their goal for the day, the oldest brother deemed himself to be the "reader" of the Pocket Encyclopedia of Snakes, thus keeping him out of the business of actually catching the snakes. Meanwhile, the middle brother—my partner and the more adventurous one—agreed to be the one to find a long pronged stick and then to pin the snakes down by the heads. That left the youngest in the default role of grabbing the snakes by the tail and getting them into the bucket. Impressively, after a long day of hard work, the three boys did fill the entire bucket full of snakes. Unsurprisingly, their mother was less impressed than horrified. And, most astonishingly, the three boys survived unharmed to tell and retell this story as adults.

From the two examples of distinctly different childhoods above, much can be learned about domestic and international law's relative differences. Most apparent is the presence of a higher authority in my story about my curfew and the creation, enforcement, and exacting of punishments for violating rules by this higher authority. In direct contrast, the rules presented by my partner's mom could be seen as suggestions or recommendations at best while she was away.

In response to this absence of a higher authority, however, the boys began to create and enforce rules governing their behavior. Though the system presented was a dangerous one, one might see the similarities between it and our current system with nuclear weapons able to destroy civilization.

The distinct nature of domestic versus international law begs the question: is international law even law? Law is a set of contractual rights and obligations among actors. If actors ignore laws blatantly, what makes them anything more than mere preferences of others written down?¶

And yet, in the boy's story collecting snakes, there was no enforcement mechanism above the three actors. However, they complied with roles and obligations under dangerous conditions until they achieved their goal. Similarly, states comply with international law most of the time.[2] To understand whether international law is law, we must reconceptualize the different approaches scholars have taken to study and analyze international law.

APPROACHES TO INTERNATIONAL LAW

This section will offer some conceptual approaches of international law from two distinct disciplines: the legal philosophy approach to international law often taught within law school programs and the political approach within international studies.[3]

In doing so, this text begins to create a conceptual framework for combining these approaches to explain when and why states choose to create, enforce, comply with (and ignore) international law.

Though international law and international politics have formed as distinct disciplines, there is considerable overlap in how both attempt to explain when and why states comply with international law. This section will review each in turn while highlighting some of the brief underlying assumptions the two disciplines have in common.

A Legal Approach to International Law

Within the legal approach to international law, there appears to be a focus on where states can make these agreements. International Natural Law scholars within this field determine rules to arise from a universally acceptable morality within our international community. As a result, these scholars tend to see the law as a moral reflection of what we as a global community aspire to be.

In contrast, other scholars (known as International Legal Positivists) argue that international law reflects how states are in the system, not what they could be. This second camp is a group of legal positivists called International Legal Realists who pay special attention to states' power distribution. Within this smaller camp, they argue that laws reflect the interests of the most powerful imposed on those least so.

And finally, there is a group of scholars in international law known as New Stream scholars who focus on the context in which actors develop international law. David Kennedy, writing about the New Stream field, explained the paradoxical nature of international law as a push-and-pull between power and morality dating back to its inception by Hugo Grotius in the seventeenth century.[4]

As the Dutch formed the East India Company and became the most powerful commercial trader globally, Grotius wrote his work, On the Law of War and Peace, to justify a universal and natural right for all states to trade freely. Though, at first glance, this work would fit into the International Natural Law scholarship, the impetus for this work was the undermining of the established colonial powers and mercantilist economies of Spain and Portugal.

Within the next centuries, the growth of international law would continue within a paradoxical context in which states in the aftermath of the Thirty Years' war sought a new secular form of morality (to weaken the authoritarian nature of more institutionalized religion) while simultaneously increasing their raw political power as sovereigns. Kennedy presents the third phase of international law growth, which focuses on international organizations and law as purveyors of justice and fairness in the process. Though the current system understands state interests, the institutional system allows states to negotiate with other states through peaceful dispute resolutions instead of old alliances.

A Political Approach to International Law in International Studies

International political scholars share a similar debate concerning the role of values versus power politics in shaping international law. Though most agree that the principle of anarchy (i.e., the guiding rule that there is no higher authority above states) shapes the global system, there is disagreement on the role anarchy plays on the motivations of states in general as well as in the choice to create and compliance with international law.

Like International Legal Realists in international law, Realists in international studies suggest that anarchy results in states' focus on power acquisition and the relative distribution of power among them. Though Realists in international studies agree with International Legal Realists that international law's substance will reflect the interest of the most powerful, Realists tend to be underwhelmed by the impact of international law within the system. In contrast, International Legal Realists emphasize the political processes by which law is perpetuated rather than its relative ineffectiveness at shaping political outcomes.

Realists' more realpolitik approach within the discipline has done much to downplay the second group of International Studies scholars. However, there are elements of their ideas within Liberalism and Constructivism (discussed below). Termed idealists, they were most narrowly associated with the inter-war period and Woodrow Wilson's promotion of the League of Nations. This camp promotes the presumption that human nature can use moral reasoning to imagine the world as it could be, instead of what it is. In this way, they most closely align with International Natural Law scholars.

The third group in International Studies are Constructivists. These scholars would align most naturally with the New Stream legal scholars as both insist that laws are shaped based on how states perceive themselves, others, and the social context in which they interact. As the credited founder of Constructivism, Alexander Wendt, concluded about the principle of anarchy, "anarchy is what we make of it."[5]

Others within International Studies, called Neoliberals, suggest that states can create mechanisms that increase cooperation, including compliance with international law. Such mechanisms include: communication of clear, consistent rules, transparency in rule compliance and violation, and time build reputations over multiple rounds of interactions. As a result, this camp allows for international law to serve as a manner by which states cooperate more with each other over time.

TOWARD A COMBINED FRAMEWORK

As reflected in the two distinct disciplines above, at the heart of all choices whether to form an agreement with others, an actor must determine their preferences, the power distribution among all actors involved, and the social context in which they make these decisions.

Preferences

Rational actors are assumed to select their preferred option from a group of choices by measuring the benefits against the costs. In doing, an actor's preference is the choice that is benefit-maximizing.

Power Distribution

Though an actor calculates preferences individually, they make agreements with other actors. Still, the likelihood of that preference being realized depends on the other actors' preferences and the relative distribution of power among all actors in a given scenario. Though power has been the focus of the Realist paradigm, there are ongoing debates within realism regarding how to conceptualize and empirically measure power theoretically. Payne defines power as "the ability to get others—individuals, groups, or nations—to behave in ways that they ordinarily would not."[6]

Suppose two actors have determined which choice is each actor's benefit-maximizing preference. In that case, power is the ability for one of those actors to shape an agreement between those two actors that reflect the first actor's preference (in absolute terms) or that reflects the first actor's will at the direct expense of the other actor's preference (in relative terms). This second scenario is more in keeping with Payne's definition of power as shifting the outcome from one in which the other might otherwise prefer.

Actors with more benefits at the onset of an agreement are more likely to have the ability to use those previous benefits (i.e., power) to secure more benefit-maximizing outcomes. They will do so by encouraging others to adopt their benefit-maximizing choices by either using their ability to take on a larger share of the costs or to forcibly transfer those costs to another actor outside of the agreement.

Social Norms

Actors do not shape their preferences within a vacuum. Humans are inherently social beings, and just as the previous positions of power at the onset of negotiations may shape outcomes between actors—the social component of actors all calculating preferences, considering prior benefit distribution (i.e., power), and then determining which choice will be benefit-maximizing based on power distributions sounds and is exhausting.

Over time, actors may undervalue or even fail to consider choices they perceive as socially inappropriate. When one peels back the layers of these normative conclusions, there is a rational calculus at play. It has just been calculated repeatedly over time and across space to the point that one's subconscious presents it as intuited rather than reasoned.

More powerful actors, those who have seen their choices realized in previous negotiations, may then tip future social norms in their favor as other actors assume that options that are unattractive to this actor may not be worth even attempting to see come to fruition. Over time and across space, the most preferential choices become circumscribed, leaving only those likely to be realized within interactions with others. As a result, instead of seeing social norms as some distinct factor explaining outcomes, it can be seen as an inter-action of preferences and power within a social framework of multiple actors in repeated negotiations.

Legal-Social Continuum

Through this new conceptual framework, domestic and international law exists on a legal-social continuum. Each actor calculates their benefit-maximizing option based on their preference and the power dynamic between or among the actors and the social norms established over time from previous interactions. As a result, the notable difference between domestic and international law within this framework is the role of power distribution among actors. In domestic law, previous benefits have been secured by the state over its citizenry for decades, if not centuries. In contrast, in international law, actors have different power measurements. Still, no one (not even the hegemon with a preponderance of power) has the monopoly on power in the international system that a state has within its territory.

This difference in the relative power distribution within the domestic and international realms shapes what norms are deemed possible, and thus acceptable, by actors. Individuals within a state consider how the state has the power because of previous benefit acquisitions over time, reinforced by social norms perpetuating its authority. As a result, it makes sense that the negotiation between state and individual will more likely reflect the state's preferences over the individuals' preferences within that state. Individuals can work to change the normative power the state has. However, to do so, they must fully appreciate the power distribution enforced within the social norms to push for the options that may not be preferable to the state.

In contrast to the more stark power distribution in domestic law, international law's power distribution is more fluid and less absolute. And this creates different dynamics among the actors. Specifically, if a stronger state wishes to see its preferences realized in a negotiation, it begins with the benefit of more power, but its power is not absolute. As a result, when powerful states work to create an outcome they prefer, they must spend some capital to do so. The more powerful the state, the more it can spend without worrying it undermines its relative power over other states. However, states must consider the finite amount of their capabilities within a crowded and ever-changing world.

As a result, even the most powerful states will encourage other states to agree to the same outcomes when negotiating international law. These states do so by communicating the benefits of an agreement for the other states (even when it is clear the choice benefits the powerful state primarily).

Meanwhile, they work to share the burden of enforcement of this agreement as well by codifying the rights and obligations of all states within a compact, over time the focus of the benefits and costs shifts away from the powerful state that promoted this agreement initially and toward the community of states that are party to the agreement. And this is what best explains why, over time, even states that no longer feel an agreement benefits them may choose to violate its terms and then insist it is not. In terms of political calculus, this state is attempting to maintain the benefits of power while avoiding any of the costs of violating an increasingly important social norm.

International organizations serve as an ideal mechanism by which states can increase an agreement's benefits while diminishing the costs by sharing the enforcement role. Neoliberalism in international studies offers tools that further enhance states' cooperation in real and lasting ways.

When returning to the question posed in the title of this text—is international law even law?—the answer is that domestic and international law begins based on the most powerful state's preferences. Over time, the authority shifts to the community as social norms become more shared and internalized by the other actors. Though the requirement for social norms is more pronounced in international law than domestic law, each contains a combination of actors seeking to have their benefit-maximizing preferences within power distributions. Over time, these preferences and power structures evolve and develop equally evolving and ever-changing norms. In essence, though domestic law can rely more on absolute power and international law is undergirded more by social norms, both are legal norms that reflect both the preferences and power of certain actors reinforced by a normative pull over time.

NOTES

1. International public law is distinguished from international private law in that at least one of the actors within international public law is a state or states. In contrast, international private law includes only agreements between non-state actors. This text will use international law to mean international public law.

2. Henkin, Louis. *How Nations Behave: Law and Foreign Policy*. Columbia University Press, 1979.

3. Broadly, the term International Studies is used to include various disciplines (e.g., Geography, International Politics, Global Affairs, etc.).

4. Kennedy, David, "A New Stream of International Law Scholarship," *Wis. Int'l LJ* 7 (1988): 1.

5. Wendt, Alexander, "Anarchy is What States Make of It: The Social Construction of Power Politics (1992)," In *International Theory*, pp. 129–177. Palgrave Macmillan, London, 1995.

6. Payne, Richard J. *Global Issues*. Longman, 2011.

Chapter 1

Anatomy of a Legal Argument

Within the same legal case, two opposing sides may use the same law source to present opposite legal conclusions. If a law can be interpreted and applied in distinctly different ways by opposing sides, how do we know when someone breaks the law? To understand the art of the law argument, one must first understand the science behind it.

This chapter will break a legal argument into its four fundamental components and even further into the integral elements to build these components. It will then explain how to use this text in an active learning setting to simulate judicial hearings. Finally, it will provide an overview of the topics covered in the remaining chapters of this text.

FOUR COMPONENTS OF A LEGAL ARGUMENT

There are four components of any legal arguments. The first two—the source of law and the major premise—address the general rules in place, guiding how actors *should* behave in given situations. The second two components—the minor premise and the legal conclusion—then examine whether the actor(s) acted in accordance with these rules.

1. Sources of Law

The first component of any legal argument should be a direct reference to the source of law being applied in a case. According to Article 38(1) of the Statute of the International Court of Justice, there are four recognized sources of international law: treaties, customs, general principles, and subsidiary sources.[1]

The first source is treaties. States negotiate, sign, and ratify treaties. Though the most well-known sources, treaties serve as only a small fraction of the laws codified at the international level.

The second source of international law is customs. Unlike treaties, which are almost exclusively written and signed and ratified by states, customary law is best described as consistent patterns of behavior consistently throughout an extended period (e.g., centuries), uniformly enacted by states, and enacted out of a perceived sense of obligation (known as *opinio juris,* shorthand for the longer phrase, *opinio juris sive necessitatis,* which means "an opinion of law or necessity."

The third source of international law is general principles. In some cases, there is no international treaty or custom that directly addresses a problem that emerges between actors at the international level. In such cases, these actors may choose to examine their domestic laws. Suppose a general principle exists within the actors' domestic law as to issue. In that case, this general principle (though written for a domestic legal framework) may be subsequently applied to identify a general principle at the international law level.

The fourth and final type of sources of law is subsidiary law. Though these laws are equally crucial to international law (i.e., there is no hierarchy among the sources), these laws are considered secondary. They do not apply directly to actors' interactions but instead identify an actor's obligations to the law's primary sources. As a result, the legal relationship within these sources is between an actor and the primary sources of law (i.e., treaties and customs). Included within these sources are judicial decisions (either at the international or national level) and the writings of "the most highly qualified publicists."

Strategies for Choosing Among Laws

When developing a strong legal position, one must first recognize which laws may apply in a given scenario. International law offers a direction on how to craft, enforce, and interpret other laws. Commonly called the "treaty on treaties," the Vienna Convention on the Law of Treaties (VCLT) of 1969[2] offers three general approaches to recognizing which sources of law (e.g., treaties) and which provisions within each source of law is the best to apply within a given legal scenario.

Context

First, context is key to choosing the correct source of international law to apply. Most importantly, international law is viewed not in isolation but within a larger context or a legal regime. As an example, one of the fundamental purposes of the United Nations, stated in the Charter of the United Nations (1945), is to "maintain international peace and security" among states.[3] Four years later, when Western powers formed the North Atlantic Treaty Organization, the founding document of this organization (the North Atlantic Treaty of 1949) reaffirmed that all members and the organization would act to reaffirm the "purposes and principles of the Charter of the United Nations."[4]

There are times when two or more comprehensive sources or specific provisions could apply within a given scenario. There are two principles to determine which law best applies in these scenarios. First is the principle of *lex posterior derogat legi priori* (Latin for "later law supersedes earlier law"). Article 30 of the Vienna Convention on the Laws of Treaties mentions this principle explicitly. With an assumption that newer laws are likely more applicable than older laws, the principle of *lex posterior derogat legi priori* suggests that when two laws address the same topics, one should prioritized the newer law over the older one. A second principle, *lex specialis derogat legi generali*, may also help determine which law is best applied. Latin for "specific law supersedes general law," this principle views the more concrete law (or provision) as superior to the vaguer.

In tandem, these two principles denote the likelihood that, over time, law evolves to be both more specific and more relevant to the actors in the present day. For example, both the United Nations and NATO Charters allow states to respond collectively if one of its members is attacked. However, the NATO Charter offers more specifics as to when and how NATO members can engage in collective defense missions and be written four years after the UN Charter.

There is some debate among scholars and interpreters of international law about what to do in situations where only one of these two principles applies (e.g., the more recent rule is more general than a previous one). However, most seem to side with the principle of *lex specialis derogat legi generali* as superior to *lex posterior derogat legi priori*.

2. The Major Premise

Once the law has been chosen, the next step in crafting a legal argument is to present the law in a series of related statements in a manner that identifies the law's four key elements: actors, rights, obligations, and conditions (or, the AROC).

Actors

Actors are the first of the four elements. Actors within the law are those to whom the rule applies. Some laws may mention a specific individual, while others may reference a larger group of actors. As examples, some laws may mention a group of actors (e.g., multilateral treaties, like the UN Charter), while others (e.g., bilateral treaties) may mention states specifically by name. When examining international public law, actors tend to be states (and at times international organizations as well). Further, as will become evident in subsequent chapters, some actors may be mentioned explicitly within the law, while others may be indirectly referenced.

Within the curfew example, the law mentions that I had the right to be gone with the car and be with my friends, so long as I met the obligation of returning home by ten at night. Though the rule mentioned me explicitly, there is an implied role (as enforcer) for my parents.

International law works much the same way. Article 2(4) of the UN Charter says that "all Members shall refrain in their international relations from the threat or use of force against the territorial integrity or political independence of any state, or any other manner inconsistent with the Purposes of the United Nations."[5] Though this provision explicitly references all the UN members as actors, this provision is an implied role for the international organization. After all, if Members of the organization fail to refrain from acts of threat or force, it would be the United Nations' responsibility to respond to such a breach.

Rights and Obligations

The next two critical elements within the major premise are the rights and obligations of actors. Rights are the benefits afforded to an actor within an agreement, and obligations are the costs for actors to enjoy the benefits. As a result, rights and obligations are the legal equivalents to benefits and costs.

In most agreements, one actor's rights are another actor's obligation and vice versa. For example, the First Amendment of the U.S. Constitution affords the "right of the people peaceably to assemble."[6] Implied in this right of the people is the state's obligation to allow them to do so without interference. In turn, the individuals assembling must do so peacefully, and it is the right of the state to prevent or interfere with unpeaceful assemblies.

In the curfew example, my right is to leave home with the car to see friends, and I must return home by ten at night. In this case, my parents have the mirror inverse rights and obligations. As a result, they have the right to ensure Leah is home safely by ten at night and responsible for allowing her to use the car and see friends before that time.

Conditions

A final element within the major premise is the conditions under which these rights and obligations apply. For example, imagine my parents allowed me to have a curfew only on weekends, and the rest of the time,

I had to stay at home. As a result, the right for me to leave the house with the car to see my friends could only apply under the condition that it was a weekend night.

In international law, a condition for actors' rights and obligations in international humanitarian law (IHL) to apply is that an armed conflict must have begun. For example, the same rights and obligations would not extend to times of peace. Instead, the protection of individuals, irrespective of whether it is a time of peace or conflict, is guaranteed under international human rights law (IHRL).

3. The Minor Premise

As noted above, the first two components of legal arguments guide how actors behave in certain situations. The source of law presents the agreement between actors. The major premise reorganizes this law into statements that explain to whom the rule applies, the rights and obligations afforded to these actors, and the conditions this law applies. The minor premise begins with the statements presented in the major premise; however, it applies these rules to the specifics of a case. As a result, one must have a clear understanding of both the elements of the major premise and the specific events of a case to develop a robust minor premise.

When deciding the most important facts of the case to include in the minor premise, it is essential to consider which facts directly explain the actions of the key actors under examination and the conditions under which those actions occur. As a result, even if a case has seemingly salient relevant facts, if these facts are not in service to determine whether an actor met their legal obligation, facts need not be included in the minor premise.

Let us return a final time to the example of the strict curfew to illustrate. As a reminder, one night during my senior year, I chose to return home with the car at the designated time my parents had dictated for me, only this time I decided to bring my friends home with me. When summarizing these events, I might choose to mention the number of friends, their names, the snacks we ate, the movie we watched, and so on. Though potentially interesting, none of these facts are relevant to determining whether I met my obligations. The essential point is what time I returned home.

Often, presenting the major premise and then substituting specific actors in place of general ones can highlight which facts are most relevant and not. An example of a minor premise for the curfew example might look like this: Leah had the right to leave home with the car to see friends, so long as she returned home by ten at night. On the night in question, Leah left home with the car, met with friends, and then returned home before the obligated time in question. As a result, she complies with the stated curfew.

If my parents were shaping the minor premise, however, they would likely focus on the fact that, when I returned home, I was not alone. As a result, when examining the differences in opposing sides' minor premises, you can begin to understand where disagreements over interpretations of law or facts occur. In most cases, the accused actor (e.g., me) will present their actions as comfortably within the major premise framework. In contrast, those accusing the actor of violating the law will argue that the same measures were outside of the obligations state under the law.

4. The Legal Conclusion

As the two sides interpret the actions in question in light of different interpretations of the major premise or various applications of the facts, each side will likely come to opposite legal conclusions. If presented clearly, an argument's legal conclusion briefly presents the critical source of law and the case's facts. It then offers an explicit statement determining whether the actor in question complied with or violated international law. The legal conclusion for the argument that I made (and lost) for my curfew would flow like this: Given the curfew stipulated that I needed to be home by ten at night and made no mention that others could not return home with me, I am in full compliance with my obligations. In contrast, my parents would conclude with an opposite statement: Given the curfew stipulated that Leah needed to be home by ten at night and made no mention that others could return home with her, she is in full violation of her obligations (and grounded forever).

This text affords classes the opportunities to practice crafting, presenting, defending, and critiquing legal arguments within moot court settings. The next section explains how to run moot courts and strategies for their success.

USING THIS BOOK IN AN ACTIVE LEARNING CLASSROOM

Setting Up Moot Courts

Engaging in moot court simulations is an excellent way for you to understand international law and international studies' concepts and build practical written and argumentation skills. Each of the subsequent chapters offers a real or fictionalized legal problem between two actors.

For court cases, divide the class into three groups: the Applicants, the Respondents, and the Justices. Some courses may wish for students to remain in the same roles throughout the semester (e.g., one student is always an Applicant). Still, others prefer one of two rotating systems: (1) students remain in the same groups but change roles (e.g., first Applicants, then

Respondents, and finally Justices), or (2) students shift both groups and positions from one moot court to the next. When deciding groups, it is also worth determining whether the instructor will assign roles or allow students to choose.

Students may work in smaller groups within each of these groups to formulate different aspects of a side's argument. As an example, there are three hypothetical proposals for the U.S. Space Force's future actions in chapter 10. The legal question posed is whether these three hypotheticals would violate the United States' obligations under outer space law. In larger classes, smaller groups within the larger roles of Justices, Applicants, and Respondents could focus on one of these three hypotheticals.

Some of the cases are historical cases (e.g., the Corfu Channel case). In contrast, others take a more current topic (e.g., the United States' decision to establish Space Force) and examine whether this choice complies with international law. For all of the courses, students' goal is to apply the concepts and sources of international law to specific facts of a case to determine whether or not a certain actor was in compliance or violation of international law.

If students are playing the Applicants' role in a case, they must demonstrate that the Respondents' actions (presented in each of the relevant chapters) violated international law. If students are in the Respondents' role, they must demonstrate that their activities comply with international law. And the Justices must weigh the two sides' arguments and be the ultimate arbiters of justice.

Depending on the course's learning objectives, courses may run only a few or all of the cases presented in this book. Most often, courses run the courts either weekly (e.g., as the Friday class in a Monday, Wednesday, Friday schedule), at two points in the semester (e.g., as midterm and final projects), or only a handful of selected times throughout the semester. The time allotment for each moot court can be adjusted. However, it is usually best to allow for at least an hour for the formal proceedings (with considerable preparation time beforehand).

To prepare for the moot courts, students must demonstrate that they understand the concepts and sources of international law and the case's facts. Once they have done so, students can begin crafting written arguments (to be presented orally). These arguments often include an introductory statement, the four components of a legal opinion, and concluding remarks.

Applicants will conclude by accusing the Respondents of violating international law. In contrast, the Respondents will emphasize their compliance with the law. The Justices are then free to determine which conclusion they think is most legally sound.

Even when working in teams, it is best to have students formulate their legal arguments independently (e.g., perhaps as an out-of-class assignment) before discussing their positions within a larger group of peers. Within the moot court, oral arguments follow closely with those written arguments prepared beforehand. After one side makes its argument, the opposing side and the Justices will have the opportunity to craft questions or rebuttals. Students must work quickly to prepare these rebuttals and then craft responses to such rebuttals when this occurs. This fast-paced back and forth offers students a chance to sharpen their points and present complex ideas quickly and eloquently.

Running Moot Courts

On the day you are running a moot court in-person, consider rearranging the classroom to have the Justices in the front, facing the other two groups, and the Applicants and Respondents on opposing sides facing the Justices. If possible, set up a podium in the center of the room facing the Justices and acquire a gavel for the Justices to initiate the proceedings. These steps allow the court to feel more formal and let the students guide the court. Below is a suggested order of procedure and a script adaptable for most moot courts.

Opening Remarks

Before the court proceedings, the Justices should each recite the preliminary declaration per Article 20 of the Statute of the International Court of Justice. "I solemnly declare that I will perform my duties and exercise my powers as judge honourably, faithfully, impartially and conscientiously." Once they have done so, they may initiate the court proceedings. A chosen Justice should bang the gavel and then state: "This court is now in session. May I please have the appearances for the case concerning [case topic here]?"

The Applicants should then stand, and at least one member of the Applicant's legal team should reply: "If it pleases the Court, your honors, the Applicants, [name of a state], appear before you for your advisement." The Respondents will then stand, and at least one member of the Applicant's legal team should reply: "If it pleases the Court, your honors, the Respondents, [name of a state], appear before you for your advisement."

Applicants' Presentation

Applicants will present their argument first. For the Respondents alleged breach of international law. To do so, they will first begin with the opening statement, "Your Honors, the Applicant requests the Court to determine the Respondents, [name of a state], to violate international law." The rest of the presentation should follow the four components of a legal argument outlined in this chapter. Specifically, one or more members of the Applicants' legal team will present (1) the sources of law, (2) their major premise, and (3) their minor premise, and (4) the conclusion.

Teams can organize their presentations various ways. Most often, moot courts work best if students refrain from reading a script. They take turns presenting different parts of the legal argument (leaving no student to carry the burden alone) when they direct their views toward the Justices using a professional yet engaging tone.

Deliberation and Responses

This next portion of the court simulation allows the opposing side and the Justices time to meet in their groups to compose clarifying questions or criticisms in response to the Applicants' argument. Students ask clarifying questions when they genuinely do not understand the Applicants' view, while the criticisms' purpose is to highlight its weaknesses.

For this time to be used most effectively, the students should be considering possible clarifying questions or criticism to pose to their groups as the Applicants are presenting their arguments. It may be advisable to encourage individual members of these groups to focus on specific components of the other team's statements (e.g., one group of Respondents would determine whether the Applicants applied the correct sources of law). Depending on your time constraints, these deliberation sessions can either be timed or can be ended once each group has generated a certain number of clarifying questions or criticisms.

Once the other two groups draft questions and criticisms, members of these groups should pose these directly to the Applicants. It is then time for the applicants to take some time to determine how they might best respond. To ensure questions and criticisms are clear and to give Applicants ample time to respond, some classes ask groups to compose their questions and criticisms on a shareable document.

Respondents' Presentation

Once the Applicants have responded to the questions posed or criticisms levied, the Respondents should present their defense. One group member should begin by stating, "Your Honors, the Respondent requests the Court to [name of Respondent's state] to comply with international law," before starting the four components of their legal arguments. Strong arguments tend to focus attention in words, inflection, speed on the distinctions the Respondents are trying to draw between their interpretations and the Applicants' interpretations.

Deliberation and Responses

Once the Respondents conclude their argument, the Applicants and Justices will discuss and present clarifying questions and criticisms, and the Respondents will need to provide their best rebuttals.

Justices Deliberation and Decision

The final portion of the moot court allows a small amount of time for Justices to discuss their opinions before calling for a vote of Justices in favor of the Respondents being in compliance with or in violation of the law. Once the Justices have tallied the final vote, one of the Justices should strike the gavel a final time before announcing, "The court has determined [the Respondent] to comply with/violation of international law in [case topic here] in a vote of ____ to ____."

Once the court has concluded, the instructor needs to offer a debrief. There are two key themes to cover within this session. First, it is essential to provide any notes on points made that were inaccurate or points missed. As the semester proceeds, these notes will decrease as students mention many of the weaknesses of each other's arguments in the rebuttal periods. A second theme to say in the debrief is what political motivations led actors to create and later comply with or violate international law.

Outline of the Book

Each of the remaining chapters will introduce fundamental legal concepts and sources of international law. Next, the chapter will present either a historical or fictional case in which the law discussed in that chapter applies. Finally, the chapter will offer a legal question to be argued by the Applicants and Respondents and adjudicated by the Justices within a judicial hearing (e.g., at the International Court of Justice or the Permanent Court of Arbitration).

Chapter 2 will combine the two fields of international public law and interactions studies into one conceptual framework. Next, this chapter will use this conceptual framework to introduce the critical components of a legal argument. Finally, this chapter will explain how to run ten moot courts (each based on the topics presented in chapters 3 through 13) using the conceptual framework introduced in chapter 1 and the components of legal arguments in chapter 2. Chapter 3 will examine the concept of statehood as codified in the Montevideo Convention of 1933 to apply it to the precarious position of the Republic of Kiribati, an archipelagic state in the Pacific Ocean, faced with rising sea levels. Chapter 4 will consider the steps that quasi-states, like Palestine, must take both politically and legally to become a state.

The subsequent four chapters will focus on one of the four international law sources: treaties, customs, general principle, and subsidiary sources. Chapter 5 will examine the well-known of the four sources of international law, the treaty, and then discuss the United States' original decision to unsign the Rome Statute, the treaty that established the International Criminal Court.

Chapter 6 will explore the concept of customs in international law (e.g., laws that states fail to codify formally but still practiced consistently and uniformly out of a sense of obligation). This chapter will then review a famous incident in international law between the United States and Great Britain concerning a ship named *The Caroline*.

Chapter 7 introduces issues that arise when there is no international law to apply to a specific situation (i.e., a legal lacuna) and how states often choose to fill in the gap by identifying general principles in international law. This chapter will then examine the omission of any legal provisions for attorney-client in the European Communities when a case arose when the European Commission attempted to seize documents from the attorneys of a multinational mining and smelting corporation, and the attorneys refused.

Chapter 8 presents the secondary or subsidiary sources of international law (e.g., court rulings, international organization procedures and rules, and the International Law Commission's publishings) and uses one of these subsidiary sources to examine whether Albania violated international law in its actions toward Great Britain in an infamous incident in the Corfu Channel in 1947 in which sea mines laid in the channel sunk two British warships.

Chapter 9 examines the different dispute resolution mechanisms states are encouraged to choose by the UN Charter. Next, the chapter will discuss which one to choose when conflict arises to a real case presented at the Permanent Court of Arbitration between the Philippines and China over competing claims to the South China Sea.

Chapters 10 through 13 explore different regimes, or topic areas, in international law. Chapter 10 examines the United States' possible plans for Space Force within the existing outer space law. Chapter 11 debates whether NATO's humanitarian intervention efforts in Kosovo as part of the larger Balkan Wars of the 1990s was in keeping with jus ad bellum, or the rights of states to go to war. Chapter 12 looks at the choice of the Brush Administration to determine alleged Al-Qaeda operatives to be "unlawful combatants," a term that offers no protection under the laws of war, specifically the Third or Fourth Geneva Conventions.

Chapter 13 focuses on the right to adjudicate international crimes committed anywhere given the egregious nature of the acts (i.e., universal jurisdiction). The chapter then investigates Spain's push to try Augusto Pinochet for crimes he committed as dictator of Chile.

Chapter 13 surveys the broad and ever-growing body of international human rights law and focuses on the right to seek asylum for refugees. The chapter focuses on the Keynan government's decision to announce that it would close its largest refugee camp and refuse to register new refugees after decades of welcoming neighboring Somalis seeking refuge from ongoing political conflict, environmental disasters, terrorism, and widespread famine and disease.

The final chapter of this text will examine the benefits of reviewing international law from a political perspective and legal one, and then discuss some career paths for students wishing to pursue a career in international law.

NOTES

1. United Nations. *Statute of the International Court of Justice*, April 18, 1946. Available at: https://www.icj-cij.org/en/statute.

2. United Nations. *Vienna Convention on the Law of Treaties*, May 23, 1969. Available at: https://legal.un.org/ilc/texts/instruments/english/conventions/1_1 _1969.pdf.

3. United Nations. *Charter of the United Nations*, October 24, 1945. Available at: https://www.un.org/en/charter-united-nations/.

4. North Atlantic Treaty Organization. *North Atlantic Treaty*, April 04, 1949. Available at: https://www.nato.int/cps/en/natolive/official_texts_17120.htm.

5. United Nations. *Charter of the United Nations*, October 24, 1945. Available at: https://www.un.org/en/charter-united-nations/.

6. United States of America. *Constitution [United States of America]*, September 17, 1787. Available at: https://www.archives.gov/founding-docs/constitution -transcript.

Chapter 2

States in International Law

The Republic of Kiribati (pronounced *kiribas*) is an archipelagic state of thirty-three island formations that stretches more than 300 square miles across the Pacific Ocean northeast of Australia. Increasing global temperatures and glaciers melting thousands of miles away from Kiribati's shores threaten its very existence. While some view a state's legal status to be irrevocable, others maintain that a state should not exist in law if it can no longer exist in practice. Still, others believe there are specific criteria a state should have and that others must have to continue to exist.

This chapter will discuss all of the actors recognized under international public law before focusing on the state as the global system's primary actor. Next, it will examine the source of law that addresses under which conditions a state is recognized. The chapter will then explain Kiribati's plight in greater detail and the government's steps to anticipate and address the crisis.

ACTORS IN INTERNATIONAL LAW

There are four different actors in the international system: (1) states, (2) international organizations, (3) non-governmental organizations, and (4) individuals. This section will give an overview of each and discuss each kind of actor's standing in international public law.

States

States are the primary actors in the international system. There are currently 193 states, with South Sudan being the youngest state (established in 2011).

States form in various ways, and how they come into existence often shapes whether they can successfully claim statehood.

Fragmentation occurs when larger empires or federations dissolve into smaller new states. Examples of this include the dissolution of the Austro-Hungarian and Ottoman Empires after World War I or the more modern dissolution of Yugoslavia and the USSR in the late-1980s and early 1990s. For fragmentation to occur, the old state or empire must cease to exist altogether.

Secession occurs when a group no longer wishes to be associated with a state and attempts to claim territory once belonging to that state as a new state. Examples of this include the failed attempt at secession by the Confederates leading to the United States' Civil War, as well as the successful attempt by the South Sudanese to secede from the northern region of Sudan.

Merging is a rare act in which two formerly independent states choose to become one. The most recent example of this was when Egypt and Syria attempted to join in 1958 into the United Arab Republic. The idea was that the more stable government in Egypt would stabilize the more chaotic one in Syria. Instead, Syria's chaos sought to destabilize Egypt while making those in power in Syria feel even less powerful and thus more chaotic. As a result, this merging lasted only three years before a divorce was finalized.

Post-colonial independence is the most common manner by which states have been created. Of the 193 states in the international system, just 10 were never under colonial rule: Saudi Arabia, Iran, Japan, Korea, Thailand, China, Afghanistan, Nepal, Bhutan, and Ethiopia.

A principle in international law is a rule that is of the utmost importance. Such is the principle of sovereignty. The principle of sovereignty is the general rule in the international system that, because there is no higher authority above states in the international system (i.e., it is anarchic), states are the ones who have absolute authority over their internal affairs and autonomy from other states. Rules, however, are often broken, and the principle of sovereignty is no exception. That said, sovereignty is almost always followed by most states most of the time and undergirds most of the other laws guiding interactions among states.

International Organizations

This text will focus on states' responsibilities and rights under international law. However, there are some additional actors as well. International organizations are entities comprised of states that meet three criteria: an establishing treaty, organs, and member-states.

Each international organization has some establishing treaty made among its members that details its purpose and structure (and the states' rights and duties as members). Examples include the UN Charter, the Rome Statute of the International Criminal Court, and the Treaty of Rome for the European Union.

In American politics, the divisions in government are called branches. In international organizations, various parts of the organization are called organs. Some international organizations only function with one organ, while others have many more. For illustration below, I will use the organs of the United Nations.

The United Nations' General Assembly serves as the United Nations' legislative organ and is responsible for making rules that bind to UN members. Though created multilaterally, however, General Assembly laws are not considered treaties, which are negotiated and assigned directly by governments instead of voted on within the UN structure. Yet, the General Assembly's laws can be seen as sources of essential norms within the international community as they require at least ninety-seven states to vote in favor of the law to be put in place.

The executive organs in international organizations are in charge of the executive functions of the international organization. Though technically, two UN organs could be considered executive organs—the Security Council and the Economic and Social Council (or EcoSoc)—the former is considerably more powerful than the latter.

Though fifteen members of the UN Security Council (UNSC) at any given time, ten rotate off after two years. The five permanent members have been on the Council since the United Nations' inception. They include the United States, China, Russia, France, and the United Kingdom. For a vote to pass, these five states must concur, meaning any of these members can choose to veto actions by the Council and indirectly the United Nations as a whole. This Council has the power to impose diplomatic measures against states (e.g., suspend membership to the United Nations), enact economic sanctions against states (e.g., forbidding trade between a given state and all other members of the United Nations, which is everyone), and even intervening militarily (much more on this later).

And many international organizations have organs that help states arbitrate disputes as they arise between (or among) states. The United Nations has the International Court of Justice (ICJ). The ICJ's rulings are binding upon member-states, though we will examine times in which the United States chose not to listen.

Though we do not have a secretariat branch in the American government, the executive bureaucracy could be considered an equivalent. As noted (right), much of the government's work occurs within the executive branch's bureaucracy. For an international organization, the secretariat serves as the headquarters or central office. Those working within the secretariat must carry out the mission of the international organization day-to-day.

And, lastly, international organizations have states as their full members. These international organizations can offer universal membership, such as the United Nations, or more exclusive membership. For example, the regional international organizations, such as the EU, African Union (AU), Organization of American States (OAS), and the Association of Southeast Asian Nations (ASEAN), all require a state to be geographically located within a given region to qualify for membership. The United Nations, as noted above, has 193 full member-states.

It also offers Permanent Observer status to two entities: the Holy See and Palestine.[1] Though the Permanent Observer's role is not included in the UN Charter, the Secretary-General to the United Nations began accepting observers after World War II before them becoming members. The Holy See was granted its role formally as Observer in 2004, though it had been a sitting Observer in the General Assembly since 1964. The General Assembly voted to recognize Palestine as an Observer in 2012.

International Non-Governmental Organizations (INGOs)

The term non-governmental organization is a catchall term in international public law to describe all other actors than states, international organizations, and individuals. Loosely, there are three broad categories of international non-governmental organizations based on their stated purpose.

Some international non-governmental organizations are service-advocacy groups. These groups form with the stated purpose of building coalitions to encourage states and international organizations to promote specific global-level policies. Examples include Greenpeace, Human Rights Watch, Oxfam, and so on. Within this category, some also directly provide a service to people as well (e.g., humanitarian aid provided by the International Red Cross and CARE (based in Atlanta).

Other international non-governmental organizations are identified as ethnoreligious groups. These groups include individuals collectively identifying as practitioners of an organized religion or ethnically identifying around a specific nationality. Examples may consist of the Muslim, Catholic, and Jewish diasporas.

Some international non-governmental organizations identify across national boundaries that advocate through conflict. Examples within this category include transnational rebels or insurgent groups, internationally organized paramilitary groups, and terrorist organizations.

Though INGOs play essential roles in shaping international political and legal outcomes, international public law does not recognize INGOs as primary actors. As an example, the Geneva Conventions offer protections to those providing aid within a conflict. Still, the right is for each providing assistance, and the state must protect these individuals. Thus they have no independent legal recognition in international law.

Individuals

Historically, individuals protected under international law served a role in a state (e.g., leaders and diplomatic corps). It has only been since World War II that the international community has committed to creating international law that protects individuals more broadly because of their essential humanness (i.e., human rights) and more specifically for individuals caught in conflict zones (humanitarian law).

Are corporations people? Though multinational corporations could be considered international non-governmental organizations, international public law tends to treat corporations as individuals, distinguishing them as legal persons instead of natural ones. (as opposed to natural ones). Domestic law tends to do so as well (e.g., the United States' Supreme Court ruled that the freedom of speech protections of the First Amendment applies to unlimited campaign contributions by corporations in *Citizens United v. Federal Elections Commission*).[2]

CRITERIA FOR STATEHOOD

Though international organizations play a crucial role in drafting and promoting international public law and other actors, such as individuals, corporations, and non-governmental organizations also play a role, as in international affairs, international public law recognizes the part of the state primary in international law.

The Declarative Approach

There is significant debate surrounding what makes a state. Generally, there are two theoretical approaches in international law about how a state can come to be. The older is the *declarative approach*. This theory supposes that if an entity meets specific criteria, it has the authority to declare itself a state, irrespective of other states' recognition.

So, what do declarativists declare are the four criteria for statehood? These scholars use the same measures first codified in Uruguay in 1933 in the first Article of the Montevideo Convention on the Rights and Duties of States: a permanent population, a defined territory, a government, and the capacity to enter into relations with other states (Text Box 2.1).[3]

TEXT BOX 2.1   MONTEVIDEO CONVENTION ON THE RIGHTS AND DUTIES OF STATES (1933) [ARTICLES 1, 3, 5-8, AND 11]

Article 1

The state, as a person of international law, should possess the following qualifications:

1. A permanent population
2. A defined territory
3. Government
4. Capacity to enter into relations with other states

Article 3

The political existence of the state is independent of recognition by the other states. Even before recognition the state has the right to defend its integrity and independence, to provide for its conservation and prosperity, and consequently to organize itself as it sees fit, to legislate upon its interests, administer its services, and to define the jurisdiction and competence of its courts. The exercise of these rights has no other limitation than the exercise of the rights of other states according to international law.

Article 4

States are juridically equal, enjoy the same rights, and have equal capacity in their exercise. The rights of each one do not depend upon the power which it possesses to assure its exercise, but upon the simple fact of its existence . . . under international law.

Article 5

The fundamental rights of states are not susceptible of being affected in any manner whatsoever.

Article 6

The recognition of a state merely signifies that the state which recognizes it accepts the personality of the other with all the rights and duties determined by international law. Recognition is unconditional and irrevocable.

Article 7

The recognition of a state may be express or tacit. The latter results from any act which implies the intention of recognizing the new state.

Article 8

No state has the right to intervene in the internal or external affairs of another.

Article 11

The contracting states definitely establish as the rule of their conduct the precise obligation not to recognize territorial acquisitions or special advantages which have been obtained by force whether this consists in the employment of arms, in threatening diplomatic representations, or in any other effective coercive measure. The territory of a state is inviolable and may not be the object of military occupation nor of other measures of force imposed by another state directly or indirectly or for any motive whatever even temporarily.

The Constitutive Approach

The second theory on statehood—the constitutive theory, however, argues that this is not enough. Instead, this approach reasons that a state cannot exist unless other states accept it in the international system. As a result, they argue that it is not merely about a state's capacity to enter into relations with other states and those other states' willingness to see the new state as a legal equal. Constitutivists disagree with one another over the details of recognition. Some say the most powerful states must accept you, while others suggest majority rules. For the most part, theorists have tended to agree that becoming a full member of the United Nations is how statehood is recognized in the present international system.

UN membership is universal and thus open to any "peace-loving" political entity. To become a UN member, a state must submit a short application letter to the UN Secretary-General. In the letter, the state-hopeful must ensure that it will meet all obligations set forth under the UN Charter. Next, once the quasi-state files the letter, the UN Security Council reviews the request and votes. For this Council to approve a nomination, no permanent members can veto, and it must garner nine affirmative votes. If the Council recommends it for admission, then the General Assembly must reach a two-thirds majority to gain full membership. If a resolution passes, then it automatically becomes a member that day. Thus, in essence, the accepted constitutive approach meets all of the concerns noted above: both the powerful states *and most* other states must recognize a state before it can exist.

THE CLIMATE CRISIS FOR THE REPUBLIC OF KIRIBATI

The Republic of Kiribati[4] is a state consisting of twenty-one inhabited islands and twelve atolls (uninhabited hardened coral reefs) located northeast of Australia in the Oceania region. Before the British, the islanders were army migrants from Southeast Asia (around 3000 BCE) and later ethnic Samoans (beginning around the fourteenth century).

In the nineteenth century, the British conquered the island nation, naming it the Gilberts, and began extracting phosphates (a key ingredient in the modern industrialized agricultural revolution occurring at the time). As a colony, the British administered the Gilbert Islands and Ellice Islands (later the Tuvalu nation) together. However, religious missionaries to the Gilberts brought Catholicism to these islands, while Protestant missionaries settled in the Ellice Islands. As a result, the two island chains viewed each other as ethnically and religiously at odds.

During World War II, the Japanese occupied one of the key islands for phosphate, Banaba, interning, killing, and deporting most of its inhabitants. After the war, the British government resettled many of the remaining Banabans on a small island in Fiji (more than 1,000 miles from their home).[5] Though the British claimed the Banabans could not return home to their island due to devastation caused by the Japanese during the war, the British continued to mine phosphates on the island.

By the mid-1970s, Britain divided the two territories into distinct colonial holdings. In an unprecedented move, the Gilberts' inhabitants launched civil actions against the United Kingdom within the British courts. They sued the colonial power, seeking a greater share in the profits of phosphate mining[6] and funding to address the environmental impact of this extractive sector (phosphorus mining removes vegetation and erodes soil to extract the rock below and creates pollutant runoff).[7] With decreasing phosphorus yields and an expensive trust payment instead of future litigation, Britain ultimately acquiesced to independence for the Gilbert Islands. In 1979, the Gilbert Islands became the Republic of Kiribati (*kiribas* is the indigenous pronunciation of the name "Gilbert").

After independence, the government formed a presidential system with a unicameral legislative branch with less than fifty representatives. With few agricultural resources and exhausted phosphate mines, Kiribati focuses primarily on fishing and remittance for seafarers. With the increased competition in these two sectors (especially from laborers from Indonesia and the Philippines[8]) over the past few decades, Kiribati must rely more heavily on foreign aid.

The United States estimates that eight foreign entities fund nearly one-third[9] of Kiribati's finances: the European Union, Australia, New Zealand, Japan, Canada, the United States, the Asian Development Bank, and Taiwan.[10] Beginning in the 1990s, Japan constructed a satellite station in Kiribati. In exchange for financial aid from Taiwan, Kiribati recognizes the Republic of China (i.e., China's ousted government that now resides in Taiwan). British Petroleum also leases oil-rig space in Kiribati's exclusive maritime economic zone.

As the global climate continues to warm, the World Bank warns that Kiribati and its more than 100,000 inhabitants will be among the most vulnerable states[11] as waves further erode any habitable land and saltwater salinates any available groundwater and dries out any available cropland.

While world powers have summit meetings to negotiate treaties on how to reduce and mitigate the effects of carbon emissions, the i-Kiribati (pronounced *ee-kiribas*) are debating how to survive as a nation-state. One option the Kiribati government has is to promote "migration with dignity."[12] These programs are aimed at preparing the i-Kiribati people for employment in other places, such as financing educational opportunities and careers in Australia for people to work in healthcare and human services.

A second step the government has taken is to purchase land in Fiji. In 2014, Kiribati purchased nearly 6,000 acres in Fiji for an estimated $9.3 million.[13] Unlike the Fijian island of Rabi, where earlier—Kiribati were displaced, this tract of land is in a more forested mountain region of the second largest island in Fiji, Vanua Levu, where the new residents are attempting to cultivate taro and coconut.

And finally, with the help of a pioneering Japanese company, Kiribati is also considering the creation of the world's first floating nation-state. One Tokyo-based engineering company, called Shimizu, is devising plans for connected "cities" they say would act like "lily pads."[14] These "cities" would be tethered to the ocean floor and then float on the surface of the water. Each island would be nearly two miles across and would have towers with residential units and shops and a central shaft where inhabitants can cultivate fruits and vegetables.[15]

The head of the scheme, Masayuki Takeuchi, says, "It would be a city immune to earthquakes and tsunamis as well as saving the islands from rising sea levels." The estimated cost of this project, however, would be more than $390 billion. That is almost 3,000 times Kiribati's annual GDP. Though the government of Kiribati does not know where the money might come from, it admits that Kiribati must find a radical solution to exist. And if Kiribati no longer has islands to call home, many wonder whether its status as a state could be in jeopardy as well.

THE MOOT COURT: *THE PEOPLE'S REPUBLIC OF CHINA VS. THE REPUBLIC OF KIRIBATI*

Though the Republic of Kiribati's statehood status is intact, the events threatening the island nation's existence are profoundly concerning. This moot court will imagine a scenario in which the international community is divided over whether to allow Kiribati to remain as a state.

With Chinese expanding naval presence in the South China Sea and beyond, this moot court will imagine that China is the Applicant wishing to advocate for Kiribati's removal as a state (with the political goal of building a Chinese naval base in its place), while Kiribati is seeking to defend its statehood status. For this moot court, the legal question before the International Court of Justice is:

If Kiribati is unable to meet all of its obligations for statehood as codified by the Montevideo Convention, does it lose its statehood status?

As this legal question is an existential one, the script for this moot court will need to be modified to reflect a question of existence rather than a violation of an obligation.

NOTES

1. United Nations, "About Permanent Observers," Available at: https://www.un.org/en/sections/member-states/about-permanent-observers/index.html.
2. Citizens United v. Federal Elections Commission, 558 U.S. 310 (2010) Available at: https://www.supremecourt.gov/opinions/09pdf/08-205.pdf.
3. The Seventh International Conference of American States. *Convention on Rights and Duties of States*, December 23, 1933. Available at: https://treaties.un.org/pages/showdetails.aspx?objid=080000020166aef.
4. Britannica Encyclopedia, "Kiribati," Available at: https://www.britannica.com/place/Kiribati/History.
5. National Geographic Society Newsroom, "Our Heart Is on Banaba: Stories From 'The Forgotten People of the Pacific'," *National Geographic*, October 14, 2015.

Available at: https://blog.nationalgeographic.org/2015/10/14/our-heart-is-on-banaba -stories-from-the-forgotten-people-of-the-pacific/.

6. Minority Rights Group International. *World Directory of Minorities and Indigenous Peoples: Fiji Islands: Banabans*, 2008. Available at: https://www.ref-world.org/docid/49749d251e.html.

7. Teaiwa, Katerina Martina. *Consuming Ocean Island: Stories of People and Phosphate from Banaba*. Indiana University Press, 2014.

8. Kiribati Minister of Labour and Human Resource Development. *Kiribati National Labour Migration Policy*. United Nations Economic and Social Commission for the Asian Pacific. Available at: https://www.unescap.org/sites/default/files/ Kiribati%20National%20Labour%20Migration%20Policy.pdf.

9. Central Intelligence Agency, "Oceania: Kiribati," *The World Factbook 2020*. Available at: https://www.cia.gov/library/publications/the-world-factbook/geos/kr .html.

10. Committee for Development Policy 20th Plenary Session, "Ex-ante Impact Assessment of likely Consequences of Graduation of Kiribati from the Least Developed Country Category," United Nations. Available at: https://www.un.org/ development/desa/dpad/wp-content/uploads/sites/45/CDP-PL-2018-5b.pdf.

11. Climate Change Knowledge Portal, "Kiribati," World Bank Group. Available at: https://climateknowledgeportal.worldbank.org/country/kiribati#:~:text=Kiribati %20is%20amongst%20the%20most,variability%20and%20sea%2Dlevel%20rise.

12. Kiribati Minister of Labour and Human Resource Development. *Kiribati National Labour Migration Policy*. United Nations Economic and Social Commission for the Asian Pacific. Available at: https://www.unescap.org/sites/default/files/ Kiribati%20National%20Labour%20Migration%20Policy.pdf.

13. Caramel, Laurence, "Besieged by the Rising Tides of Climate Change, Kiribati Buys Land in Fiji," *The Guardian*, June 20, 2014. Available at: https://www.the-guardian.com/environment/2014/jul/01/kiribati-climate-change-fiji-vanua-levu.

14. Dalton, Matthew, "How a Floating Island Could Save Pacific Nation From Rising Seas," *Wall Street Journal*, December 8, 2015. Available at: https://www .wsj.com/articles/how-a-floating-island-could-save-pacific-nation-from-rising-seas -1449589251.

15. Hurtes, Sarah, "What Happens to a People When Their Land Sinks Into the Ocean?," *Vice*, September 5, 2019. Available at: https://www.vice.com/en/article/ gyzxd7/what-happens-to-a-people-when-their-land-sinks-into-the-ocean-v26n3.

Chapter 3

Quasi-States in International Law

The territory known as Palestine has changed hands throughout history and has been the backdrop for millennia's religious and political conflicts. In 1947, the United Nations attempted to offer a two-state solution, dividing Israel's territory into one Jewish and one Arab state. Conflict and violence ensued. The result is that Israel claims the territory known as Palestine to fall within its legal jurisdiction, while claimed by many Palestinians to be a territory illegally occupied by Israel.

This chapter returns to the question of statehood by examining the role of a quasi-state or entity that shares some (if not most) of the legal qualities of a state but has not received full statehood status. It will examine at what point and under what conditions a quasi-state achieve full statehood status.

The first section in this chapter will explore the legal ambiguity for quasi-states throughout history, evolving from loosely administered colonies to self-governing territories. The next sections will explore the historical evolution of the Palestinian territory. One will focus on the period of the region before the UN General Assembly proposed a two-state solution in 1947.[1] The other section will then explore the period after the partition to determine if the status of Palestine changed as a result of this document.

QUASI-STATES IN INTERNATIONAL LAW

Territory under Empires

For a review, our current international system consists of sovereign states. The principle of sovereignty has guided the international system since the Peace of Westphalia ended the Thirty Years' War (1618–1648).

This war broadly included two factions: on one side were kingdoms in Europe that wished to have complete sovereignty over their territory, including their decision to allow religious freedoms, while on the other hand were the political and religious allies of the Catholic Church who wishes to see Catholicism resurrected as the religion across Europe via the Holy Roman Empire (which as many have pointed out in history books was neither that holy, nor Roman, nor even really an Empire). It was a bold name for a desire many wished to see come to fruition.

The war began when the Catholic Church declared that all Europeans must adhere to Roman Catholicism. In protest, the Bohemian nobility in present-day Austria and the Czech Republic rejected this decree by throwing four Catholic priests out of Prague Castle's window in 1618 (might I recommend visiting Prague—it is lovely, and you can see this very spot).

The Bohemian states, calling for greater freedom from the Church and the Holy Roman Empire, soon had the backing of Sweden and Denmark-Norway, and the Thirty Years' War began. At the end of the three decades, a peace treaty was signed in Westphalia, Germany, that stated that each sovereign leader could have absolute and exclusive decision-making power over how their state would be governed (including the practice of religion). Ultimately, the Peace of Westphalia in 1648 laid the groundwork for forming the modern nation-state and the international system, built on the principle of sovereignty (though it never explicitly mentioned the term).

The term "quasi-state" describes entities with some of the statehood criteria but have not obtained full sovereignty.[2] Historically, many quasi-states have existed under the control of a sovereign state's empire as colonies.

Some scholars of colonialism have focused on the strategy of political governance of the colonies by different states. For example, some have focused on two colonial strategies, direct and indirect rule. Whereas direct rule would replace pre-existing governance structures with those systems and procedures of the home state, indirect control was meant to serve as a more extractive system that organized economic activity within the governance system being built insomuch as the extraction of resources and labor was protected under the rule of law. Even under indirect control, the colonies' territory was under the legal possession of the imperial state. Colonies did not have absolute and exclusive political sovereignty over their territories. Colonial powers forbid their colonies from entering into relations with other states (e.g., mercantilism).

League of Nations Mandates

After World War I, the international community moved away from colonies. The fifth of President Woodrow Wilson's Fourteen Points called for "a free, open-minded, and impartial adjustment of all colonial claims, based upon a strict observance of the principle that in determining all such questions of sovereignty the interests of the populations concerned must have equal weight with the equitable claims of the government whose title is to be determined."[3]

In practice, however, the victors of the war formed the League of Nations with a somewhat paternalistic view of the areas once controlled by powerful states (including, as we shall learn below, the territory called Palestine that had been under Ottoman control).

Article 22 of the establishing treaty of the League of Nations, called the Covenant of the League of Nations, created a temporary "mandate" status for territories deemed (by its members) to not yet "have reached a stage of development where their existence as independent nations can be provisionally recognized."[4] Legally, these lands would under the legal jurisdiction of the League of Nations and then administered by certain states.

UN Territories

After World War II, the League of Nations failed to exist because it could not prevent or effectively respond to the Axis Powers' mobilization before World War II. Though WWII tested the will of all political leaders' will responding to German, Japanese, and Italian expansionism, the League of Nations proved wholly ineffective as it required consensus to act. Since both Germany and France were members, however, and later France and other League members (Denmark, Norway, Luxembourg, Belgium, and the Netherlands) were all occupied by Germany in 1940, a consensus was unlikely. Switzerland became nervous about hosting an organization perceived as an anti-German, and its members soon dismantled the League (whose headquarters was in Geneva).

In the depths of fighting, the United Nations' concept was conceived in 1941 after a bibulous late-night brainstorming session. President Roosevelt presented the idea of the structure and roles of Member-States to Churchill after he had retired for the evening and then had been taking a bubble bath. While dripping naked, Roosevelt explained the organization need not be consensus-based. Still, two-tiered: with one tier meant to represent all states (i.e., the General Assembly) and the other meant to take action in times of crisis (e.g., the UN Security Council). There are other organs (i.e., branches of international organizations) of the United Nations as well, but FDR understood these two were the nexus of normative (former) and real (latter) power.

The details of the United Nations were worked out in 1945 at the Yalta Conference. One of the agreements made at Yalta was that the former League of Nations' mandates would need to be administered by the United Nations. Instead of referring to these former mandates as such, the UN Charter re-classified these mandates as "trusteeships" and created a Trusteeship Council (which was for a time its organ) to oversee their functioning. Though legally under the UN jurisdiction, the Palestinian territory was under the post-war administrative control of Great Britain and would remain so until 1947.

Unlike in the League of Nations' Covenant, there was no direct mention of the Palestinian territory's status. However, Article 77 of the UN Charter transferred all domains "now held under mandate" to this new UN trustee-ship system. In Article 76(b), the Charter stated that the trusteeship system would promote the "progressive development" of these territories toward "self-government or independence as may be appropriate to the particular circumstances of each territory and its peoples and the freely expressed wishes of the peoples concerned, and as may be provided by the terms of each trusteeship agreement."[5]

Self-Governance, But Not Full Independence

Since World War II, the international system has seen a burgeoning of new states. Below is a map that shows all 193 states in the current global system, more than two-thirds of which were created after World War II (just seventy-five years ago). As a result, though the concept of statehood is quite old, the realization of a world filled with almost two hundred states is relatively new.

The UN Charter offered two pathways the trusteeship system would promote for territories: self-government or independence. Palestine began under the Ottomans and then the British. In 1947, the UN General Assembly resolved to have this territory divided into two states: Israel and Palestine. After 1947, conflict ensued over for decades (with Israel in de facto con-trol) until a peace agreement in 1992 made the Palestinian territories self-governing with the potential for independence. Violence, politics, and strife, however, have only continued. As a result, we must decide for ourselves what is the status of Palestine today.

Palestinians refer to the territory as an Occupied Territory. A territory classified as occupied is under the control of a belligerent army. Occupation does not imply a legal status for the territory (i.e., de jure), but instead is a political status (i.e., de facto). As the International Red Cross (IRC) notes in its commentary surrounding the Fourth Geneva Convention,[6] the occupation of another's territory does not deprive that territory of its political authority over people and the territory. It "merely interferes with its power to exercise its [political] rights."

As opposed to an annexation, which is the act of acquiring territory to absorb it under one's sovereignty, occupation is considered more of a tem-porary denial of rights for a territory. Further, the occupation does not afford a state the right to annex the territory, even if it occupies the whole of the region concerned. The IRC concludes that a decision of annexation after occupation can only be reached within the peace treaty.

PALESTINE BEFORE 1947

One of the lasting questions in international law is over the Palestinian territories within the State of Israel. Though the United Nations has formally recognized Israel as a state, the region was slated (by the United Nations) to be two states: one Palestinian and one Jewish. As you will read below, the turn of events that led to Israel's creation and later the creation of territories within Israel controlled by Palestinians leaves lasting questions to be answered: what is the legal status of the Palestinian territories and thus the Palestinian people within those territories?

Palestine under the Ottoman Empire

The Ottoman Empire's founders can be traced back to the Central Asian Muslim group, called the Turkmen, who adopted Islam as they migrated westward into the Middle East in the seventh century. One independent group of these Turkmen—known as the Ottomans—defeated the independent Turkish principalities in Anatolia. Then, beginning in the fourteenth century, the Ottomans took advantage of the weakened Eastern Orthodox Byzantine Empire, then pushing south into North Africa in the fifteenth century, and finally expanding into the Middle East in the sixteenth century.

As the Ottomans expanded into the Middle East territory, they consolidated power by aligning with Sunni Muslims in the region—and sharply dividing their loyalties against Sufis and Shiites. These sects were more closely aligned with the Persian Empire. Thus it was in the expansion into the Arabian Peninsula that the Ottomans solidified their identity, not just Islam, but with Sunni Islam.

During the Ottomans' control of the Middle East, they ruled over present-day Israel. Though demographics are often rough estimates, it is believed that the territory today known as Israel was home to approximately 690,000 people in 1914, five years before World War I. Of the nearly 700,000 people, 76 percent were Muslim, 10 percent were Christian, and around 14 percent were Jewish.

The Jewish population had grown steadily throughout the late 1880s and into the 1900s, as an academic movement, called Zionism, spread throughout Jewish communities worldwide. Zionism is a nationalist call for Jews worldwide to return to Jerusalem's holy city and surrounding lands.

The Zionist movement encouraged the resettlement of Jews into the region far more than had been there previously. Rough estimates suggest that, at the turn of the nineteenth century, around 7,000 Jews lived in the territory. By 1890, that figure had grown almost fivefold to 43,000 (and would nearly double again by 1914). In 1897 an Austrian Jewish journalist named Theodor Herzl worked to turn the Zionist movement into a political organization. To do so, he created a World Zionist Organization, comprised of Jews worldwide. Their first act was to make a declaration (known as the Basel Program, as the first meeting was held in Basel, Switzerland) to state the Zionists' desire "to create a publicly guaranteed homeland for the Jewish people" in Palestine.

The following year, Herzl went to the Ottoman sultan to negotiate the grant of a charter declaring autonomy for the territory, but to no avail. Before his death (and before World War I broke out), Herzl went to Great Britain to negotiate a Jewish state in the British-controlled Sinai Peninsula (bordering present-day Israel in Egypt). However, this project failed (as did an offer from the British for 6,000 square miles of uninhabited land in Uganda) as the Zionists held out for Palestine. As a result, more Jewish settlers moved into the territory to the Ottomans and Muslim residents' concern.

British Promises during World War I

Before World War I, the great powers of Europe and beyond had formed two rigid alliances. On one side was the Triple Entente—the French, the British, and the Russians. Though these states had their tense past, all feared the Germans' growing might and wished to claim resources and shipping routes of the Ottoman and the Austro-Hungarian Empires. As a result, the Triple Entente was formed against the Triple Alliance (comprising Germany, Austro-Hungarian Empire, and the Ottoman Empire).

If you notice, Italy is also in the mix. That was because Italy first aligned with the Triple Alliance, then switched to the Triple Entente, and ultimately sat World War I out (oh, Italy). Not to give World War I away, but the Triple Entente (composed of France, Great Britain, and Russia) won! But before that was clear, Great Britain was the main fighting force against the Ottomans in the region because of its territorial claims in Egypt, its great power status in the world, and its interest in the oil reserves potentially available to it was it to free the Arabian Peninsula from the Ottomans.

In this war, the British made three distinct promises to different actors in the war. To the Arab people on the peninsula, one British High Commissioner, Sir Henry McMahon, offered one local leader independence for the entire peninsula if Arabs collectively fought against the Ottoman rule. This set of letters would collectively be known as McMahon-Hussein Understanding. The British's second agreement was with the French and Russians, dividing the territory among the three great powers. And the final deal that the British made during World War I was to Zionists, promising them a Jewish home-land in the territory.

The McMahon-Hussein Understanding

Beginning in July of 1915, the British began to employ the assistance of Arab leaders to oust the Ottomans from the Arabian Peninsula. To do so, the British High Commissioner in Egypt, Sir Henry McMahon, was instructed to reach out to those on the Arabian Peninsula who may be willing to work with the British against the Ottomans. He soon found a partner in the governor over Mecca and Medina, Hussein ibn 'Ali. In these letters, Hussein expressed to McMahon the Arabian people's full desire for independence from the Ottomans and discussed with McMahon a plan to work with the British to oust the Ottomans in exchange for British acknowledgment of independent Arab confederation, known as the Arab Caliphate of Islam, to replace Ottoman rule once victory is theirs.

In response, McMahon agreed to the Arab Caliphate, though he determined that it would be premature to draw the boundaries before victory was theirs. After Hussein responds that this is an essential point to be worked out before any conflict, McMahon creates clear exclusion zones around Palestine (e.g., the Arab state would not include the oil-rich Turkish sea towns Mersina and Alexandretta and key western regions in present-day Syria. Many, including Hussein, interpreted this letter to mean that the Arab people would control the Palestinian territory to the south of these locations. In response, Hussein commits to the plan to overthrow the Ottomans on New Years' Day of 1916, and McMahon breathes a sigh of relief in response.

The Arab revolt, led by Hussein's son Faisal with British Colonel T. E. Lawrence ("Lawrence of Arabia"), began on June 10, 1916. Three months later, the revolt successfully defeated the Ottomans, and Britain took control over much of the Arabian Peninsula by September of that year.

The Sykes-Picot Agreement

But Britain made other promises during the war that conflicted with the Hussein-McMahon understanding. Just two months after the McMahon-Hussein correspondence concluded and a month before the British assisted the Arabs in their revolt against the Ottomans, Britain, France, and the Russian Empire made a secret agreement that they would divide the Arabian Peninsula among themselves. The Russians, they had all agreed at a previous meeting, would get Istanbul and the surrounding areas.

It was in May of 1916 that the three powers negotiated a carving up of Turkey and the northern portion of the peninsula for themselves, with Russia gaining Armenian territories between it and Istanbul, the French taking full control of Lebanon and Western Syria (areas left ambiguous in the McMahon-Hussein letters), Britain laying either full or partial claim to the oil-rich regions of Iraq and Kuwait and the coastal regions needed to transport oil from the Middle East back to Britain. The territory, collectively known by the British as the Palestinian territory, determined that the holy sites were best administered as an international protectorate (international, meaning only these three powers).

However, this agreement was exposed to the world in November of 2017 when the Bolsheviks toppled the Russian Empire. Angered by this back-door agreement made by international elites, the Bolsheviks published this agreement in three national newspapers. It soon reached Hussein, his son Faisal, and the other Arab leaders and revolutionaries.

The Balfour Declaration

Around the same time that Sykes-Picot was being laid bare, the British made the third promise in November of 1917 in a letter from the British foreign minister, Lord Arthur Balfour (pictured left), to Britain's most illustrious Jewish citizen and international financier and leader of the UK's Zionist Federation, Baron Lionel Walter Rothschild. The foreign minister expressed Britain's support for a Jewish homeland in the Palestinian territory (most likely looking for further financial assistance for Britain through the now-prolonged war).

The Palestinian Mandate

After the Bolsheviks overturned the Russian Empire and went public with the Sykes-Picot Agreement news, Hussein demanded the British explain. Just four days before the armistice was signed, the British and French offered the Anglo-French Declaration, assurances of "the complete and final liberation of the peoples who have for so long been oppressed by the Turks, and the setting up of national governments and administrations deriving their authority from the free exercise of the initiative and choice of the indigenous population."[7]

The Paris Peace Conference, however, showed which of the promises would be upheld. For the Arabs, Hussein's son and favored fighter by the British, Faisal, would attend the conference. In a memorandum before the peace conference, Faisal expressly asked for independence for all "Arabic speaking peoples" in the Middle East along the boundaries agreed upon by McMahon and his father, Hussein. During a meeting in February of 1919, Faisal reiterated to the group that his and his father's ideals were the same as "all Arabic patriots:" to form a loose federation of Arab states (or emirates) in which former Ottoman provinces would not be independent of colonial rule and under one Arab king.

In a preliminary meeting, however, the British and French colonial rule had been proposed. President Woodrow Wilson of America was highly opposed to colonial rule on principle (as he had noted in his Fourteen Points). He did, however, also have a paternalistic view of Arabs and compromised with the British and French instead of considering a mandate.

During the meeting with Faisal, President Wilson spoke to Faisal, offering him only one of two options, neither of which was his first choice. As the U.S. secretary present at the Conference historian described it, Wilson asked the Emir whether, "seeing that the plan of mandatories on behalf of the League of Nations had been adopted, he would prefer for his people a single mandatory or several." And so, the Western powers decided the mandate system for the Middle East.

At the Conference, France obtained a mandate over Syria, carving out Lebanon as a separate state with a (slight) Christian majority. Meanwhile, Britain received a mandate over Iraq and the area that now comprises Israel, the West Bank, the Gaza Strip, and Jordan. In 1921, the British divided this latter region in two: East of the Jordan River became the Emirate of Transjordan. This was to be ruled by Faisal with some autonomy from British rule. West of the Jordan River became the Palestine Mandate. This was ruled directly by the British.

European Jewish immigration to Palestine increased dramatically after Hitler's rise to power in Germany in 1933, leading to new land purchases and Jewish settlements. Palestinian resistance to British control and Zionist settlement culminated in the Arab revolt of 1936–1939, which Britain suppressed with Zionist militias' help.

After crushing the Arab revolt in 1939, the British reconsidered their governing policies to maintain order in an increasingly tense environment. After failing to encourage both Jews and Arabs to reach an agreement in a peace conference, Britain issued the 1939 White Paper, declaring "unequivocally that it is not part of [British government's] policy that Palestine should become a Jewish State."[8] This statement limited future Jewish immigration and land purchases, which would have resulted in a majority-Arab Palestinian state. The Zionists regarded the White Paper as a betrayal of the Balfour Declaration and a particularly egregious act in light of the desperate situation of the Jews in Europe, who were facing extermination. The White Paper marked the end of the British-Zionist alliance. At the same time, the defeat of the Arab revolt meant that the Palestinians were politically disorganized, and the future of Palestine was decided for them.

PALESTINE AFTER 1947

Following World War II, hostilities escalated between Arabs and Jews over the fate of Palestine and between the Zionist militias and the British army. Britain, exhausted by WWII and intent on withdrawing from the Middle East, requested the United Nations handle the Palestinian trusteeship issue.

In response to Britain's request, the UN General Assembly held three sessions in May, September, and finally November of 1947. Following the third meeting, the General Assembly voted (with thirty-three in favor, including the United States and USSR, thirteen opposed, and ten abstentions) to pass the Palestinian Partition Resolution (GA Resolution 181).[9]

The United Nations General Assembly Partition Plan of 1947

There are three essential divisions of the territory included in the UN Partition plan. Part II, Section A denotes the boundaries of a Palestinian Arab state. Part II, Section B designates the boundaries of a Jewish state, Part III indicates how Jerusalem would become an international city administered by the United Nations. The boundaries of each state mentioned in Part II are shown in Figure 3.1.

Part III explains how the United Nations was to administer Jerusalem. Part III designated the city to be a *corpus separatum*, (Latin for "separated body"), and it tasked the UN Trusteeship Council with administering it. Specifically, the Trusteeship Council had to "protect and to preserve the unique spiritual and religious interests located in the city of the three great monotheistic faiths" to ensure that "order and peace, and especially religious peace, reign in Jerusalem."[10] As a result, the United Nations' goal was to guarantee equal access to Jerusalem for all.

Part I presented a timeline for these steps. It stated that the Mandate for Palestine would terminate nine months after the Partition passed in the General Assembly (i.e., no later than August, 1st 1948). At that time, Part I required the British military to withdraw from the territory before the two states (and Jerusalem) came into existence no later than October 1, 1948.

To achieve these milestones, Part I, Section B offered steps toward independence, including creating a provisional government for each state to work with the United Nations to create a constitution and permanent administrative organs. Though the Partition allowed each provision government to "recruit an armed militia from the residents of the State," the "general political and military control" of each state "shall be exercised by the [United Nations]" until the states were formed.[11] The section makes clear that, though the General Assembly is guiding these steps, each measure was taken by it "shall become immediately effective" unless the Security Council expressly states otherwise.

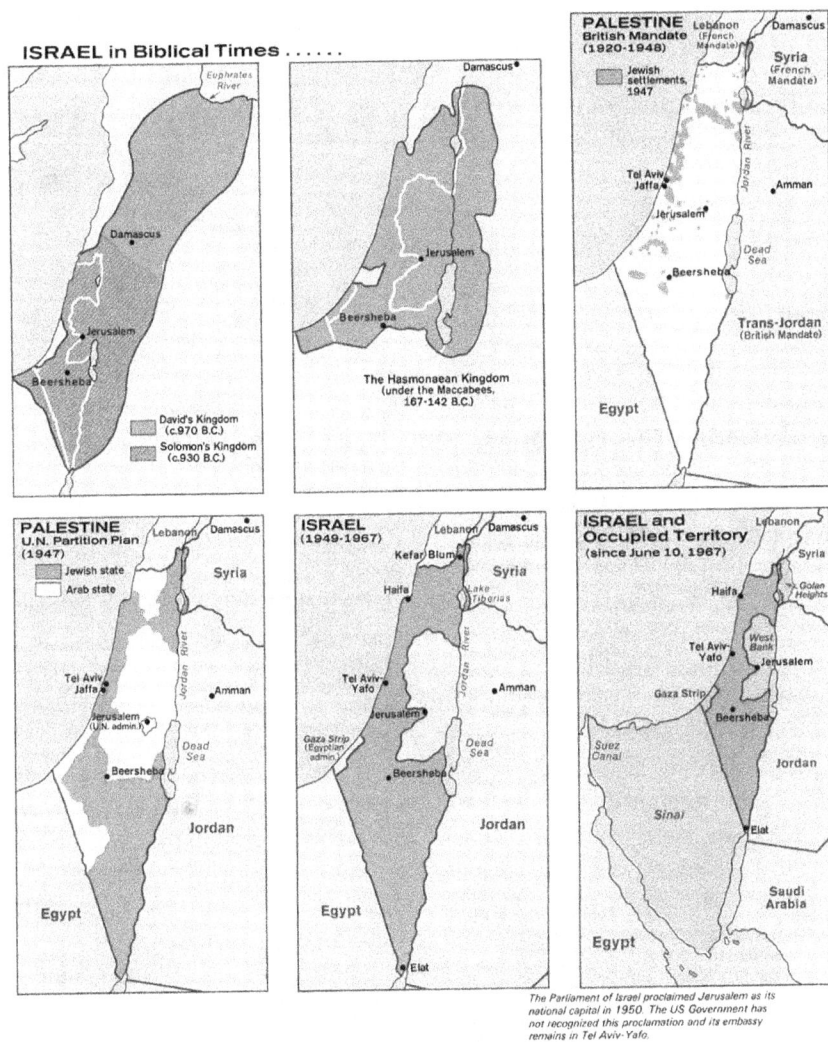

Figure 3.1 United Nations Partition Plan of 1947. *Source:* Courtesy of University of Texas Libraries.

After the General Assembly passed the partition, six nations—Egypt, Lebanon, Iraq, Saudi Arabia, Syria, and Yemen—walked out in protest. One *New York Times* article about the walkout suggested that "if the Arabs carry out their threats to fight rather than agree to partition," the Commission on Palestine will be responsible to the Security Council. Fighting began between the Arab and Jewish residents of Palestine days after adopting the UN Partition plan.[12]

Statehood and War: 1948–1949

Within the following two years, events unfolded quickly. First, Israel unilaterally declared statehood. Next, the Arab states surrounding Israel launched an attack on the newly declared state. Israel won this war, and Jordan, Egypt, and Israel divided the territory slated to be Palestine. After much reluctance and assertion that this would not preclude a future Palestinian state, the United Nations welcomed Israel as a member in 1949.

Israel Declares Independence March 4, 1948

The Arab military forces were poorly organized, trained, and armed. In contrast, although numerically smaller, Zionist military forces were well organized, trained, and armed by the British during WWI and then later forming the Israeli Defense Force (IDF). By early April 1948, the Zionist forces had secured control over most of the territory allotted to the Jewish state in the UN plan and begun to go on the offensive, conquering territory beyond the partition borders in several sectors.

On May 14, 1948, the Israeli people unilaterally declared the establishment of the State of Israel. This declaration did not follow the legal steps outlined in the Partition plan. The declaration deemed the right to exist on the historical and religious claims to the territory based on "national and universal significance" offered in the "eternal Book of Book" (e.g., the Torah)[13] and promises made in the Balfour Declaration. Interestingly, the declaration references that the Partition Plan called "for the establishment of a Jewish State" and the "General Assembly required [its] inhabitants . . . to take such steps as were necessary on their part for the implementation of that resolution," but it did not follow the steps included in the Partition Plan.[14] The declaration ends by noting that This recognition by the United Nations of the right of the Jewish people to establish their State is irrevocable."[15]

Arab-Israeli War (1948-1949)

Arab neighbors invade Palestinian territory to reclaim land from the newly formed State of Israel. On May 15, 1948, British evacuated Palestine, and Zionist leaders proclaimed the State of Israel. The neighboring Arab states of Egypt, Syria, Jordan, and Iraq then invaded Israel, claiming that they sought to "save" Palestine from the Zionists. Lebanon declared war but did not invade. The Arab rulers had territorial designs on Palestine. Upon hearing of the initial UN partitioning, the Arab League concluded that they would annex the territory slated for Israel (and the Palestinians) per the Hussein-McMahon Understandings.

During May and June 1948, when the fighting was most intense, this first Arab-Israeli War was in doubt. But due to the well-organized Israeli army, the uncoordinated efforts of Syria, Egypt, and Jordan, and arms shipments from the United States, Israel established superiority. They conquered additional territories beyond the borders the UN Partition plan had drawn up for the Jewish state.

In 1949, the war between Israel and the Arab states ended with the signing of armistice agreements. An armistice is viewed in international customary law as a "suspension of military operations by mutual agreement between the belligerent parties, either for a fixed period or without an expiry date."[16]

The UN's vision of the Palestinian Arab state never existed. Instead, Jordan occupied East Jerusalem and annexed the hill country of central Palestine known as the West Bank. Egypt took control of the coastal plain around the city of Gaza in the southwest (known as the Gaza Strip), and the State of Israel took control of the remainder of the land, including West Jerusalem (dividing the city into two).

Israel Member of UN (March 1949)

After Israel agreed to an armistice with Egypt and Lebanon (but not Jordan), the UN passed General Assembly Resolution 272, accepting Israel's membership. In December 1949, the General Assembly adopted a proposal reaffirming the 1947 Partition proposal to have Jerusalem placed under trusteeship in the United Nations. In response, the Israelis moved their government into West Jerusalem.

As for east Jerusalem and the West Bank, it was formally annexed by Jordan on April 24, 1950. This annexation, however, was recognized only by Great Britain, Iraq, and Pakistan. From 1950 until Israel occupied it in the Six-Day War of 1967, Jordan governed the West Bank as part of Jordan and granted the Palestinians Jordanian citizenship. Through this, many Palestinians continued to aspire for self-determination.

The Six-Day War (1967)

In the spring of 1967, the Soviet Union misinformed the Syrian government that Israeli forces were massing in northern Israel to attack Syria. Initially supportive of Israel at the time of its founding, by the early 1950s, the Soviets no longer regarded the Zionist state as useful for extending their influence into the Middle East (mainly due to the Zionists' warm relations with the United States). Transferring their support to the Arab side, the Soviets took on arming both Syria and Egypt, supplying them with modern tanks, aircraft, and later missiles.

The Soviet Union exerted a troublesome influence on the events leading up to the war by feeding Arab suspicions about Israel, culminating in the Syrians and Egyptians' delivery of a false alert in 1967 that Israel had massed troops near the Israeli-Syrian border in preparation for an attack on Syria. There was no such Israeli mobilization, but Israel and Syria's clashes had been escalating for about a year. Further, Israeli leaders had publicly declared that it might be necessary to bring down the Syrian regime if it failed to end Palestinian guerrilla attacks from the Golan Heights territory in the southwest corner of Syria and on the northeastern border of Israel.

Believing that an Israeli attack was imminent, Syria requested Egypt's assistance against their common neighbor, and Jordan soon joined in. Thus the Six-Day War involved three distinct battlefronts for Israel on its borders with Egypt, Syria, and Jordan.

In May of 1967, Egyptian troops moved into the Sinai Peninsula just across from the Israeli border. They blocked the Israelis' only direct access to the Red Sea through the Gulf of Aqaba. in response, Israel launched a pre-emptive strike against the Egyptian army and air force. Egypt's air force was quickly crippled, and a well-executed Israeli ground offensive routed the Egyptian forces in Gaza and the Sinai Peninsula in four days.

Buoyed by false reports of Egyptian success, Jordan initiated offensive actions against Israel from the eastern portion of Jerusalem and the West Bank. Israeli forces responded by attacking Jordanian military positions. After three days of fierce fighting, especially in and around Jerusalem, Israeli forces defeated the Jordanians. They gained control of Jerusalem and the West Bank, the Jewish people's historical heartland known to Israelis as Judea and Samaria.

Following an air attack by the Syrians on the first day of the war, Israel dealt a shattering blow to the Syrian air force. Hostilities continued in the days that followed, and on the fifth day of the action, the Israelis mustered enough forces to remove the Syrian threat from the Golan Heights. Israel completed the difficult operation the following day, bringing the war's active phase to a close.

By June 11, 1967, six days after the battles began, the Egyptian, Syrian, and Jordanian armies were quickly and decisively defeated (thus the name "Six Days War"). As a result of this war, Israel increased its territorial gains significantly. Specifically, it gained the Golan Heights from Syria, the Gaza Strip and the Sinai Peninsula from Egypt, and the West Bank and East Jerusalem from Jordan (thus gaining full control of the city).

After the 1967 war, the UN Security Council adopted Resolution 242, which notes the "inadmissibility of the acquisition of territory by force."[17] The Resolution then directly calls for Israel to withdraw from all lands seized in the war based on "the right of all states in the area to peaceful existence within secure and recognized boundaries." Another issue addressed in Resolution 242 was that it calls for a "just settlement" of the refugee problem, but it does not indicate any other specifics.

The Resolution calls for the "respect for and acknowledgment of the sovereignty, territorial integrity, and political independence of every State in the area." The Palestinians argue that this means that Palestinians should recognize Israel, but Palestinians (as a nation, not a state) do not also receive reciprocal recognition by Israel.

After Israel won Gaza and the West Bank in 1967, it established a military administration to govern over Palestinian residents and began encouraging Jewish settlements in these territories. The UN's 1947 partition plan advocated that Jerusalem become an international zone. After the 1948 Arab-Israeli War, however, Israel took control of the western part of Jerusalem. Jordan took the eastern part, including the old walled city containing important Jewish, Muslim, and Christian religious sites.

During the Six-Day War, Israel captured East Jerusalem from Jordan and immediately annexed it. In 1980, the Israeli government passed a law declaring Jerusalem as its capital. However, the UN Security Council passed Resolution 478, claiming that law to be null and void. The United States abstained as it sees an international city as the best future for Jerusalem (a significant contention between the United States and Israel). Israel still regards Jerusalem as its "eternal capital," moving its political capital to West Jerusalem in 1949, though the international community accepts Tel Aviv as its capital.

Agreements and Uprisings

The next decades offered moments of peace between the Palestinians and Israelis, followed by moments of violence and bloodshed. Though the two parties fought each other, violent attacks also occurred within the Palestinian and Israeli factions as moderates advocated for peace, and extremists chose violence instead.

First Intifada (1987)

Some Palestinians began to organize their nationalistic aspirations around the Palestine Liberation Organization (PLO), a militant group promoting Palestinian nationalism. The PLO's military wing most often gathered recruits from Palestinian refugees' descendants in Lebanon, Syria, and Jordan. Its original goal was the destruction of the "Zionist entity." Further, backed by the Arab states, it refused to recognize Israel's right to exist.

From its inception until the 1990s, the PLO's paramilitary wing advocated guerrilla warfare tactics to weaken and demoralize the Israelis. The PLO instigated incursions into Israel from the border countries of Jordan, Lebanon, and Syria and inside Israel as well, entering from the Gaza Strip and the West Bank. In 1968, Yasser Arafat became chairman of the PLO, and he served until he died in 2004.

The largest, most powerful faction of the PLO to emerge in this diplomatic role was Arafat's Fatah. Other significant groups within the PLO include the Popular Front for the Liberation of Palestine (PFLP), the Democratic Front for the Liberation of Palestine (DFLP), and The Palestinian People's Party (PPP, formerly the Communist Party). Each of these parties often criticized the Fatah for failing to lead the PLO to reach its paramilitary goals. That said, under Fatah, the international community began to perceive the PLO as the more moderate and international legitimate representative of the Palestinian people.

In December 1987, the Palestinian population in the West Bank and Gaza began a mass uprising against the Israeli occupation. This uprising, or intifada (which means "shaking off" in Arabic), was not started or orchestrated by the PLO leadership in Tunis, but it was a popular mobilization. The intifada involved hundreds of thousands of people, many with no previous resistance experience. It took many different forms. Some non-violent forms include mass demonstrations, strikes, refusal to pay taxes, boycotts of Israeli products, political graffiti, and underground "freedom schools" (alternative schooling options after regular schools were closed by the Israeli military). Some violent forms included: stone throwing, Molotov cocktails, and the erection of barricades to impede the movement of Israeli military forces. Under the leadership of Defense Minister Yitzhak Rabin, Israel responded with force. From 1987 to 1991, Israeli forces killed over 1,000 Palestinians and engaged in arrests and detainments.

The Oslo Accords (1993 to 1995)

The United States, under the administration of President George H. W. Bush, attempted to establish talks with Palestinians and the right-leaning Israeli government under the Likud Party in 1991. The Israeli government, headed by Prime Minister Shamir, argued that the PLO should be excluded from the talks as they were a terrorist organization and that the Palestinian desires for statehood not be directly addressed. Thus the Palestinians were represented by a non-PLO delegation of citizens from the West Bank and Gaza.

After Yitzhak Rabin, the defense minister who led the Israeli military in violently suppressing the demonstrations during the First Intifada became prime minister in 1992, conditions in the West Bank and the Gaza Strip deteriorated dramatically. Hamas began employing suicide bombing against Israeli citizens, and Israel increasingly returned military force. Many argue that the fear of rising power of the radical Islamists among the Palestinians and the stalemate in the Washington talks brought the Israeli government to reverse its long-standing refusal to negotiate with the PLO.

Israeli prime minister Yitzhak Rabin initiated secret negotiations directly with PLO Negotiator Mahmoud Abbas. The talks were conducted in Oslo, Norway. They produced the Israel-PLO Declaration of Principles on Interim Self-Government, which was signed in Washington in September 1993 and 1995 is commonly referred to as the Oslo Accords.

The Oslo Accord offered notable concessions on the part of the Israelis and Palestinians. The Israelis promised to acknowledge the PLO as *the* Palestinians' representative if the PLO promised to renounce violence. If the PLO did so, both sides agreed to create "subnational governing responsibilities in the West Bank and Gaza Strip" called the Palestinian Authority. This subnational governance would control the territories for five years (under the national control of Israel). After five years, "permanent status talks on borders, refugees, and Jerusalem would be held." A second accord in 1995 (i.e., Oslo II) detailed how elections and bilateral cooperation would occur between the two entities.

After Oslo

In November 1995, Rabin was assassinated by a right-wing Israeli who opposed the Oslo Accords on religious grounds. Following Rabin's murder, a string of terrorist attacks by Hamas undermined the Labor Party's support in Israel's May 1996 elections.

New prime minister Binyamin Netanyahu hailed from the Likud Party, which had historically opposed Palestinian statehood and withdrawal from the occupied territories. Worried that the peace process might collapse, the Clinton administration involved itself more actively in Israeli-Palestinian negotiations.

In Israel's May 1999 elections, the Labor Party's Ehud Barak decisively defeated Netanyahu. Barak predicted that he could reach agreements with both Syria and the Palestinians in 12 to 15 months. At the prime minister's insistence, Clinton convened a summit at Camp David in July 2000, where he, Barak, and Arafat attempted to reach a final agreement on the West Bank and the Gaza Strip. Accounts differ as to why Camp David failed, but it is clear that despite additional concessions by Barak, the Israelis and Palestinians remained firmly at odds over Israeli's reluctance to withdraw from the West Bank and the Gaza Strip, the future of Jerusalem, recognition of statehood, and the "right of return" (a legal question as to whether

Palestinian refugees could return to their property lost during the Arab-Israeli War in 1948).

Clinton would blame Arafat for its failure, and Arafat left Camp David with enhanced stature among his constituents because he did not yield to American and Israeli pressure. Barak returned home to face a political crisis within his government, including the departure of coalition partners who felt he had offered the Palestinians too much.

Second Intifada (2000)

On September 28, riots erupted following a visit of Likud Party leader Ariel Sharon to the Temple Mount. Accompanied by 1,000 armed guards, Sharon's visit to the holy site within East Jerusalem aggravated the issue of Israel's complete control of Jerusalem for Palestinians in Jerusalem and the West Bank.

The following day, Palestinians threw rocks at Jews praying at the Western Wall. In response, Israeli police stormed the Temple Mount and killed seven and wounded approximately 200 protesters. This conflict soon escalated into a wave of Israeli-Palestinian violence known as the Second Intifada, spread throughout the West Bank and into Gaza. The Second Intifada was much bloodier than the first. During the first three weeks of the uprising, Israeli forces shot one million live bullets at Palestinian demonstrators, and in some cases, Palestinian Authority police officers returned fire.

It was a conscious escalation in the use of force designed to avoid a protracted civil uprising like the first intifada. Israel also expanded its use of force to include tanks, helicopter gunships, and F-16 fighter planes. The IDF shelled civilian neighborhoods and launched aerial bombardments over both the West Bank and Gaza. The Israeli government justified the use of force in these areas because these were under semi-autonomous control (and therefore outside the jurisdiction of the Israeli police and within the jurisdiction of the Israeli army).

In November 2000, Hamas and Islamic Jihad (and groups connected to Fatah) began conducting suicide bombings and other armed operations. Over 150 such attacks from 2000 through 2005, compared to twenty-two incidents from 1993 to 1999 by Islamist opponents of the Oslo process. In December 2000, Clinton put forward his proposals for an Israeli-Palestinian agreement. However, the president was leaving office by this point, Barak faced electoral defeat, and Israeli-Palestinian violence continued unabated.

Ariel Sharon handily won the 2001 election. Sharon's first term as premier coincided with a particularly violent stretch of the Second Intifada. A cycle of targeted killings of Palestinian militants and Palestinian attacks inside Israel culminated in a suicide bombing in Netanya on March 27, 2002, during the Passover holiday. The attack killed thirty Israelis. In retaliation, Israel launched Operation Defensive Shield, a full-scale tank invasion of the West Bank that lasted for several weeks. Armored Caterpillar bulldozers razed swathes of the Jenin refugee camp, and tanks ringed the Church of the Nativity in Bethlehem.

Meanwhile, Israeli forces imposed all-day curfews in seven of the West Bank's eight major towns. Israel justified this offensive as the pursuit of terrorist suspects, with George W. Bush administration's full backing in Washington. The United States bucked the trend of international opinion, which was generally critical of Israel's operation. A second, shorter tank invasion occurred in June. The Likud Party dominated Israeli politics for the next decade. Its ascendancy marked Oslo's end for all practical purposes since the Likud unequivocally opposed establishing a Palestinian state or making any territorial compromises.

Palestinian Division (2006 to the Present)

In January 2005, following Yasser Arafat's death, Mahmoud Abbas was elected president of the Palestinian Authority with support from the Fatah party. In the January 2006 elections for the Palestinian Legislative Council, Hamas won a majority of 77 out of 122 seats.

In response to the Hamas victory, America cut off its financial support for the Palestinian Authority and, Israel began to withhold the tax revenue collected on behalf of the government. These measures further weakened the already embattled Palestinian economy.

Ignoring the legitimacy of Hamas' victory in the elections, the United States provided $84 million in military aid to improve the fighting ability of the Presidential Guard loyal to Mahmoud Abbas. Palestinian security forces in the West Bank were retrained under a U.S. Marine Lt. Gen. Keith Dayton. In June 2007, with backing from the United States, Fatah moved to carry out a coup to oust Hamas from the Gaza Strip.

Hamas preempted the move and, after a pitched battle, established its sole control over the territory. Since then, governance of the West Bank and the Gaza Strip has now been divided between Fatah and Hamas. In the aftermath of the failed coup, Mahmoud Abbas dissolved the Palestinian Authority cabinet. He appointed Salam Fayyad, a U.S.-trained economist with experience in the International Monetary Fund, as prime minister. Fayyad undertook to transform the Palestinian economy along neoliberal lines, hoping that this "good governance" and the more aggressive pursuit of Hamas and Islamic Jihad by the "Dayton Brigades" would convince the West that the Palestinians deserved a state. Fayyad, however, resigned in frustration in April 2013.

On September 19, 2007, Israel declared that Gaza had become a "hostile territory." With support from Egypt under President Husni Mubarak, Israel tightened its blockade of the Gaza Strip. Israel's 2008 to 2009 and 2012 assaults on the Gaza Strip enhanced Hamas' stature and popularity among Palestinians and internationally. In May 2010, the moderate Islamist party ruling Turkey expressed its sympathy for Hamas by permitting the Mavi Marmara, sponsored by the Islamist Humanitarian Relief Foundation, to join a flotilla to relieve the besieged population of the Gaza Strip. Israel attacked the Mavi Marmara, killing eight unarmed Turkish citizens and one unarmed U.S. citizen of Turkish origin. (A tenth victim fell into a coma and died in May 2014.) This incident led to the freeze of the previously warm relations between Turkey and Israel.

2011: "Palestinian Papers" Revealed

Ariel Sharon suffered a stroke that put him in a permanent coma in January 2006. (He would die eight years later.) Ehud Olmert replaced him as prime minister and leader of Kadima. From December 2006 to September 2008, Prime Minister Olmert and the Fatah leader, Abbas, conducted secret negotiations that came close to an agreement. The contents of those talks were revealed to Al Jazeera and published as "the Palestine Papers" in January 2011.

Since then, Olmert and Abbas have publicly confirmed that they agreed on demilitarization of the Palestinian territories, the stationing of an American-led international security force on the border between Palestine territories and Israel, sharing Jerusalem with an international committee to oversee its holy sites, the return of 10,000 Palestinian refugees to Israel and compensation and resettlement for the rest. The fundamental disagreement was over the extent of Israeli annexations via settlements in the West Bank, though Israel did acquiesce to a tunnel from the West Bank to Gaza for Palestinians to access both territories.

Before these talks could work through this contention, Israel invaded Gaza militarily in 2007–2008. Then in December of 2008, Olmert was indicted on corruption charges. With new elections for prime minister in 2009, Benjamin Netanyahu and the Likud returned to power. Netanyahu refused to continue the negotiations from where they had left off.

Palestinians Gain Observer Status in the UN (2012)

As chairman of the PLO, Mahmoud Abbas has twice petitioned the United Nations to accept Palestine as a member state. In September 2011, he approached the Security Council and asked for full membership for Palestine.

The petition did not receive the nine required votes. In any case, the United States would have vetoed the petition, preventing it from being passed on to the General Assembly for a vote.

On November 29, 2012, the sixty-fifth anniversary of UN General Assembly Resolution 181 partitioning Palestine, Abbas asked the General Assembly to accept Palestine as a non-member observer state, the same status enjoyed by the Vatican (and Switzerland before it joined the United Nations). One hundred-thirty-eight General Assembly members voted in favor and nine against, with forty-one abstentions. Two of the key no votes came from Israel and the United States.

Subsequently, the Palestine Authority ratified the four Geneva Conventions and an array of international human rights and other treaties, including the ICCPR, ICESCR, UN Convention against Torture, and the Rome Statute recognizing the jurisdiction of the International Criminal Court in the Occupied Palestinian Territories.

These steps, however, have had no political effect on the ground. Israel continues to control the West Bank and the Gaza Strip. However, it did open the possibility that Palestine could approach the International Criminal Court to pursue Israeli officials for crimes committed in the occupation. International opinion is nearly unanimous that a two-state solution, including a sovereign Palestinian state, is the best, if not the only way forward in the century-old conflict over historical Palestine. Yet, there is no visible movement toward achieving this outcome.

2017: Fatah-Hamas Unified Palestinian Authority Government

Since 2006, elections within the Palestinian Legislative Council have kept Hamas in control of the Palestinian Authority's legislative branch. In contrast, the executive branch, which held its last election in 2008, is run by President Mahmoud Abbas, a Fatah member. Thus, for nearly two decades, the Palestinian Authority has been divided between Fatah and Hamas, unable to hold even primary elections. Instead, Fatah has focused its efforts on providing services for the West Bank, leaving Hamas to rule over Gaza.

After the last round of attacks by Hamas militants, President Abbas applied political pressure on Hamas by cutting everyone's salary on the Palestinian Authority's payroll (e.g., bureaucrats, teachers, and police) by thirty percent. Moreover, it cut off energy subsidies to the Gaza Strip. Abbas made this threat, Gaza residents were getting on average only three or four hours of electricity per day. The Gaza Strip, the most densely populated territory globally (1.8 million inhabitants live in an area that is 140 square miles), is facing a 50 percent unemployment rate, the water quality is dangerous, and the air reeks of raw sewage.

In response, Fatah leaders agreed to work with Hamas to form a unity government, though details remain unclear. One Fatah official, Rami Hamdallah, remarked that unification works in the best interest of all Palestinians in their negotiations with Israel: "The world will not pay attention to a torn people. The main winner of a continued split is the occupation [Israel]."[18]

The Islamist Hamas party has an armed wing, known as the Al-Qassam Brigades, and is considered a terrorist group by the United States, the European Union, and Israel. It remained unclear what would happen to Hamas' armed wing and whether its 25,000 members would relinquish military control over Gaza. In a new charter announced earlier in 2017, Hamas dropped its wording of "destroying" Israel and said it would recognize a Palestinian state within the Palestinian Authority's role1967 Arab-Israeli War's borders.[19] The charter, however, says Hamas would continue armed resistance as a legitimate right.

Today

The West Bank is currently home to almost half of the 5.6 million Palestinians that remain in Israel. It is also home to nearly 400,000 Jews, who have been encouraged to live in settlements within the territory. The West Bank has changed hands several times.

Initially planned to be part of the Palestinian state in the UN Partition of 1947, Jordan took control of it in the Arab-Israeli War of 1948. After the Six-Day War in 1967, Israel gained full control over the West Bank and began encouraging settlements as civilian defensive outposts against neighboring aggressors. Though Israel has retained control over the West Bank, it offered Palestinians a subnational autonomy to govern it and the Gaza Strip during the Oslo Accords of the 1990s. At that point, the Palestinian Authority (the Palestinian subnational government) took control of the area. Since then, the more moderate Palestinian political party (and the former terrorist group's political wing, the Palestinian Liberation Organization) has maintained control over the West Bank. In 2002, the more conservative Sharon government of Israel began constructing a wall around the West Bank to further divide it from the rest of Israel's land surrounding it. Any questions of the West Bank territory then must address issues of Israeli settlements, the wall, and the role of the Palestinian Authority in the region.

Almost half of the 5.6 million Palestinians who remain in Israel live in the West Bank, another third live in the Gaza Strip. The Gaza Strip, however, is only 139 square miles, making it the most densely populated place in the world. Further, whereas almost 60 percent of the West Bank is rural (with only about eight medium-sized towns throughout the 2,100 square miles),

Gaza consists of cities, towns, and eight crowded refugee camps, home to over 800,000 people (i.e., 60% of the population).

Like the West Bank, the Gaza Strip has changed hands several times. Initially planned to be part of the Palestinian state in the UN Partition of 1947, Egypt took control of it during the Arab-Israeli War of 1948. Then, after the Six-Day War in 1967, Israel gained full control over the Gaza Strip. It too offered Palestinians the Gazan territory during the Oslo Accords of the 1990s to be governed by the Palestinian Authority. However, the overcrowded conditions in Gaza have created a more extremist sentiment than in its more moderate counterpart, the West Bank (e.g., the rise of Hamas during the Second Intifada in the early 2000s).

Hamas has used Gaza as its organizational headquarters. After Hamas gained a majority of the seats in the Palestinian Authority of 2006, Israel and the United States attempted to back the more moderate Fatah in the West Bank as it entered Gaza to expel Hamas. Hamas responded by firing rockets at Israel in 2007. Since then, the Palestinian Authority and Israel have continually left Hamas out of peace talks. It has chosen to continue to fire rockets from Gaza at Israeli civilian targets (e.g., towns and airports) and an Israeli nuclear reactor near Gaza in Dimona. As Israel returns fire into Gaza, it has been responsible for killing many Palestinian civilians. In the last clash between Hamas and Israel in 2014, nearly 2,100 civilians (of whom 495 were children and 253 women) in Gaza were said to have died in the crossfire compared to about sixty Israeli soldiers.

As a result, Gaza's discussion must address the human rights concerns of overcrowding (both in and outside of refugee camps) and attacks on civilians from rocket fire. Further, any issues of political sovereignty must address Hamas's control over Gaza and its extreme views.

Jerusalem has been a holy site to both the Jews and Arabs (Muslims and Christians) who live within Israel. The original partitioning plan by the United Nations sought to make Jerusalem an "international city" under the legal jurisdiction of the United Nations and open to all visitors. This status was never realized, however, as the Arab-Israeli War soon broke out. After the armistice between Israel and its neighbors, Israel established control over West Jerusalem, and Jordan controlled East Jerusalem (home of the Western Wall and the Dome of the Rock). After the Six-Day War in 1967, Israel took complete control over East Jerusalem and has encouraged settlers to expand their presence in the area.

As noted above, in 1980, the Israeli government passed a law declaring Jerusalem as its capital. However, the UN Security Council passed Resolution 478, stating that the law to be null and void. The United States abstained as it sees Jerusalem's best future as an international city (a significant contention between the United States and Israel). Israel still regards Jerusalem as its "eternal capital," moving its political capital to West Jerusalem in 1949, though the international community accepts Tel Aviv as its capital.

About 200,000 Palestinians live in East Jerusalem and about the same number of Jewish settlers (with the Netanyahu government encouraging thousands of new settlement homes in 2014). Currently, most moderate Palestinians in the West Bank see East Jerusalem as the future capital of a Palestinian state. However, Jerusalem's future is a significant area of contention with Israel as this would mean the Western Wall would be inaccessible to Jews. Any discussion of peace talks must include an agreement over the future of Jerusalem, specifically East Jerusalem.

On December 5, 2017, President Trump announced his intention to move the U.S. Embassy from Tel Aviv to Jerusalem. Following the announcement, Pope Francis said he was "profoundly concerned" about recent developments and called for Jerusalem's status quo to be respected. The Saudi Press Agency reported having told Trump that King Salman of Saudi Arabia warned: "Such a dangerous step is likely to inflame the passions of Muslims around the world due to the great status of Jerusalem and the al-Aqsa Mosque."

In his first public remarks since confirmation of a change in U.S. policy, Netanyahu avoided any mention of the development, instead emphasizing in general terms Israel's "irreplaceable and unique alliance" with the United States during a speech in Jerusalem. On December 21 of 2017, 128 UN member countries voted on a resolution expressing condemnation at President Trump's decision to recognize Jerusalem as Israel's capital. The U.S. Embassy opened in Jerusalem in May of 2018.

THE MOOT COURT: *PALESTINE VS. ISRAEL*

In 2004, the International Court of Justice issued an advisory opinion on the Israel-Palestinian conflict. The Court determined Israel's choice to build a wall in the West Bank to violate international law. With the legal victory and the recognition of Observer status by the United Nations, this fictional scenario will have Palestine as the Applicant pushing for full recognition as a state before the International Court of Justice. In defense of the status quo, Israel will serve as the Respondent, arguing against Palestinian statehood. For this moot court, the legal question posed before the International Court of Justice is: *Does the Palestinian territory meet the criteria for statehood under the Montevideo Convention?*

As this legal question is an existential one, the script for this moot court will need to be modified to reflect a question of existence rather than a violation of an obligation.

NOTES

1. United Nations General Assembly, "Future Government of Palestine," A/Res/181(II), November 29, 1947. Available at: https://unispal.un.org/DPA/DPR/unispal.nsf/0/7F0AF2BD897689B785256C330061D253.

2. Oxford Encyclopedic Dictionary of International Law, "Quasi-State," Oxford University Press. Available at: https://www.oxfordreference.com/view/10.1093/acref/9780195389777.001.0001/acref-9780195389777.

3. Wilson, Woodrow, "Wilson's Fourteen Points," *Woodrow Wilson Presidential Library Retrieved* 12, no. 05 (1918): 2007.

4. The Avalon Project, "Covenant of the League of Nations," Yale Law School. Available at: https://avalon.law.yale.edu/20th_century/leagcov.asp.

5. United Nations, "Charter of the United Nations," October 24, 1945. Available at: https://unispal.un.org/DPA/DPR/unispal.nsf/0/7F0AF2BD897689B785256C330061D253.

6. International Committee of the Red Cross, "Convention (IV) Relative to the Protection of Civilian Persons in Time of War," August 12, 1949. Available at: https://ihl-databases.icrc.org/ihl/COM/380-600054.

7. "Anglo-French Declaration," Woodrow Wilson Presidential Library, November 9, 1918. Available at: http://presidentwilson.org/items/show/27610.

8. The Avalon Project, "British White Paper of 1939," Yale Law School. Available at: https://avalon.law.yale.edu/20th_century/brwh1939.asp.

9. United Nations General Assembly, "Future Government of Palestine," A/Res/181(II), November 29, 1947. Available at: https://unispal.un.org/DPA/DPR/unispal.nsf/0/7F0AF2BD897689B785256C330061D253.

10. Ibid.

11. Ibid.

12. United States Congress, "Proceedings and Debates of the 85th Congress: First Session 1957," Indiana University Press, 2013.

13. Israel Ministry of Foreign Affairs, "Declaration of Establishment of State of Israel," December 14, 1948. Available at: https://mfa.gov.il/mfa/foreignpolicy/peace/guide/pages/declaration%20of%20establishment%20of%20state%20of%20israel.aspx.

14. Ibid.

15. Israel Ministry of Foreign Affairs, "Declaration of Establishment of State of Israel," December 14, 1948. Available at: https://mfa.gov.il/mfa/foreignpolicy/peace/guide/pages/declaration%20of%20establishment%20of%20state%20of%20israel.aspx.

16. Lachenmann, Frauke, and Rüdiger Wolfrum, eds. *The Law of Armed Conflict and the Use of Force: The Max Planck Encyclopedia of Public International Law.* Oxford University Press, 2016.

17. United Nations Security Council, "Middle East," S/Res/242, November 22, 1977. Available at: https://www.un.org/securitycouncil/content/resolutions-adopted-security-council-1967.

18. Human Right Watch, "Two Authorities, One Way, Zero Dissent," October 23, 2018. Available at: https://www.hrw.org/report/2018/10/23/two-authorities-one-way-zero-dissent/arbitrary-arrest-and-torture-under.

19. Federation of American Scientists, "The Covenant of Hamas: main Points," Available at: https://fas.org/irp/world/para/docs/880818a.htm.

Chapter 4

Treaties

Treaties serve as the least ambiguous indication of each states' rights and obligations under international law. Dating back to the first treaty, etched into clay and codified the terms of a peace agreement between rival city-states in Mesopotamia over four millennia ago, treaties have been honored as a key instrument in making lasting agreements between parties. Part of this is a sense of obligation on the parties of a treaty that the agreements should be honored. The question to be explored in this chapter is at what point in the negotiations between parties does an actor become obligated to the treaty's terms?

In the late 1990s, the United States joined 120 states in adopting the Rome Statute of the International Criminal Court. This treaty would establish a permanent judicial organ to try individuals for the most egregious crimes committed (including genocide, crimes against humanity, and other serious war crimes). After noting some reservations, the Clinton administration chose to sign the statute but not ratify it, which it has done with other treaties in the past. After George W. Bush came to power, his government chose the unprecedented choice to "unsign" the statute, noting that the signing of a treaty gives no "legal obligation" for an actor to be accountable to it. America's choice led to several legal questions. At what point is a state bound to it? Can a state legally unsign a treaty once signed? And, if it does so, what is the legal effect of this "unsigning?"

This chapter will examine the Treaty on Treaties, a—well, treaty—offers guidance for when states become bound to treaties. Next, it will look at the purpose and jurisdiction of the International Criminal Court. And finally, this chapter will investigate the devolving relationship the United States had with the International Criminal Court leading up to its decision to unsign its founding document.

WHEN IS A STATE BOUND TO A TREATY?

In 1969, the international community took their love of treaties to a new level, creating a treaty that was all about—you guessed it—treaties. The Vienna Convention on the Law of Treaties is a treaty signed by 131 states.[1] As the topic is all about treaties, the Vienna Convention on the Law of Treaties has been lovingly called the "Treaty on Treaties" or the VCLT. The Vienna Convention on the Law of Treaties offers insights into the two distinct steps that most states must take to become a party to a treaty. The first is to sign the treaty, and the second step is to ratify it.

Signing a Treaty

The United Nations interprets Article 12 of the VCLT to read that most treaties require a *signature ad Referendum.*[2] This signature expresses a state's willingness to continue the treaty-making process. In rare cases (mentioned in Article 12, section 1, subsection c of the Vienna Convention on the Laws of Treaties), there may exist a treaty in which signatures can be *definitive* without a second step. Still, these treaties are rare, and a treaty must expressly mention that a signature alone binds that state to the treaty's provisions for it to do so.

Further, Article 7 of the Vienna Convention on the Laws of Treaties places the power of signing a treaty firmly in the hands of the executive branch of states, unless otherwise appointed. Article II, Section 2, of the U.S. Constitution states that "the President shall have Power, by and with the Advice and Consent of the Senate to make Treaties, provided two-thirds of the Senators present concur."[3]

Ratifying a Treaty

In its broadest sense, ratification is the process by which a state legally consents to be bound by a treaty. Whereas the signatory first step is almost always the executive's role, the ratification process means different things for each state. Most often, though, both the executive and legislative organs participate in the ratification process.

Here is where things get a little tricky. Though technically the president's power to make a treaty requires the Advice and Consent of the Senate, the Senate's vote does not determine the United States to be bound by the agreement (i.e., ratification). Instead, the Senate votes on accepting a ratification resolution (thus voting in ratification support).

Though many treaties that are signed by the United States get ratified, many notable ones do not. Some significant treaties the United States failed to ratify are the Convention on Discrimination against Women (CEDAW) (1981),

Convention on the Rights of the Child (1995), the Comprehensive Test Ban Treaty (1996), and the Kyoto Protocol (1998). There was a perceived failure to get the two-thirds votes to support its ratification in each of these cases. In each case, the executive sends the treaty to the Senate Committee on Foreign Relations, but it never makes it to a floor vote.

The second paragraph of Article VI of the U.S. Constitution is known as the supremacy clause. It states that "the laws of the United States which shall be made in pursuance thereof; and all treaties made, or which shall be made, under the authority of the United States, shall be the supreme law of the land." This clause asserts that both Congressional acts (and other federal laws) *and international treaties* shall be considered supreme to any other laws (e.g., state, local, and municipal laws) and are considered equal. As a result, after the Constitution, the ranking of law in the United States is (1) federal laws *and international treaties*, (2) then state laws, and (3) finally local laws.

In practice, treaties tend to be accepted legally as equal to Congressional acts so long as (1) they are not in direct conflict with Congressional acts, or (2) they require Congress to do something new. In such cases, Chief Justice Marshall explained that treaties that do not need anything of Congress are self-executing. In non-self-executing treaties, they may be theoretically equal to Congressional acts, but they will not have the financial and political support of Congress (Text Box 4.1).

TEXT BOX 4.1   VIENNA CONVENTION ON THE LAW OF TREATIES (1969) [ARTICLES 1, 7, AND 12]

Article 1

The present Convention applies to treaties between States.

Article 7

A person is considered as representing a State for the purpose of adopting or authenticating the text of a treaty or for the purpose of expressing the consent of the State to be bound by a treaty if he produces appropriate full powers . . . [or] in virtue of their functions and without having to produce full powers, the following are considered as representing their State:

1. Heads of State, Heads of Government and Ministers for Foreign Affairs, for the purpose of performing all acts relating to the conclusion of a treaty;

2. Heads of diplomatic missions, for the purpose of adopting the text of a treaty between the accrediting State and the State to which they are accredited;

3. Representatives accredited by States to an international conference or to an international organization or one of its organs, for the purpose of adopting the text of a treaty in that conference, organization or organ.

Article 12

1. The consent of a State to be bound by a treaty is expressed by the signature of its representative when:
   a. the treaty provides that signature shall have that effect;
   b. it is otherwise established that the negotiating States were agreed that signature should have that effect; or
   c. the intention of the State to give that effect to the signature appears from the full powers of its representative or was expressed during the negotiation.
2. For the purposes of paragraph 1:
   a. the initialing of a text constitutes a signature of the treaty when it is established that the negotiating States so agreed;
   b. the signature ad referendum of a treaty by a representative, if confirmed by his State, constitutes a full signature of the treaty.

When Does *Pacta Sunt Servanda* Apply?

In the preamble of the Vienna Convention, it mentions three fundamental principles undergirding all treaties. The first is the principle of free consent (i.e., that actors enter into agreements freely). The second is the principle of good faith (i.e., that actors are honest about their ability and willingness to meet their obligations). And the final principle is *pacta sunt servanda* (Latin for "agreements must be kept"), which creates a sense of responsibility for parties to comply with the agreement).

The preamble mentions these principles as being "universally recognized," and Article 18 of the VCLT explicitly obligates all states to "refrain from acts which would defeat the object and purpose of a treaty" in two circumstances. First, the article discusses the time in which a state has signed a treaty (or some equivalent act) but has not yet ratified it. In this case, the article states that a state cannot act in a manner that would defeat the object and purpose of a treaty "until it shall have made its intention clear not to become a party to the treaty." Second, the article mentions that a state cannot defeat a treaty's object and purpose once it has ratified it.

Most fascinatingly, the United States signed the Vienna Convention on the Laws of Treaties on April 24, 1970. Then in November of 1971, President Nixon submitted the Vienna Convention for the advice and consent of the Senate to ratification, stating that "The international community as a whole will surely benefit from the adoption of uniform rules on such subjects as the conclusion and entry into force of treaties, their interpretation and application, and other technical matters."[4] Though Nixon sent the VCLT to Congress, it died in committee, last being considered April 30, 1974.

As for the current status of the United States toward the Vienna Convention, the State Department notes that, though the United States is not a party to the Vienna Convention, "it considers many of the provisions of the Vienna Convention on the Law of Treaties to constitute customary international law on the law of treaties."[5] Pacta sunt servanda is a principle that has existed in international customary law for centuries (Text Box 4.2).

TEXT BOX 4.2   VIENNA CONVENTION ON THE LAW OF TREATIES (1969) [PREAMBLE AND ARTICLE 18]

Preamble

Noting that the principles of free consent and of good faith and the pacta sunt servanda rule are universally recognized.

Article 18

A State is obliged to refrain from acts which would defeat the object and purpose of a treaty when:

1. It has signed the treaty or has exchanged instruments constituting the treaty subject to ratification, acceptance or approval, until it shall have made its intention clear not to become a party to the treaty; or
2. It has expressed its consent to be bound by the treaty, pending the entry into force of the treaty and provided that such entry into force is not unduly delayed.

Once a state ratifies and is bound by a treaty, it must make a formal declaration to withdraw from it. If a state wishes to leave a treaty, it must follow steps for termination based on provisions outlined in the treaty or present its written desire to leave the treaty at least one year before doing so.

THE INTERNATIONAL CRIMINAL COURT

The Rome Statute of the International Criminal Court is the establishing treaty for the international organization, the International Criminal Court.[6] The organization's mandate is to serve as a court to prosecute and adjudicate individuals accused of the most serious crimes in international law: genocide, war crimes, and crimes against humanity.

On July 1, 2002, after sixty states (i.e., the requisite number) ratified the agreement, the Rome Statute entered into force, and the ICC was established as the first permanent criminal court to exist. The ICC's headquarters is in the Netherlands in a small beach town that has become the center of international public law, the Hague.

The Legal and Judicial Precedents for the ICC

Before the ICC, temporary international judicial bodies existed to adjudicate criminal acts within specific conflicts. There were two tribunals established by the victors of World War II and later two tribunals established in the 1990s to adjudicate crimes committed during the Rwandan genocide (1994) and the Yugoslav Wars (1992 to 1995).

The Nuremberg & Tokyo Trials

The Nuremberg Trials took place from 1945 to 1946, and the Tokyo Trials took place from 1946 to 1948. The London Agreement, signed by the United States, the United Kingdom, France, and the Soviet Union, established the Nuremberg Trials. Later, the Nuremberg Charters allowed each of these states to appoint two justices to serve on the tribunals and outlined the crimes for which the Allies prosecuted German officials. In 1946, the U.S. government issued a second identical Charter, the Tokyo Charter, which established the International Military Tribunal for the Far East. The three crimes—crimes against peace, war crimes, and crimes against humanity—all had legal precedence in the Hague Convention of 1907.

The Geneva Conventions (1948)

Nation-states held various meetings between 1864 and 1949, attempting to codify the laws of war (*jus in bello*). These meetings produced various earlier treaties (e.g., Convention for the Amelioration of the Wounded in Time of War in 1964, Hague Conventions of 1899 and 1907, and the Convention Relating to the Treatment of Prisoners of War in 1929) that built upon one another, culminating in the four Geneva Conventions of 1948. As a result, much of what we know about the Geneva Conventions was not drafted in

1948. Instead, most were created over eight decades of negotiation among the great powers.

Thus, in 1949, the International Red Cross conference in Stockholm extended and codified the existing provisions. The conference developed four conventions, which were approved in Geneva on August 12, 1949: (1) the Convention for the Amelioration of the Condition of the Wounded and Sick in Armed Forces in the Field, (2) the Convention for the Amelioration of the Condition of the Wounded, Sick, and Shipwrecked Members of Armed Forces at Sea, (3) the Convention Relative to the Treatment of Prisoners of War, and (4) the Convention Relative to the Protection of Civilian Persons in Time of War.

The importance of the Geneva Conventions in 1948 was twofold. Following World War II, there was a moral push to codify the international laws of war across all states. As a result, every state in the world is a party to the four Geneva Conventions. Second, the fourth convention sought comprehensive protection for civilians in war—something the previous treaties failed to do.

The same year the Geneva Conventions went into force, the UN General Assembly tasked the International Law Commission (ILC) with drafting a statute for a future international criminal court to hold individuals accountable for crimes committed that violated crucial provisions within the Geneva Conventions. Three years later, the commission submitted a draft statute, but the General Assembly postponed the vote. In 1989, the project was resurrected and became a primary goal of the General Assembly, however, following the atrocities in Yugoslavia and Rwanda.

The International Criminal Tribunal of Yugoslavia & Rwanda (the 1990s)

From the end of WWII to the 1990s, the concept of the rights afforded to human beings (international human rights) and specifically the rights within war (international humanitarian law) had grown significantly. Many, outraged at the scale of atrocities committed in two separate conflicts—one in the Socialist Federation of Yugoslavia and the other in Rwanda—led the UN Security Council to create two temporary tribunals to address crimes committed within these two conflicts. The UN Security Council created the International Criminal Tribunal for Rwanda (ICTR) to address "serious violations of international humanitarian law committed in Rwanda" from January 1st, 1994, to December 31st, 1994.[7] Similarly, the UN Security Council created International Criminal Tribunal for Yugoslavia (ICTY) had jurisdiction over the territory of the former Yugoslavia from 1991 to the present to "prosecute and try individuals on four categories of offenses: grave breaches of the 1949 Geneva conventions, violations of the laws or customs of war, genocide, and crimes against humanity."[8]

The Rome Statute of the International Criminal Court

The success of the previous courts led the UN General Assembly to pass a resolution to convene a diplomatic conference (held in Rome) to establish a permanent international criminal court. The conference would conclude in Rome in July of 1998. After sixty states become a party, the treaty would enter into force on July 1st, 2002.

Most Serious Crimes

The International Criminal Court can hear cases only on crimes considered the "most serious crimes of concern to the international community." Article 5 of the Rome Statute lists four crimes, three of which were automatically adopted when the ICC was established. The fourth was conditional under the adoption of a future provision (and is still being debated). The four crimes are genocide, crimes against humanity, war crimes, the crime of aggression.

Article 6 of the Rome Statute defines genocide as "acts committed with intent to destroy, in whole or in part, a national, ethnical, racial or religious group." The intent to enact genocide is enough to be charged with this crime. Though commonly genocide is understood to be conducted against a large group of people, there is no final consensus on how many people must be targeted for an act to be considered genocidal (as opposed to mass murder). Moreover, actions that can be deemed genocidal may not be directly intended to kill people but may have an indirect effect of the intent to destroy a group of people (e.g., imposing measures intended to prevent births and forcibly transferring children of one group to another).

Article 7 of the Rome Statute defined and prohibited any crimes against humanity. Like genocidal acts, crimes against humanity are also crimes considered a "widespread and systematic" nature. The difference between these two crimes was intent. In genocide, the acts are to destroy a group of people. In contrast, crimes of humanity include actions that psychologically deprive a group of their essential humanity (e.g., enslavement, enforced disappearance of persons, and torture).

The third crime included in the Rome Statute, and thus able to be tried by the ICC, is war crimes. This is a broad category and must be understood strategically. In terms of which war crimes the Rome Statute includes, these are best viewed as a list of offenses chosen from the larger Geneva Conventions for their importance and that there was consensus around these by states (e.g., no attack on civilian food supply). Moreover, this list was one that could be added to by the member-states in the future.

The fourth and final crime included in the Rome Statute is the crime of aggression, or in essence, the crime of starting a conflict. IN keeping with the UN Charter, a state may only launch an attack if attacked. Thus all acts of force other than self-defense are forbidden in international law.

The ICC jurisdiction to try crimes of aggression was not automatic, but it requires the negotiation of a future provision to occur. Politically, this crime's inclusion brought many states to the table as a check on powerful states' interventions into other states. In practice, this crime category has been debated without much progress in the court's history.

How Does a Case Go Before the ICC?

As noted above, only allegations of the above crimes are investigated by the ICC. Further, because the Rome Statute did not go into force until July 1, 2002, no one can be held accountable for crimes committed before that day.

The ICC is a "court of last resort" meant to complement national courts rather than supersede them. Based on the complementarity principle, Article 17 of the Rome Statute states that the ICC can only try a case when a state "is unwilling or unable genuinely to carry out the investigation or prosecution." The ICC cannot hear a case if (1) a state has investigated the matter and determined it was not worth prosecuting, (2) any national court already tried the accused individual, or (3) the case does not meet the threshold of alleged violations of "most serious crimes." Article 17 makes exceptions for situations in which proceedings were unjustifiably delayed or conducted in a manner that appears inconsistent with their purpose.

Even if the allegations stem from acts after July 1, 2002, and the court has determined no other court has begun the process of adjudicating the alleged crime, then there are other concerns of jurisdiction. Below are the scenarios in which the ICC's jurisdiction might apply. Once a state becomes a party to the Statute, it *must* accept the court's jurisdiction over all of the acts both within its territory or by its nationals (i.e., Article 12) after a seven-year transition period. State parties may also recommend crimes committed outside of their territory or by foreign nationals (i.e., Article 14).

The UN Security Council's role in determining which cases came to trial was a contentious issue in Rome. The original draft of the ILC granted the UN Security Council's permanent members (P5) veto over which cases went before the ICC.

Instead, negotiating states made a compromise, disallowing an outright veto by the P5 but allowing a deferral of any case for twelve months (noted in Article 12). It does not, however, prevent the possibility of one of these states continually deferring a case not to allow it to appear before the ICC. Though the P5 cannot veto a case outright, the UN Security Council does have the power to refer any matter to the ICC (see Article 13b). One final way in which a case can come to court (mentioned in Article 15). The ICC Prosecutor may begin a case *proprio motu* (Latin for "on her impulse").

As a result, individuals alleged of committed serious crimes in international law may appear before the ICC if a state party, the UNSC, or the ICC prosecutor submits evidence for a case to the international organization. Further, if the ICC issues a warrant for an individual, a state must assist in arresting that individual *unless* this assistance would go against the state's obligations under international law (Article 98) (Text Box 4.3).

TEXT BOX 4.3   ROME STATUTE OF THE INTERNATIONAL CRIMINAL COURT (1998) [ARTICLE 98]

Article 98

Cooperation with respect to waiver of immunity and consent to surrender

1. The Court may not proceed with a request for surrender or assistance which would require the requested State to act inconsistently with its obligations under international law with respect to the State or diplomatic immunity of a person or property of a third State, unless the Court can first obtain the cooperation of that third State for the waiver of the immunity.
2. The Court may not proceed with a request for surrender which would require the requested State to act inconsistently with its obligations under international agreements pursuant to which the consent of a sending State is required to surrender a person of that State to the Court, unless the Court can first obtain the cooperation of the sending State for the giving of consent for the surrender.

THE U.S. DECISION TO "UNSIGN" THE ROME STATUTE

The Clinton administration was divided on the issue of the ICC during the negotiation of the Rome Statute. On the one hand, Clinton seemed to be a strong proponent for deterring and punishing egregious criminal acts rhetorically. For example, he established the first-ever Office of War Crimes Issues in the Department of State to report on directly and investigate criminal atrocities. On the other hand, when faced with the genocide in Rwanda, Clinton was criticized for failing to prevent the genocide from occurring and later spreading. Initially, the Clinton administration was quite supportive of the ICC when it arrived in Rome to discuss the details of the court.

However, soon it began criticizing what it saw as a shift in power away from the UN Security Council. According to the State Department, the representatives from the United States "stressed that the ICC must operate in coordination, not in conflict, with the UN Security Council."[9] Specifically, they opposed that other states and ICC Prosecutor could bring forth investigations without a referral from the UN Security Council and that the Security Council could only defer, and not veto, investigations.

On the day the treaty was opened for signatures, December 31st, 2000, President Clinton announced that the United States would sign the Rome Statute but would not submit it to the Senate for ratification. In a statement about his choice to sign the treaty, Clinton stated that he was concerned with "significant flaws in the treaty," including the power it had to "claim jurisdiction over personnel of states" that had not ratified the Rome Statute.[10] Ultimately, however, Clinton chose to sign the Rome Statute. He reasoned that "with signature . . . we will be in a position to influence the evolution of the court. Without [a] signature, we will not." As he would leave office just three weeks later, Clinton also included that he would not recommend that his successor submit the treaty to the Senate "until our fundamental concerns are satisfied."

After taking office, President George W. Bush also began working to protect U.S. personnel from the ICC's jurisdiction. Starting in April of 2002, the Bush administration created a template for bilateral non-surrender agreements. The administration made these agreements with other states who were party to the International Criminal Court. In these agreements, other states promised that they would not assist nor allow U.S. nationals in their territory to be surrendered or transferred to the ICC for prosecution. The United States argued these agreements complied with Article 98 of the Rome Statute, which allows states not to comply with a "request for surrender or assistance" if this request requires the state to "act inconsistently with its obligations under international law." The United States concluded more than 100 of these agreements, even calling them Article 98 Agreements, after the Rome Statute provision they sought to exploit.

Then, in May 2002, President Bush's Under Secretary of State for Arms Control and International Security, John R. Bolton, sparked controversy in the international community when he penned a letter to the UN Secretary-General. In the letter, Bolton explained that the "United States does not intend to become a party to the treaty" and has "no legal obligations arising from its signature" and thus the intention not to become a party should be "reflected in the depositary's status lists relating to this treaty." In essence, the Bush administration was asking the United Nations to remove the United States from Rome Statute signatories. In an op-ed article in the Washington Post, Bolton advocated this action, referring to this step as "unsigning."[11]

The problem is that no state has ever "unsigned" a treaty before or since.[12] Before the rise of modern democracies, legislative branches did not exist to play a role in the treaty-making process. With the advent of a division of powers within governments, the treaty-making process allows for more voices, and more roadblocks, to eventual ratification. The United States has a particularly high threshold for treaty-making as it requires the executive and two-thirds of the Senate to be in favor of a treaty for ratification to occur. As a result, many treaties have been signed by the U.S. executive. However, the Senate votes against a resolution of ratification, or the treaty resolution is never presented for a vote. The step to unsign a treaty made clear, however, that the United States wished to no longer be a signatory to the treaty (instead of signing it and not ratifying it). In response, some argued this step met the obligation of the right to *pacta sunt servanda*, codified in the Vienna Convention of Laws and Treaties and present in customary law, while others argued it directly violated it.

After "unsigning" the Rome Statute, the United States took three additional steps to protect its military personnel, officials, and nationals from ICC claims of jurisdiction. In June of 2002, the United States vetoed a UN Security Council Resolution to extend UN peacekeepers' presence to Bosnia. To overturn this veto, the United States required a stipulation that guaranteed U.S. military personnel stationed in Bosnia were not subject to ICC jurisdiction. Following tense negotiations, the UN Security Council passed Resolution 1422 in July of 2002. This Resolution invoked the power of the UNSC to defer any cases for one year. Though the ICC has not investigated U.S. operations, this Resolution protected "current or former officials or personnel from a contributing State not a Party to the Rome Statute over acts or omissions relating to a United Nations established or authorized operation" from "investigation or prosecution of any such case, unless the Security Council decides otherwise."

Second, in August 2002, the American Service Member Protection Act was passed with strong bipartisan support. Some of the critical provisions make it illegal for U.S. federal and state law enforcement agencies to cooperate with the ICC directly, including sharing evidence, extradition of those alleged crimes by the court, and even providing any financial assistance to it—without exception from a presidential waiver. The act further noted that U.S. nationals' participation in UN peacekeeping missions would first need to be waived from ICC jurisdiction. Finally, one of the more controversial pieces of the statute noted that the U.S. "President is authorized to use all means necessary and appropriate to bring about the release of any person described in subsection who is being detained or imprisoned by, on behalf of, or at the request of the International Criminal Court." This led the act to be nicknamed "the Hague Invasion Act" by opponents of it.[13]

THE MOOT COURT: *THE NETHERLANDS VS. THE UNITED STATES*

When the United States made the unprecedented decision to withdraw its signature (i.e., unsign) the Rome Statute of the International Criminal Court, there was a mix of responses from the international community. Some claimed the act was not allowed, others were worried about the precedence it set, and still others congratulated the United States for taking steps to free itself from a treaty with which it no longer wished to be associated and even encouraged it to do so with other treaties as well.

Though the real-world scenario ends there, this chapter will present a case in which the international community took the legal question of unsigning a treaty to the International Court of Justice. Though in a real-world situation, the General Assembly would have most likely requested an advisory opinion, this moot court will imagine that the Netherlands served as the Applicants in a contentious case against the United States. The Netherlands was distinctly displeased with the American Service Members Protection Act (terms "the Hague Invasion Act"). It, therefore, would seem the most vocal opponent to the steps chosen by the Bush administration.

For this moot court, the legal question presented before the International Court of Justice is: *Though the U.S. argued that a signature offers "no legal obligations" to a treaty, others interpret customary law and the Vienna Convention on the Laws of Treaties to suggest otherwise. In your opinion, is the United States in violation of its obligations under customary law and the Vienna Convention on the Laws of Treaties by "unsigning" the Rome Statute.*

NOTES

1. United Nations. *Vienna Convention on the Law of Treaties*, May 23, 1969. Available at: https://treaties.un.org/doc/publication/unts/volume%201155/volume-1155-i-18232-english.pdf.

2. United Nations Dag Hammarskjold Library, "What is the Difference Between Signing, Ratification and Accession of UN Treaties?," Available at: https://ask.un.org/faq/14594.

3. United States of America, Constitution, September 17, 1787. Available at: https://www.refworld.org/docid/3ae6b54d1c.html.

4. The American Presidency Project, "Message to the Senate Transmitting the Vienna Convention on the Law of Treaties," November 22, 1971. Available at: https://www.presidency.ucsb.edu/documents/message-the-senate-transmitting-the-vienna-convention-the-law-treaties.

5. U.S. State Department Archives, "Vienna Convention," Available at: https://2009-2017.state.gov/s/l/treaty/faqs/70139.htm

6. United Nations General Assembly, *Rome Statute of the International Criminal Court*, June 17, 1998. Available at: https://www.icc-cpi.int/resource-library/documents/rs-eng.pdf.

7. United Nations International Residual Mechanism for Criminal Tribunals, "International Criminal Tribunal for Rwanda," Available at: https://unictr.irmct.org/.

8. United Nations International Residual Mechanism for Criminal Tribunals, "International Criminal Tribunal for the former Yugoslavia," Available at: https://www.icty.org/.

9. Bellinger, John. B. "The United States and the International Criminal Court: Where We've Been and Where We're Going," April 25, 2008. Remarks to the DePaul University College of Law. Available at: https://2001-2009.state.gov/s/l/rls/104053.htm.

10. Associated Press, "Clinton's Words: "The Right Action,'" *New York Times*, January 1, 2001. Available at: https://www.nytimes.com/2001/01/01/world/clinton-s-words-the-right-action.html.

11. Bolton, John, "Unsign That Treaty," *The Washington Post*, January 4, 2001. Available at: https://www.washingtonpost.com/archive/opinions/2001/01/04/unsign-that-treaty/36e310be-072d-44df-9aa4-6cff7ef098ce/.

12. McLaurin, Luke A, "Can the President "Unsign" a Treaty? A Constitutional Inquiry," *Wash. UL Rev* 84 2006): 1941. Available at: https://heinonline.org/HOL/LandingPage?handle=hein.journals/walq84&div=73&id=&page=.

13. Human Rights Watch, "U.S.: 'Hague Invasion Act' Becomes Law," August 3, 2002. Available at: https://www.hrw.org/news/2002/08/03/us-hague-invasion-act-becomes-law.

Chapter 5

International Customary Law

Though not all international law is formally codified in a written agreement, some are agreed upon through consistent observable and uniform practices by states enacted out of a sense of obligation. One of the most notable international customs is the right of self-defense by a state if threatened by another state. And yet, without clear provisions detailing the nature of this right, the obligations included with this right, and the conditions under which this right can apply, there can be some wiggle room among interpretations sounding the right to self-defense.

This chapter will focus on a famous incident between the United States and Great Britain in the early 1800s surrounding a commercial steamship named the *Caroline*. The *Caroline* incident, as it has been called since, illustrates the distinct difficulty for states in interpreting and applying unwritten law while a case is still unfolding and tensions run high. Next, this chapter will examine customary law in greater detail, presenting its benefits and challenges. Next, it will provide the background of the events leading to the *Caroline* and how the incident unfolded on December 29, 1837. Finally, the chapter will offer the exchange of letters between the United States and Great Britain that ultimately led to an easing of tensions and a clearer interpretation of the right to self-defense.[1]

WHAT IS CUSTOMARY LAW?

Article 38 of the Statute of the International Court of Justice includes "international custom" to be one of the accepted sources of international law. Unlike treaties, which are explicitly agreed upon, international customs are agreed upon through consistent and uniform practices of states, enacted out of a sense of obligation. How does someone know if a practice has reached the threshold of international custom?

First, a custom is an observable behavior of a state. It can be an action (e.g., responding to the threat of force with force), or it can be refraining from acting in the face of an action (e.g., not responding to a threat before the use of force is considered to be imminent). A second criterion that should be met for a behavior to be considered an international custom is the consistency of a behavior occurring for an extended period of time. The time period has been debated, but a common requirement is a century. A third criterion that should be met for a behavior to be considered an international custom is that this behavior is observed across multiple states. The criteria for uniformity have also been debated. Some suggest it needs to have at least a majority of states. Others suggest a majority is not needed if the major powers are included in the states who engage in this behavior.

It is not enough, however, for a state to enact a behavior out of habit. Instead, for a behavior to be an international custom, there must be supportive evidence that this behavior was enacted out of a sense of obligation to comply with the previous agreement. At times it is difficult, even for a state, to know what motivates it to act.

Though international customary law has existed for centuries, if not millennia, and the effects of customary law on international law's evolution are profound, questions surrounding this more amorphous set of laws. For example, though an act must be observed consistently over a period of time, just how long must this act be observed to be a custom? Does the same timeframe apply to relatively new and quickly evolving issue areas, such as cyberspace?

Similar questions surround the criteria of uniformity. How many states must act in a certain way for it to be considered uniformly customary? Are powerful states weighted more than weaker ones? And, finally, how can one be assured a state is acting out of a sense of obligation to the international custom and not out of inducements or coercion placed upon them by other states?

The right to use force (i.e., *jus ad bellum*, or "right to war") is justified in cases of the defense of existence to your territory and people. This is part of international customs and has been for millennia. The issue at hand is that, though this was an accepted custom, the conditions under which the right to use force for self-defense could be invoked were not codified in any international treaty. As a result, those claiming self-defense as their justification for conflict had no exact provision in a treaty they could rely upon to determine whether conditions were in place to justify violence.

Though we have provisions in an international treaty in which the right to self-defense is now codified, our case this week returns to a dispute between the British and Americans in the early nineteenth century when no such provision was formalized. You must instead investigate whether there existed an agreement on what conditions needed to be present for a state to be able to defend itself. At the time of the *Caroline* incident, there was an international scholar, Emmerich de Vattel, who wrote a tome called *The Law of Nations*.[2] In this work, Vattel defined the right of states to self-preservation when threatened by other states.

THE *CAROLINE* INCIDENT

William Lyon Mackenzie, a parliamentary representative from Ontario, returned home to Canada from Britain after failing to seek reform efforts within the royal government. In early December of 1837, Mackenzie attempted an uprising by invading the British armory and marching the streets of Toronto to city hall. When the British army fired shots to disperse the uprising, some of the rebels returned fire. After reaching city hall, Mackenzie demanded "independence and a convention to arrange details" from the British government.[3] In response, the British sent for more reinforcements. On December 7, 1,837, around 300 rebels gathered outside of a tavern in Toronto called Montgomery's. There more than 1,000 royal soldiers and militiamen marched toward the tavern. After overwhelming the rebel forces, these royalists torched the tavern to the ground.

After this standoff at Montgomery's in Toronto, William Lyon Mackenzie and nearly some 200 followers retreated to Navy Island, an uninhabited island off the coast of Ontario on the Canadian side of the Niagara River. On December 5, 1837, Mackenzie declared the island the Republic of Canada.

To arm the Canadian rebels, Mackenzie soon sought American citizens' assistance who were sympathetic to the revolutionary fight against the British. Though the U.S. government remained officially neutral, private American citizens began assisting Mackenzie and the other rebels in this effort. One New York businessman named William Wells purchased 75-foot-long cargo ships called the *Caroline* to help ferry armaments to the island from the United States.

On December 29, 1837, a Royal Navy officer, Andrew Drew, led around seventy Canadian militia members loyal to the British in seven ships from the Ontario mainland across the Niagara River Navy Island in search of the *Caroline*. According to the Niagara Falls Museum, the officers were in search of the *Caroline* as they believed Mackenzie would use this vessel to launch his invasion of the Canadian mainland.[4]

On their way to Navy Island, however, the loyalists sighted the *Caroline* on the American bank of the river. The British loyalists chose to cross the river to Fort Schlosser. When they reached the bank, the loyalists fired a musket at the watchmen, an African American crew member named Amos Durfee.

They then boarded the ship with swords and bayonets, scattering the other thirty-two crew members toward the shore (but killing none). Once emptied of its crew, the loyalists unmoored the *Caroline* from the dock, set it ablaze, and sent it adrift over Niagara Falls.

Though New York newspapers would claim more fatalities than Durfee, the loyalists' treatment of Durfee was quite brutal. After taking his body, they publicly displayed it in front of a recruiting tavern in Buffalo, New York, days later.

GOVERNMENT EXCHANGE OF LETTERS

Though the Canadian revolution led by Mackenzie died out when he was convicted and imprisoned in 1839, the U.S. response to the incident continued when an Englishman drinking in a tavern in New York claimed he had been present and responsible for the acts that occurred on the *Caroline*. Though a New York court case would ultimately prove he was not present on the *Caroline* and only boasting drunkenly, tensions reignite over this and other skirmishes along the U.S.-British-Canadian border.

In 1842, then U.S. secretary of state, Daniel Webster, lodged diplomatic protests with the British government's foreign minister, Lord Ashburton, claiming that the destruction of the *Caroline* violated the national sovereignty of the United States and requested a formal apology to be given. In response, Lord Ashburton asserted the right to self-defense as justification for the actions on the part of the loyalists. Snippets of this correspondence between the secretary of state—Daniel Webster—and his British counterpart—Lord Ashburton—are below. These letters illustrate how two states discussed the details of the international custom of self-defense in the nineteenth century before it was codified within a treaty and amid rising tensions between them (Text Box 5.1).

TEXT BOX 5.1   LETTER FROM U.S. SECRETARY OF STATE DANIEL WEBSTER TO BRITISH FOREIGN MINISTER LORD ASHBURTON ON APRIL 21, 1842

[It] will be for Her Majesty's Government to show, upon what state of facts, and what rules of national law, the destruction of the "*Caroline*" is to be defended. It will be for that Government to show a necessity of self-defense, instant, overwhelming, leaving no choice of means, and no moment for deliberation. It will be for it to show, also, that the local authorities of Canada,—even supposing the necessity of the moment authorized them to enter the territories of the United States at all,—did nothing unreasonable or excessive; since the act justified by the necessity of self-defense, must be limited by that necessity, and kept clearly within it.

It must be strewn that admonition or remonstrance to the persons on board the *"Caroline"* was impracticable, or would have been unavailing; it must be strewn that daylight could not be waited for; that there could be no attempt at discrimination, between the innocent and the guilty; that it would not have been enough to seize and detain the vessel; but that there was a necessity, present and inevitable, for attacking her, in the darkness of the night, while moored to the shore, and while unarmed men were asleep on board, killing some, and wounding others, and then drawing her into the current, above the cataract, setting her on fire, and, careless to know whether there might not be in her the innocent with the guilty, or the living with the dead, committing her to a fate, which fills the imagination with horror. A necessity for an this, the Government of the United States cannot believe to have existed.

When Webster did not get any serious response from the British, he sent a follow-up letter that July (Text Box 5.2).

TEXT BOX 5.2   LETTER FROM BRITISH FOREIGN MINISTER LORD ASHBURTON TO U.S. SECRETARY OF STATE DANIEL WEBSTER ON JULY 27, 1842

That act is of itself a wrong, and an offense to the sovereignty and the dignity of the United States, being a violation of their soil and territory-a wrong for which, to this day, no atonement, or even apology, has been made by Her Majesty's Government. Your Lordship cannot but be aware that self-respect, the consciousness of independence and national equality, and a sensitiveness to whatever may touch the honor of the country-a sensitiveness which this Government will ever feel and ever cultivate-make this a matter of high importance, and I must be allowed to ask for it your Lordship's grave consideration.

In 1840, as tempers remained high and the issue of the *Caroline* remained unresolved, a new issue further exacerbated the tensions.

Alexander Macleod, a former member of the British Royal Navy, visited the United States two years after the *Caroline* incident. While in a bar in

New York state, he drunkenly boasted that he had been a part of the attack on the *Caroline*. Some who overheard his drunken boast told New York state authorities, and he was arrested and charged with murder in a New York court.

Britain protested Macleod's arrest, stating that he was not responsible for criminal acts of murder in his official role as an officer in the British Royal Navy (but instead, he participated in the act as a private citizen participating in a loyalist militia). After the British government chose to pay Macleod's bail, an American mob formed outside of the prison and blocked his release. In the face of mounting tensions, both the British and American public called for their government to remain uncompromising.

This issue was further exacerbated by the lack of an extradition treaty (i.e., a treaty on how criminal acts by the national of one state would be handled by the state holding said national) agreed upon between the two states. After much back and forth, in which the British complained about the American inability to enforce order on their side of the border, Lord Ashburton finally threatened war if Macleod was found guilty of murder. Below are the key correspondences between Lord Ashburton and Secretary Webster concerning the *Caroline* incident in general and MacLeod in specific (Text Box 5.3).

TEXT BOX 5.3 LETTER FROM U.S. SECRETARY OF STATE DANIEL WEBSTER TO BRITISH FOREIGN MINISTRY LORD ASHBURTON ON JULY 28, 1842

It is so far satisfactory to perceive that we are perfectly agreed as to the general principles of international law applicable to this unfortunate case. Respect for the inviolable character of the territory of independent nations is the most essential foundation of civilization . . . you may be assured, Sir, that Her Majesty's Government set the highest possible value on this principle, and are sensible of their duty to support it by their conduct and example for the maintenance of peace and order in the world. If a sense of moral responsibility were not a sufficient surety for their observance of this duty towards all nations, it will be readily believed that the most common dictates of interest and policy would lead to it in the ease of a long conterminous boundary of some thousand miles with a country of such great and growing power as the United States of America, inhabited by a kindred race, gifted with all its activity and all its susceptibility on points of national honor.

Every consideration therefore leads us to set as highly as your Government can possibly do this paramount obligation of reciprocal respect for the independent territory of each. But, however, strong this duty may be it is admitted by all writers, by all Jurists, by the occasional practice of all nations, not excepting your own, that a strong overpowering necessity may arise, when this great principle may and must be suspended. It must be so for the shortest possible period, during the continuance of an admitted overruling necessity, and strictly confined within the narrowest limits imposed by that necessity. Self-defense is the first law of our nature and it must be recognized by every code which professes to regulate the condition and relations of man. Upon this modification, if I may so call it, of the great general principle, we seem also to be agreed, and on this part of the subject I have done little more than repeat the sentiments, though in less forcible language, admitted and maintained by you in the letter to which you refer me.

Supposing a man standing on ground where you have no legal right to follow him has a weapon long enough to reach you, and is striking you down and endangering your life, how long are you bound to wait for the assistance of the authority having the legal power to relieve your or, to bring the facts more immediately home to the ease, if cannon are moving and setting up in a battery which can reach you and are actually destroying life and property by their fire. If you have remonstrated for some time without effect and see no prospect of relief, when begins your right to defend yourself, should you have no other means of doing so, than by seizing your assailant on the verge of a neutral territory?

After some tumultuous proceedings in Upper Canada, which were of short duration and were suppressed by the Militia of the Country, the persons criminally concerned in them took refuge in the neighboring state of New York, and with a very large addition to their numbers openly collected, invaded the Canadian territory taking possession of Navy Island.

This invasion took place December 16, 1837; a gradual accession of numbers and of military ammunition continued openly, and though under the sanction of no public authority, at least with no public hindrance until the 29th of the same month, when several hundred men were collected, and twelve pieces of ordnance, which could only have been procured from some public store or arsenal, were actually mounted on Navy Island and were used to fire within easy range upon the unoffending inhabitants of the opposite shore. Remonstrances, wholly ineffectual were made; so ineffectual indeed that a Militia regiment, stationed on the neighboring American island, looked on without any attempt at interference, while shots were fired from the American island itself.

This force, formed of all the reckless and mischievous people of the border, formidable from their numbers and from their armament, had in their pay and as part of their establishment this steamboat Caroline, the important means and instrument by which numbers and arms were hourly increasing. I might safely put it to any candid man acquainted with the existing state of things, to say whether the military commander in Canada had the remotest reason on the 29th of December to expect to be relieved from this state of suffering by the protective intervention of any American authority. How long could a Government, having the paramount duty of protecting its own people be reasonably expected to wait for what they had then no reason to expect? What would have been the conduct American officers-what has been their conduct under circumstances much less aggravated? I would appeal to you, Sir, to say whether the facts which you say would alone justify this act, via: "a necessity of self defence, instant, overwhelming, leaving no choice of means and no moment for deliberation," were not applicable to this case in as high a degree as they ever were to any case of a similar description in the history of a nation.

It appears from every account that the expedition was sent to capture the *Caroline* when she was expected to be found on the British ground of Navy island, and that it was only owing to the orders of the rebel leader being disobeyed, that she was not so found. When the British officer came round the point of the island in the night, he first discovered that the vessel was moored to the other shore . . . I mention this circumstance to show also that the expedition was not planned with a premeditated purpose of attacking the enemy within the jurisdiction of the United States, but that the necessity of so doing arose from altered circumstances at the moment of execution.

The time of night was purposely selected as most likely to ensure the execution with the least loss of life, and it is expressly stated that, the strength of the current not permitting the vessel to be carried off, and it being necessary to destroy her by fire, she was drawn into the stream for the express purpose of preventing injury to persons or property of the inhabitants at Schlosser.

Although it is believed that a candid and impartial consideration of the whole history of this unfortunate event will lead to the conclusion that there were grounds of justification as strong as were ever presented in such cases, and above all that no slight of the authority of the United States was ever intended, yet it must be admitted that there was in the hurried execution of this necessary service a violation of territory, and I am instructed to assure you that Her Majesty's Government consider this as a most serious fact, that far from thinking that an event of this kind should be lightly risked, they would unfeignedly deprecate its recurrence. Looking back to what passed at this distance of time what is perhaps most to be regretted is that some explanation and apology for this occurrence was not immediately made: this with a frank explanation of the necessity of the case might and probably would have prevented much of the exasperation and of the subsequent complaints and recriminations to which it gave rise.

For his part, Daniel Webster returns Lord Ashburton's letter with a curt response. He calls for Great Britain to reconsider the loyalists' actions as acts of self-defense, and he refuses to release Alexander MacLeod from jail per Ashburton's wishes (Text Box 5.4).

TEXT BOX 5.4 LETTER FROM BRITISH FOREIGN MINISTER LORD ASHBURTON TO U.S. SECRETARY OF STATE DANIEL WEBSTER ON AUGUST 6, 1842

The President sees with pleasure that your Lordship fully admits those great principles of public law, applicable to cases of this kind, which this Government has expressed; and that on your part, as on ours, respect for the inviolable character of the territory of independent States is the most essential foundation of civilization. And while it is admitted, on both sides, that there are exceptions to this rule, he is gratified to find that your Lordship admits that such exceptions must come within the limitations stated.

Undoubtedly it is just, that while it is admitted that exceptions growing out of the great law of self-defense do exist, those exceptions should be confined to cases in which the necessity of that self-defense is instant, overwhelming, and leaving no choice of means, and no moment for deliberation.

Understanding these principles alike, the difference between the two Governments is only whether the facts in the case of the "Caroline" make out a case of such necessity for the purpose of self-defense.

As to that part of your Lordship's note which relates to other occurrences springing out of the ease of the "Caroline" with which occurrences the name of Alexander McLeod has become connected. This Government has admitted, that for an act committed by the command of his sovereign . . . an individual cannot be responsible, in the ordinary courts of another state. It would regard it as a high indignity if a citizen of its own, acting under its authority, and by its special command, in such cases, were held to answer in a municipal tribunal, and to undergo punishment, as if the behest of his Government were no defense or protection to him.

But your Lordship is aware that, in regular constitutional Governments, persons arrested on charges of high crimes can only be discharged by some judicial proceeding.

I have the honor to be, my Lord, with great consideration, your obedient servant,

DAN WEBSTER.

THE MOOT COURT: *THE UNITED STATES VS. GREAT BRITAIN*

Though the historical events following the *Caroline* incident ended with the exchange of letters, this court will present an imaginary arbitration proceeding between the two parties (though the Permanent Court of Arbitration would not be established until 1899).

In this scenario, each group will first present a standard for the custom of self-defense. Though the UN Charter formally codifies the right to self-defense, the Charter was not codified until 1948, one century after the *Caroline* affair occurred and well after our fictional case.

As a result, for this case, the actors involved are tasked with creating their criteria for self-defense based on mutual understandings revealed in the exchange of letters between Secretary Webster and Lord Ashburton. Thus the groups for this case must define self-defense before arguing whether the incidents surrounding the destruction of the *Caroline* meet the criteria for self-defense. Further, once an attack occurs, what acts constitute an appropriate self-defense response. For this moot court, there are two legal questions posed before the Permanent Court of Arbitration:

1. *Using the correspondence between the two statesmen, what is the agreed-upon interpretation of the conditions under which a state has the right to use force within customary law?*
2. *Based on an application of this interpretation, were the actions of the British against The Caroline and its crew on December 29, 1841 in compliance with their rights to self-defense?*

NOTES

1. The Avalon Project, "British-American Diplomacy," Yale Law School. Available at: https://avalon.law.yale.edu/subject_menus/brtreaty.asp.

2. de Vattel, Emer. *The Law of Nations Or The Principles of Natural Law Applied to the Conduct and to the Affairs of Nations Adn of Sovereigns*. Oceana Publications, 1964.

3. John Charles Dent. *The Story of the Upper Canadian Rebellion: Largely Derived from Original Sources and Documents*, Vol. 2. CB Robinson, 1885.

4. Ibid.

Chapter 6

General Principles

Treaties, and to a lesser extent customary law, provide a source of clear agreements among states on various issues. There are scenarios, however, in which international law is silent on a subject. In the 1980s, the European Court of Justice, the judicial organ of the European Communities (the name of the European Union at that time), heard a case on which no law existed. The issue concerned an alleged cartel formed among multinational corporations to price-fix iron ore products (e.g., steel). As free trade is a cornerstone of the European Communities, it launched an investigation into alleged cartel behavior among European mining and smelting corporations.

When the European Commission demanded documents from one of the cartel members' legal team, the Australian Mining & Smelting Europe Limited Corporation (AMSE), the lawyers refused to hand over the documents, citing client-attorney privilege. Most confoundingly, there was no mention—either for or against—the right of attorneys to protect the information given to them by their client within European law. A gap in the law is known as a legal lacuna.

As a result, the European Court of Justice heard the case between the European Commission and the AMSE. Within this case, the European Court of Justice needed first to determine if there was evidence of a general principle within its ten member-states' domestic laws. If so, its next task was to decide whether this general principle could be apple to the case between the European Commission and the AMSE.

This chapter will first explain the notion of general principles in international law in greater detail. Second, it will offer a review of the European Union's evolution from its founding organization to its present form, including its stated purpose to ensure the free trade of goods and services. Third, it will focus on the issue between the European Commission and the Australian Smelting Europe Limited Corporation (AMSE) over the investigation into alleged cartel behavior and the legal teams of AMSE's assertion attorney-client privilege protected them from turning over any documents. And finally, it will present the domestic laws of each of the ten-member states of the European Communities at the time of the case (i.e., 1982) so that the simulated European Court of Justice might determine if a general principle exists with the European Communities.

LEGAL LACUNAE AND GENERAL PRINCIPLES

When you think of International Law, you might imagine agreements made between states only. However, according to the International Court of Justice Statute mentioned in previous chapters, one international law source can come from domestic law. The notion of "general principles" in international law is that widely accepted domestic laws apply at the international level. However, the issue with a general principle is that it is unclear how many states must agree to it and how closely they need to agree to be fully applicable in international law.

HISTORY OF THE EUROPEAN UNION

The European Union started as an international organization meant to coordinate economic policies around coal and steel between Western European states after World War II. Over time the European Coal and Steel Community became the European Economic Community (in 1957), then the European Communities (1965), before finally being reorganized and renamed the European Union in 1993. Below is a quick look at the treaties associated with each state of the EU's development, as well as changes made at each stage.

Previous Organizations

The Treaty of Paris, ratified in 1952, created the European Coal and Steel Community as an administrative agency designed to integrate the coal and steel industries in Western Europe through a free trade area. The original members of the ECSC were France, West Germany, Italy, Belgium, the Netherlands, and Luxembourg.

The same members extended this free trade agreement five years later to create a common market, called the European Economic Community (EEC).

The EEC promoted the elimination of most trade barriers and prohibited monopolies and other agreements that might inhibit market competition. In 1965, the European Community combined with two separate organizations (one for atomic energy and the original European Coal & Steel Community) under the same international organization. The same members of the EEC signed the Brussels Treaty, creating the European Communities (ECs). The new organization also included the European Court of Justice as its judicial organ and an executive-legislative body, known as the European Commission.

The Treaty on European Union (TEU), also known as the Maastricht Treaty, created the European Union on February 7th, 1992, and came into force in 1993. The significant changes that distinguished the new European Union from its predecessors were that every citizen within the member states became EU citizens, and the introduction of a European Central Bank and the common currency, the Euro.

Waves of Enlargement

Initially beginning with only six member states, the European Union currently has twenty-seven member states (i.e., approximately 500 million people). This section will explore the motivations of states to join this ever-evolving union.

Though informally, the European Union has always been open to expanding its membership based on the following criteria, the Treaty on the European Union of 1993 codified the membership requirements, known as the Copenhagen criteria. First, a state must demonstrate the capacity to effectively implement the rules, standards, and policies of the EU law. Second, a state must guarantee democracy, the rule of law, human rights, and respect for and protect minorities. And finally, a state must have a functioning competitive market economy and be able to cope with competitive pressure and market forces within the European Union.

The original six European Coal & Steel Community members were France, West Germany, Italy, Belgium, the Netherlands, and Luxembourg. Following World War II, many saw the organization as a victory for liberalism. It created cooperation between France and Germany, Europe's historic rivals (though the Allied powers occupied West Germany at the time).

In 1973, Denmark, Ireland, and the United Kingdom joined. After the member-states in the European Economic Communities became key players on the economic stage, even a sovereignty-loving Britain changed its mind to not lag in economic growth. However, when Britain applied for membership, France vetoed twice (many argue because it wished to be the institution's leading power). Ireland and Denmark, heavily dependent upon the United Kingdom for their economic imports, followed it for the short-term so as to keep pace with it and with the long-term goal of developing independently from it.

In 1981, Greece gained membership after decades of military rule ended, and the member states found new economic markets attractive in a mounting recession. The same motivations (plus Greek precedence) motivated the ECs to allow for Portugal and Spain to become members three years later, bringing its membership to twelve.

After the fall of the Soviet Union, membership greatly expanded. Austria, Finland, and Sweden joined in 1995, and nine years later, ten more states joined (i.e., Czech Republic, Estonia, Hungary, Latvia, Lithuania, Malta, Poland, Slovakia, Slovenia, and Cyprus). In 2007, the two members, Bulgaria and Romania, joined after their accession was delayed over concerns about corruption, organized crime, human trafficking, and focus on the rule of law and concerns about the ability to be a participating member in Europe's free-market. In 2013, Croatia was able to join as well, after facing similar problems.

In 2016, Britain held a referendum on whether or not to leave the European Union, and many were shocked when the "leave" option won by 52 percent. Negotiations between the European Union and Britain have resulted in the British exit from the organization "Brexit," bringing the membership to twenty-seven.

The Rules against Tariffs, Monopolies, and Cartels

As noted earlier, the European Union, and all the organizations that preceded it, promoted free trade between member-states. One of the main goals of these organizations was to repeal any domestic laws that artificially increased the price of goods and services (e.g., tariffs, monopolies, and cartels). All the treaties that established and reorganized the European Union and its predecessors shared these common goals. As our case is from 1982, this chapter will focus on the treaty in force during this time: the Treaty of Rome.[1]

The Treaty of Rome requires all member-states of the ECs to repeal all tariffs (Article 18) and dismantle all monopolies (Article 37). Even after monopolies were no longer allowed, there would remain concerns that several smaller corporations might attempt to coordinate their prices by forming a cartel. Article 85 declares cartels to be "incompatible with the common market," while Article 86 prohibits specific acts, including imposing unfair costs or limiting production to drive up prices. Article 89 allows the European

Commission the right to assist in investigating any "alleged infringement of the above-mentioned principles."[2]

EUROPEAN COMMISSION VS. AUSTRALIAN MINING & SMELTING EUROPE LIMITED CORPORATION (AMSE)

Zinc is mined. It is then supplied to smelters, which melt it to extract impurities from it and combine it with other metals to form primary zinc ore. A secondary zinc ore can also be created by melting down zinc dust, ash, scraps, and even full products, thus recycling this material into a new product. Zinc metal is then used in various semi-finished and finished products such as paints, rubber, cosmetics, pharmaceuticals, plastics, inks, soaps, batteries, textiles, and electrical equipment.

In 1964, the major Western zinc mining and smelting companies joined together to create a zinc cartel, known as the Zinc Producer Group (ZPG). As the ECs produced about 20 percent of the world's zinc ore, at the time, many of the corporations operating within Europe joined this group. This group's goal was to keep zinc prices relatively high by determining how much zinc should be supplied on the global market. The miners agreed to never sell their zinc to speculators, who would likely buy the materials when demand was low and then resell them at a higher price when demand was high.

Some smelting corporations with mines outside of Europe, such as the Australian Mining & Smelting Europe Limited Corporation (AMSE), had an even more significant advantage over the market than others. These corporations would combine the mining part of the process and the smelting portion of the process into the same corporation to increase efficiency (noted in the name: Australian Mining & Smelting). This process is known as forwarding integration. It allows the smelting part of the process to be guaranteed a regular supply of mined zinc from their sister operations to use in their facilities. Meanwhile, other corporations without mining operations had to buy zinc on the open market.

In the late 1970s, the European Commission began investigating this larger cartel. As part of an investigation, the European Commission required each of the corporations that were members of the Zinc Producers Group to submit documents concerning price-fixing allegations. When the Commission requested documents from the AMSE, the corporation first delayed sending any documents, explaining its managing director was in Australia on business. Ten days later, the corporation sent only some of the documents requested, and the corporation's in-house counsel had heavily redacted passages within these documents. As for the other documents requested, the counsel had determined them unnecessary to send as they were "of no relevance."[3]

When the Commission insisted it had the right to investigate the corporation's premises in the United Kingdom to acquire the documents requested, the corporation refused to allow any Commission officials to enter their headquarters, citing attorney-client privilege. In response, the corporation applied for the European Court of Justice to determine the lawfulness of the Commission's actions under Article 173 of the Treaty of Rome, which states that "The Court of Justice shall review the lawfulness of acts other than recommendations or opinions of the Council and the Commission."[4]

Though the ECs had dozens of treaties and agreements, these treaties did not cover every issue. One area in which there is a legal lacuna was the issue of attorney-client privilege. In its broadest definition, the principle of attorney-client privilege rests on the assumption that an attorney can best help their client if they are privy to all the case's relevant facts. The logical reasoning for attorney-client privilege is that a client needs to divulge all information to their attorney without fear that a court can use the information given to the attorney as evidence. The European Court of Justice had to decide whether attorney-client privilege existed as a general principle in European law. If so, could it be applied to this particular case?

THE MOOT COURT: *THE AUSTRALIAN MINING & SMELTING EUROPE LIMITED CORPORATION (AMSE) VS. THE EUROPEAN COMMISSION*

To address the question of whether the Australian Smelting Europe Limited Corporation's legal team had a right to invoke attorney-client privilege, Justices of the European Court must first determine what threshold is needed for a general principle to exist. Does there need to be consensus across all states or just most for a general principle to exist? Moreover, does the consensus need to present the same rights and obligations under the same conditions, or can various conditions apply?

To determine whether a general principle existed, the European Court of Justice needed to examine the legal codes for each of the ten members of the European Community in 1982: Germany,[5] French,[6] Belgium,[7] Luxembourg,[8] Italy,[9] the Netherlands,[10] Denmark,[11] Ireland,[12] the United Kingdom,[13] and Greece.[14] Even when a state grants some attorney-client privilege, the wording and conditions vary across the states (Text Box 6.1).

TEXT BOX 6.1   EUROPEAN COMMUNITY MEMBER-STATES' PENAL CODES FROM 1982

German Penal Code (Sections 203 and 204)

Section 203: Violation of Private Secrets

Whoever unlawfully discloses another's secret, in particular a secret relating to that person's personal sphere of life or to a business or trade secret which was revealed or otherwise made known to them in their capacity as:

1. a physician, dentist, veterinarian, pharmacist or member of another healthcare profession which requires state-regulated training to engage in the profession or to use the professional title,
2. a professional psychologist with a state-recognised final academic examination,
3. a lawyer, non-lawyer provider of legal services who has been admitted to a bar association, patent attorney, notary, defence counsel in statutorily regulated proceedings, certified public accountant, sworn auditor, tax consultant, tax representative, or organ or member of an organ of a law, patent law, accounting, auditing or tax consulting firm,
4. a marriage, family, education or youth counsellor or addiction counsellor working in a counselling agency which is recognised by an authority or body, institution or foundation under public law,
5. a member or agent of a counselling agency recognised under sections 3 and 8 of the Act on Pregnancies in Conflict Situations (Schwangerschaftskonfliktgesetz),
6. a state-recognised social worker or state-recognised social education worker or
7. a member of a private health, accident or life insurance company or a private medical, tax consultant or lawyer invoicing service incurs a penalty of imprisonment for a term not exceeding one year or a fine.

Section 204: Exploitation of Another's Secrets

Whoever, without being authorized to do so, exploits another's secret, in particular a business or trade secret which they are obliged to keep secret as required by section 203 incurs a penalty of imprisonment for a term not exceeding two years or a fine.

French Penal Code (Chapter I, Article 378)

The physicians, surgeons, and other officers of health, likewise the apothecaries, midwives, and all other persons, to whom, in consequence of their state or profession, secrets are confided, and who, except in cases in which the law obliges them to give information, shall have disclosed such secrets; shall be punished with imprisonment from one month to six months, and a fine of from 100 to 500 francs.

Belgian Penal Code (Article 458)

Doctors, surgeons, health officers, pharmacists, midwives and all other persons, by state or by profession, of secrets entrusted to them, which— except in the case where they are called to bear witness in court (or before a parliamentary committee of inquiry) and [other places] where the law, decree or ordinance obliges or authorizes them to publicize these secrets - have revealed them, will be punished with imprisonment from one year to three years and a fine of one hundred euros to one thousand euros or one of these penalties only.

Luxembourg Penal Code (Article 458)

Doctors, surgeons, health officers, pharmacists, midwives, and all other persons, by state or by profession, entrusted with the secrets entrusted to them, which, except in the case where they are called to testify in court and that where the law obliges them to make known these secrets, will have revealed them, will be punished with imprisonment of eight days to six months and a fine of 500 euros to 5,000 euros.

Italian Penal Code (Article 622)

Disclosure of professional secrecy. Anyone who, having knowledge of a secret, because of their state or office, or their profession or art, reveals it, without just cause, or uses it for their own or others' profit, is punished, if harm can result from the fact, with imprisonment of up to one year or with a fine from € 30 to € 516. The crime is punishable by lawsuit from the offended person.

The Dutch Penal Code (Section 273)

1. Any person who intentionally:
   a. discloses specific information related to a commercial, industrial, or service enterprise in which he is or has been employed, which he was obliged to keep secret or
   b. discloses or, in pursuit of profit, uses data that has been obtained by means of a criminal offence from a computerised device or system of a commercial, industrial or service enterprise and that is

related to such enterprise, if the data, at the time of disclosure or use, was not in the public domain and if any loss or disadvantage may follow from such disclosure or use

   c. shall be liable to a term of imprisonment not exceeding six months or a fine of the fourth category.

2. Any person who could have believed in good faith that disclosure was in the public interest shall not be criminally liable.
3. Prosecution shall take place only on complaint of the management board of the enterprise.

The Danish Penal Code (Article 152)

1. Any person who is exercising or who has exercised a public office or function, and who unlawfully forwards or exploits confidential information, which he has obtained in connection with his office or function, shall be liable to a fine or to imprisonment for any term not exceeding six months.
2. If the offence as mentioned in Subsection (1) is committed with the intent to obtain an unlawful gain for himself or for others, or if other particularly aggravating circumstances are present, the penalty may be increased to imprisonment for any term not exceeding two years. Considered as particularly aggravating circumstances are especially instances where the forwarding or exploitation has occurred under such circumstances that it causes others serious damage or implies a distinct risk of such damage.
3. Information is confidential when made so in an Act or by other stipulations, or when it is necessary to keep it a secret in order to protect important public or private interests.

Irish Common Law

In Ireland, lawyers and clients benefit from privilege in terms of correspondence between them that gives advice and or documents created prior to litigation. This privileged information can only be communicated to others with consent of the client.

British Common Law

English courts have such a robust view of attorney-client privilege that they maintain that "the privilege continues to exist after the death of the client" and thus a client's communications with her lawyer takes place in "a condition of perfect security."

Greek Law

In Greece, the protection between attorneys and clients is protected, whether the attorneys are in-house counsel or independent. Moreover, all communications held within the scope of the professional relationship of attorney-client are regarded as privileged. Even after the termination of the legal relationship, no information can be used in judicial proceedings. The only exception, however, is if disclosure is the ultimate means of protecting against potential harm or the only manner by which illegal activity can be prevented.

Once these questions have been answered, the Justices must then apply the notion of a general principle of attorney-client privilege to the case between the European Commission and the Australian Mining & Smelting Europe Limited Corporation. The Applicants, the Australian Mining & Smelting Europe Limited Corporation, will argue that attorney-client privilege does exist at the European level, and as a result, their attorneys are protected from divulging any documents to the European Commission. In response, the European Commission will be advocating that attorney-client privilege does not exist at the European level and/or does not apply in this case. For this moot court, there are two legal questions posed before the European Court of Justice:

1. *Does a general principle of attorney-client privilege exist in the European Communities?*
2. *If so, can this principle be used to determine the legal team of the Australian Mining & Smelting Europe Limited Corporation to be in compliance with international law when they refused to turn over documents to the European Commission?*

NOTES

1. European Union. *Treaty Establishing the European Community, Treaty of Rome*, March 25, 1957. Available at: https://www.europarl.europa.eu/about-parliament/en/in-the-past/the-parliament-and-the-treaties/treaty-of-rome.
2. Ibid.
3. European Economic Communities European Commission, "Commission Decision of 6 July 1979 on an investigation pursuant to Article 14 (3) of Regulation No 17 into AM & S Europe Ltd, Bristol (Dossier IV/AF 379)," 9/670/EEC, July 7, 1979. Available at: https://eur-lex.europa.eu/legal-content/EN/ALL/?uri=CELEX%3A31979D0670.

4. Ibid.

5. German Criminal Code. Available at: https://www.gesetze-im-internet.de/englisch_stgb/englisch_stgb.html.

6. French Criminal Code. Available at: https://www.legal-tools.org/doc/418004/pdf/.

7. Belgian Criminal Code. Available at: https://www.legislationline.org/documents/section/criminal-codes.

8. Luxembourg Criminal Code. Available at: https://www.legislationline.org/documents/section/criminal-codes.

9. Italian Common Law. Available at: https://www.altalex.com/documents/news/2014/10/28/dei-delitti-contro-la-persona.

10. Dutch Criminal Code. Available at: https://www.legislationline.org/documents/section/criminal-codes.

11. Danish Criminal Code. Available at:: https://www.oecd.org/daf/anti-bribery/anti-briberyconvention/37472519.pdf.

12. Irish Common Law. Available at: https://www.sgrlaw.com/ttl-articles/916/.

13. Pike, Richard S., "The English Law of Legal Professional Privilege: A Guide for American Attorneys," *Loy. U. Chi. Int'l L. Rev.* 4 (2006): 51.

14. Greek Criminal Code. Available at: https://www.iadclaw.org/assets/1/7/17.13_Greece_2011.pdf.

Chapter 7

Subsidiary Sources

The fourth type of international law is subsidiary sources, mentioned by the International Court of Justices as legal rulings and notable legal scholars' writings. One of the most important subsidiary sources of international law is the "Draft Articles on the Responsibility of States for Internationally Wrongful Acts" (2001),[1] which was written by a legal community within the framework of the United Nations, called the International Law Commission. This document serves as an etiquette book for states to follow when determining how best to resolve disputes that arise in cases of alleged breaches of other primary sources of law. Though the "Draft Articles" were not concluded until 2001, they began five decades early and are based on long standing principles of international customary law.

This chapter will first explain the notion of subsidiary sources of international law and review the details of the "Draft Articles" in greater detail. Next, this chapter will present details on the first contentious case before the International Court of Justice. The case focused on the status of the Corfu Channel, a narrow waterway between the island of Corfu (claimed by Greece) and the territory of the People's Republic of Albania. This chapter will examine the customs and treaties relevant to the Corfu Channel in 1946. Finally, the chapter will outline the details of a Cold War escalation in the Corfu Channel between the United Kingdom and the People's Republic of Albania that culminated in the sinking of two British warships. Though the customs and treaties of 1946 offer some guidance in the right and obligations of each actor within the Corfu Channel incident, the "Draft Articles" will be needed to verify which party was in breach of its obligations under international law.

SUBSIDIARY SOURCES OF INTERNATIONAL LAW

Article 38(1) of the Statute of the International Court of Justice identifies four sources of international law: treaties, customs, general principles, and subsidiary sources (i.e., "judicial decisions and the teachings of the most highly qualified publicists of the various nations"). Whereas the other three sources are primary sources or created by states at the international (e.g., treaties and customs) or domestic (e.g., general principles) level, subsidiary sources are secondary sources meant to provide evidence of existing rules that apply to states, though they are not created directly by states.

One of the key bodies that develop these secondary sources of law is the International Law Commission (ILC). When the United Nations was first established in 1945, it created the Commission of seventeen international law scholars who are elected for five-year terms. Article 13(1) of the UN Charter created the Commission with the goal of initiating studies and making recommendations "for the purpose of . . . encouraging the progressive development of international law and its codification."[2] As a result, the ILC is an organ of the United Nations, and its work fits neatly under the subsidiary sources of international law.

One of the defining documents of this commission has been the "Draft Articles on the Responsibility of States for Internationally Wrongful Acts" (2001). Initially begun in 1956, the fifty-nine articles were finally finished in 2001. Below is a summary of the most important provisions of this document. Think of this source of law as an etiquette book for states. It offers how to do the right thing, and when you do not, how to make things right again.

WHAT ACTS CAN BECOME BREACHES OF INTERNATIONAL LAW?

Three articles of the Draft Articles outline the types of acts for which states can be held accountable under international law. The articles explain that these acts must be recognized as the state's obligations at the international level (Article 1), can be either an action or inaction on the part of a state (Article 1 and 2) and meets the standard of "not in conformity" of that state's obligation (Article 12) (Text Box 7.1).

TEXT BOX 7.1   DRAFT ARTICLES ON RESPONSIBILITY OF STATES FOR INTERNATIONALLY WRONGFUL ACTS (2001) [ARTICLES 1, 2, AND 12]

Article 1

Every internationally wrongful act of a State entails the international responsibility of that State.

Article 2

There is an internationally wrongful act of a State when conduct consisting of an action or omission:

(a) is attributable to the State under international law; and.
(b) constitutes a breach of an international obligation of the State.

Article 12

There is a breach of an international obligation by a State when an act of that State is not in conformity with what is required of it by that obligation, regardless of its origin or character.

As the state is a construct and it is individuals and groups that act, Articles 7 through 11 and 16 of the Draft Articles explain which individuals and groups can act on behalf of a state with international repercussions. These articles suggest that acts by (1) a state organ (i.e., federal or sub-national), (2) anyone not part of a governmental organ but "empowered by the law of that State to exercise elements of the governmental authority," (3) a governmental organ of another state placed at the disposal of a state, (4) a person or group "acting on the instructions of, or under the direction or control of, that State," (5) a person or group acting "in the absence or default of the official authorities," (6) a new government installed through insurrection in all or part of a state's territory, (7) a state is in direct control of another state, or in cases in which a state adopts conduct as its own can be attributed to a state (Text Box 7.2).

TEXT BOX 7.2   DRAFT ARTICLES ON RESPONSIBILITY OF STATES FOR INTERNATIONALLY WRONGFUL ACTS (2001) [ARTICLES 7-11 AND 16]

Article 7

The conduct of an organ of a State or of a person or entity empowered to exercise elements of the governmental authority shall be considered an act of the State under international law if the organ, person or entity acts in that capacity, even if it exceeds its authority or contravenes instructions.

Article 8

The conduct of a person or group of persons shall be considered an act of a State under international law if the person or group of persons is in fact acting on the instructions of, or under the direction or control of, that State in carrying out the conduct.

Article 9

The conduct of a person or group of persons shall be considered an act of a State under international law if the person or group of persons is in fact exercising elements of the governmental authority in the absence or default of the official authorities and in circumstances such as to call for the exercise of those elements of authority.

Article 10

1. The conduct of an insurrectional movement which becomes the new Government of a State shall be considered an act of that State under international law.
2. The conduct of a movement, insurrectional or other, which succeeds in establishing a new State in part of the territory of a pre-existing State or in a territory under its administration shall be considered an act of the new State under international law.
3. This article is without prejudice to the attribution to a State of any conduct, however related to that of the movement concerned, which is to be considered an act of that State by virtue of articles 4 to 9.

Article 11

Conduct which is not attributable to a State under the preceding articles shall nevertheless be considered an act of that State under international law if and to the extent that the State acknowledges and adopts the conduct in question as its own.

Article 16

A State which directs and controls another State in the commission of an internationally wrongful act by the latter is internationally responsible for that act if:

a. that State does so with knowledge of the circumstances of the internationally wrongful act; and
b. the act would be internationally wrongful if committed by that State.

Articles 13 and 14 of the Draft Articles determine the temporal nature of acts considered to be breaches of the law. Article 13 highlights that a state must be first obligated to this act or inaction in international law before it can be found in breach of it. This is a specific codification of the principle of *Nulla poena sine lege praevia* ("no penalty without law"), which forbids laws to be created *ex post facto* ("after the fact").

Article 14 notes that acts that occur in an instance cannot be considered an ongoing breach, even if the repercussions from the breach continue. Imagine a factory dumped pollutants into a river. The action of dumping would be the act that could be considered a breach, even if the pollutants caused lasting, devastating effects (Text Box 7.3).

TEXT BOX 7.3   DRAFT ARTICLES ON RESPONSIBILITY OF STATES FOR INTERNATIONALLY WRONGFUL ACTS (2001) [ARTICLES 13 AND 14]

Article 13

An act of a State does not constitute a breach of an international obligation unless the State is bound by the obligation in question at the time the act occurs.

Article 14

1. The breach of an international obligation by an act of a State not having a continuing character occurs at the moment when the act is performed, even if its effects continue.
2. The breach of an international obligation by an act of a State having a continuing character extends over the entire period during which the act continues and remains not in conformity with the international obligation.
3. The breach of an international obligation requiring a State to prevent a given event occurs when the event occurs and extends over the entire period during which the event continues and remains not in conformity with that obligation.

In Monopoly, players may find themselves heading to jail if they land on the "Go to Jail" square on the board, draw a Chance card that reads, "Go Directly to Jail," or roll doubles three times in a row (I did not know this last one). In each of these cases, the player had met the criteria to be jailed in the game. However, the game also offers "GET Out of Jail Free" cards for players to have met the criteria for jail but not have to go.

Articles 20 to 25 explain conditions in which a state can admit that the act did not meet its obligations under international law and still not be found in breach. Here the Drafts draw a distinction between noncompliance (not meeting one's obligation) and breach (being legally responsible for not meeting one's obligation). There are six circumstances by which a state can be in noncompliance but not in breach.

First, there are cases in which other states have allowed this act. Second, the act can be done if it is in self-defense. Third, states may not comply with a law in order to punish another state's breach of that same law. The limits of these countermeasures are described in detail in Articles 52 and 54. Fourth, a state may need to act in noncompliance with the law if there is a *force majeure,* or the "occurrence of an irresistible force or of an unforeseen event, beyond the control of the State, making it materially impossible in the circumstances to perform the obligation." Fifth, there are times when an act can be seen as noncompliance but not a breach when the act is judged to be the only "reasonable way, in a situation of distress, of saving the author's life or the lives of other persons entrusted to the author's care." And finally, an act can be seen as noncompliance but not a breach when the act is meant "to safeguard an essential interest against a grave and imminent peril (Text Box 7.4).

TEXT BOX 7.4   DRAFT ARTICLES ON RESPONSIBILITY OF STATES FOR INTERNATIONALLY WRONGFUL ACTS (2001) [ARTICLES 20-25, 52, AND 54]

Article 20: Consent Valid

Consent by a State to the commission of a given act by another State pre cludes the wrongfulness of that act in relation to the former State to the extent

Article 21: Self-Defense

The wrongfulness of an act of a State is precluded if the act constitutes a lawful measure of self-defense taken in conformity with the Charter of the United Nations.

Article 22: Legitimate Countermeasures

The wrongfulness of an act of a State not in conformity with an international obligation towards another State is precluded if and to the extent that the act constitutes a countermeasure taken against the latter State in accordance with Article 52 & 53.

Article 23: Force Majeure

1. The wrongfulness of an act of a State not in conformity with an international obligation of that State is precluded if the act is due to force majeure, that is the occurrence of an irresistible force or of an unforeseen event, beyond the control of the State, making it materially impossible in the circumstances to perform the obligation.
2. Paragraph 1 does not apply if:
   a. the situation of force majeure is due, either alone or in combination with other factors, to the conduct of the State invoking it; or
   b. the State has assumed the risk of that situation occurring.

Article 24: Distress

1. The wrongfulness of an act of a State not in conformity with an international obligation of that State is precluded if the author of the act in question has no other reasonable way, in a situation of distress, of saving the author's life or the lives of other persons entrusted to the author's care.
2. Paragraph 1 does not apply if: (a) the situation of distress is due, either alone or in combination with other factors, to the conduct of the State invoking it; or (b) the act in question is likely to create a comparable or greater peril.

Article 25: Necessity

1. Necessity may not be invoked by a State as a ground for precluding the wrongfulness of an act not in conformity with an international obligation of that State unless the act:
   a. is the only way for the State to safeguard an essential interest against a grave and imminent peril; and
   b. does not seriously impair an essential interest of the State or States towards which the obligation exists, or of the international community as a whole.
2. In any case, necessity may not be invoked by a State as a ground for precluding wrongfulness if:
   a. the international obligation in question excludes the possibility of invoking necessity; or
   b. the State has contributed to the situation of necessity.

Article 52: Conditions Relating to Resort to Countermeasures

1. Before taking countermeasures, an injured State shall:
   a. call upon the responsible State . . . to fulfill its obligations.
   b. notify the responsible State of any decision to take countermeasures and offer to negotiate with that State.
2. Notwithstanding paragraph 1 (b), the injured State may take such urgent countermeasures as are necessary to preserve its rights.
3. Countermeasures may not be taken, and if already taken must be suspended without undue delay if:
   a. the internationally wrongful act has ceased; and
   b. the dispute is pending before a court or tribunal which has the authority to make decisions binding on the parties.
4. Paragraph 3 does not apply if the responsible State fails to implement the dispute settlement procedures in good faith.

Article 54: Conditions Relating to Resort to Countermeasures

Countermeasures shall be terminated as soon as the responsible State has complied with its obligations under Part Two in relation to the internationally wrongful act.

INTERNATIONAL CUSTOMS THAT APPLIED TO THE CORFU CHANNEL IN 1947

Subsidiary sources like the Draft Articles are meant to explain how states are obligated to primary sources of international law (e.g., treaties and customs). One of the key areas in which states have had disagreements throughout history is at sea. As a result, we will spend several weeks focusing on maritime law in this course. Though maritime law has evolved since 1946, our case occurs just after World War II ends, and at this time, there was no treaty on maritime law in general (instead, states relied on international customs). The only treaty worth note for this case that was codified at the time was the Hague Convention of 1907 on weapons of war (more on why this matters in section 2, the Corfu Channel Case).

WHAT ARE THE CUSTOMARY LAWS OF THE SEA IN 1946?

There are both international customs and treaties that can apply to the Corfu Channel Incident. Before examining the details of the events that unfolded between Great Britain and Albania, this section will examine the customary laws in maritime law and a treaty that addresses the rights and obligations for states wishing to submerge mines with their coastal waters as codified in the Hague Conventions of 1907.

International Customary Maritime Law in 1946

Though maritime law was codified in a treaty in 1982, this case takes place before there was written consensus on international maritime law. As such, this section will review the international customs of law with concern to waterways. Generally, waterways may be divided into three broad categories. The first is water that is exclusively under the control of a coastal state (i.e., territorial waters). The second designation is for water that is shared by all (i.e., the high seas). And a more elusive third designation of waterways is an international strait. This third category describes frequently trafficked channels (i.e., maritime superhighways) in which some exclusions apply, while others do not (Text Box 7.5).

TEXT BOX 7.5   INTERNATIONAL CUSTOMARY MARITIME LAW IN 1947

Territorial Waters

All coastal states have a maritime buffer off their coasts. Due to the expansive nature of oceans and how maritime transportation was conducted historically, they are measured slightly differently than landmasses. That is, water distance is measured using nautical miles. Nautical miles are slightly longer than regular miles and are calculated by dividing the circumference of the Earth into 360 degrees and then further dividing each of those degrees into 60 minutes of arc. Each arc is one nautical mile (roughly 1.1 miles).

During this time, there was no full consensus during this time as to how far a state's territorial waters could extend. Historically, it had been three nautical miles (as that's how far a cannon from a ship could fire and reach land). That said, by 1940, the distance had been extended to around 12 nautical miles off one's coast (though some states, like the United States, claimed around 200 nautical miles as their territorial waters). If your state is close enough to another state as to be within each other's territorial waters, then the two states honor the median line between the two coasts. Within this buffer area, a state's full legal jurisdiction can be enacted, and an attack within this maritime buffer is equal to an attack on a state's land with one exception: the right to *innocent passage* by other states.

There are two types of ships recognized in international customary law: merchant ships and warships. International maritime law has perpetuated the notion that the seas should be open to innocent passage, or the passing of all ships through all bodies of water, even territorial waters of states to promote trade and commerce, and even defense.

The only obligation for a ship under the right of innocent passage is to notify a state when the ship is entering its waters, to not cause any harm, and to not dwell within the waters but continue where it is bound. As a result, the criteria of innocent passage allows for a warship to enter territorial waters so long as (1) it respects coastal state regulations and (2) does not interfere with or "threaten the tranquility of the coastal state." As for coast state regulations, most coastal states require that a ship within its territorial waters notify the coastal state of the entry and state its purpose. In terms of concerns of threats to the tranquility of the coastal states, these states saw it their right to determine whether a ship was "innocent" and then to "suspend, deny, or impede the innocent passage of certain types of vessels, particularly warships" they deemed to be "non-innocent."

The High Seas

Maritime law has distinguished all areas of seas and oceans that are not within the territorial waters of a state are almost always considered to be the high seas, open to all ships at all times. During this time, states had equal access to the high seas with few restrictions placed on their activities.

International Straits

There are some strategic pathways around the globe that states have determined meet the third categorization of waterways: international straits. Straits are considered to narrow waterways that link to larger bodies of water. When a strait is deemed international in nature, it is because the strait offers a convenient route for international transportation, generally between two water bodies designated as high seas.

If a strait is designated as an international strait, international customary law allows for all ships—both merchant and warships—to have the right to *transit passage* or to move through the strait without being impeded by a coastal state. Though this may sound closely related to innocent passage, in practice, a coastal state has far more rights to designate what is innocent passage and not in its territorial waters than to delimit transit passage in an international strait. Instead, the general practice is that these states can impede, but not prohibit, the passage of merchant or warships within international straits.

The Hague Convention (1907) and Naval Mines

A primary source of international law worth noting, in this case, is the Hague Convention of 1907, more formally called the "Convention Respecting the Laws and Customs of War on Land." In this convention, special attention was made to the laying of naval mines. Articles 3 and 4 allow for the right to lay mines off one's coast during a conflict but assert that "every possible precaution must be taken for the security of peaceful shipping," including informing shipowners where mines have been laid (Text Box 7.6).

TEXT BOX 7.6   CONVENTION RESPECTING THE LAWS AND CUSTOMS OF WAR ON LAND, "THE HAGUE CONVENTION" (1907) [ARTICLES 3 AND 4]

Article 3

When anchored automatic contact mines are employed, every possible precaution must be taken for the security of peaceful shipping. The belligerents undertake to do their utmost to render these mines harmless within a limited time, and, should they Cease to be under surveillance, to notify the danger zones as soon as military exigencies permit, by a notice addressed to ship owners, which must also be communicated to the governments through the diplomatic channel.

Article 4

Neutral Powers which lay automatic contact mines off their coasts must observe the same rules and take the same precautions as are imposed on belligerents. The Neutral Power must inform ship-owners, by a notice issued in advance, where automatic contact mines have been laid. This notice must be communicated at once to the Governments through the diplomatic channel.

THE *CORFU CHANNEL* CASE

The island of Corfu is off the coast of Greece and Albania (see maps below). The island was ceded to Greece's constitutional monarchy by the British Empire in 1864, mostly as an attempt to counter the sprawl of the British adversary, the Ottoman Empire. The Corfu Channel (shown in the highlighted yellow box) runs between the island of Corfu and the coasts of Albania (to the north) and Greece (in the south).

As WWII came to an end, Churchill sent the British navy to assist the monarchy's return to Greece as the Nazis were evacuating. As the Greek island of Corfu has been heavily armed with explosives by the Nazis

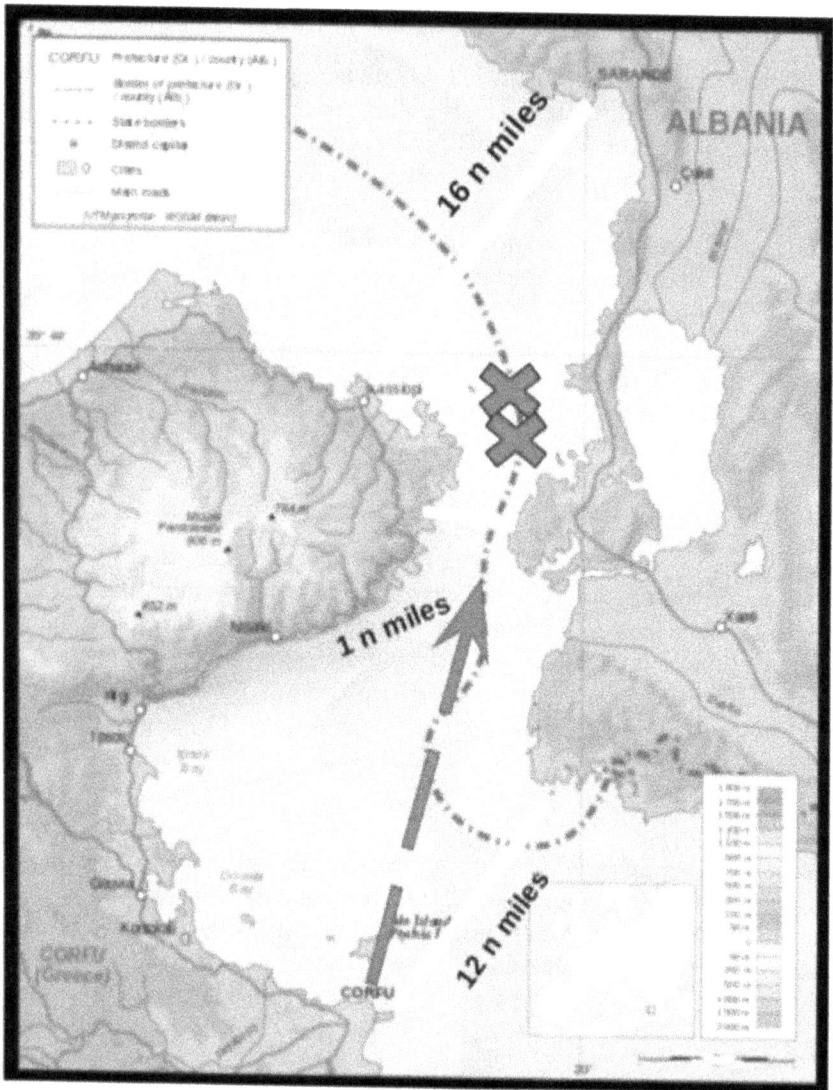

Figure 7.1 Most Likely Course and Location of Mines in the Corfu Channel Incident.
Source: Created by Author.

during the war, one of the British's roles during this time was to sweep the Corfu Channel, looking for landmines left by the Nazis. Two sweeps—one in 1944 and another in 1945—showed the Corfu Channel to be free of landmines.

Though the British planned for Greece to return to monarchical constitutional rule, Greece's largest military presence was the Communists. By the eve of 1946, Greece was on the cusp of a Civil War—divided between right-leaning royalists (backed by the British) and left-leaning Communists.

Unlike Greece, the Albanian population had supported the Axis powers' presence during WWII. After the Italians lost the Greco-Italian War in 1941 (losing their foothold in Albania), and the Nazis took control of Albania in 1943, the Communists began to increase in power (and only as a counter to Nazi control, and not Italian control). While the Allies focused their efforts elsewhere, the Albanian Communist Party maintained control of the government. By the end of WWII, when Zog I attempted to return from exile in Greece, the Communist government refused his entry.

Corfu Channel Incidents of 1946

Three separate incidents occurred in the Corfu Channel between Britain and Albania in 1946: one on May 15th, one in October, and a third in November.

May 15, 1946: Shots Fired at the Orion *and* Superb

On May 15, 1946, two British cruisers—*Orion* and *Superb*—were traveling southward through the Corfu Channel off the coast of Albania, close to Saranda, when shots were fired from Albanian shore guns at the two cruisers. Neither cruiser was hit, nor did they return fire. Both ships were ordered to change direction away from the Albanian coast.

In his report of that day, the Albanian commander of the Saranda military unit claimed that the ships were unidentified and that the shots fired were meant as warning shots as these ships were: (1) warships, (2) in territorial waters, (3) without prior notification.

Three days later, a report clarified that the flag on the ship was initially thought to be Greek and only later deemed to be "the English war banner."[3]

Following the altercation, Great Britain sent a diplomatic note on May 18th, 1946, demanding a "rapid and public apology for this violent act of the Albanian batteries" as well as "assurances that the persons responsible would be severely punished."[4] In Albania's response, on May 21st, 1946, it assured Britain that "it was never the purpose of our coastal command in Saranda to attack ships of our ally, Great Britain, if they had been recognized and if they hadn't been in our territorial waters going toward the harbor of Saranda."[5]

Britain sent a second note to Albania on May 30th, 1946, referring to international law on "the right of passage both in peace and war" for both warships and merchant ships. Britain continued by countering Albania's asserting that the channel waters belonged to Albania. Instead, Britain explained that the channel formed an international strait as it serves as a highway "of international traffic and connecting two parts of the open sea.["]6 As a result, Britain explained that it did not need to notify Albania of its passage through the channel.

On June 13th, Albania responded that it normally had "neither had, nor has the intention of hindering navigation" in the Straits of Corfu by any "kind of ship of any nationality" so long as "the ship respects the rights and laws of our country."[7] As a result, Albania reasserted its original claim that the channel was within its territorial waters and thus argued that no ship can head "toward our coast, without fulfilling the appropriate formalities and without the permission of the Albanian authorities." In a final response, on August 2nd, 1966, Britain once again rejected Albania's claim to the channel and threatened to retaliate militarily if Albanian ever opened fire again "on any of His Majesty's vessels passing through the Corfu Channel," promising "fire will be returned by His Majesty's ships."[8]

Diplomatic exchanges stopped at this point. However, Britain did not chance the Straits again until October. In the meantime, however, Greece notified the British that a ship from Communist Yugoslavia (i.e., an ally of Albania) that had regularly passed through the Channel stopped its route through the Channel beginning around September 26th, 1946.

Around the same time, British Admiralty sent a letter to its Mediterranean Command asking it "whether the government of Albania has learned how to behave [for the purposes of establishing diplomatic relations with it]." In the letter, dated September 21st, 1946, the Admiralty stated that if the Mediterranean Command had not yet attempted to pass through "Straits of the Corfu Channel since August, [they should] plan to do so as soon as possible."[9]

October 22nd, 1946: The Sinking of the **Saumarez** and **Volage**

On October 22, 1946, the British cruisers *Mauritius* and *Leander*, accompanied by the destroyers *Saumarez* and *Volage*, left the Port of Corfu on the island of Corfu, which was controlled by Greece. In a column formation, the four British warships moved northwards directly through the middle of the Corfu channel. At the narrowest portion, these ships were instructed to cross the Straits toward the Albanian coastline (heading toward the Albania town of Saranda). They were directed to respond with fire if Albania fired upon them. Soon the crews heard the firing of machine guns from the Albanian shore, but the shots missed.

Before the four ships could respond with fire, the *Saumarez* struck a submerged mine (see red X on map below), and an explosion followed, killing thirty-six sailors instantly. An Albanian launch then came out from Saranda under the white flag. Though it did not assist, it asked the *Saumarez* why the ships were in the channel. The reply is not recorded. For about half an hour, the Albanian launch kept observation, without attempting to help or being asked to do so.

During this time, a second warship, the *Volage,* moved toward the *Saumarez,* intending to tow it back to the Port of Corfu. As it was towing it away from the Albanian shore, the *Volage* hit a second submerged mine, and eight of its sailors were killed instantly. Though both ships were eventually able to return to the Port of Corfu, they had lost two additional sailors, and forty-two were suffering from injuries.

The first letter came from the British four days later. On October 26th, 1946, the British faulted the Albanians for the mines "of which the Albanian authorities will doubtless be aware," and let the Albanians know that the British mine authorities would be returning to the Channel very soon to "clean the Channel."[10]

In response, Albania submitted a letter to the UN Security Council, condemning the British for "such provocations against [it]," and asking the Security Council (with Britain as a member) to hold the state accountable.[11] The same day, Albania sent an angry letter to the British government directly: "for the second time warships of Great Britain have violated our territorial waters, without having any authorization from our government, and in this way have violated the integrity of our country."[12] It further noted that it had no issue with the British clearing mines outside of Albania's territorial waters. When the British government announced that the clearing of the mines would be done on November 12th, the Albanian government answered with a counter-proposal to set up a mixed commission to determine the area involved. The British saw the Albanian government's proposal as an attempt to delay the mine-clearing operation and refused.

November 13, 1946: Sweeping the Channel for Mines

On November 13th, British authorities sent minesweepers to the Channel to conduct a search called "Operation Retail." Twenty-three mines in all were found. One exploded in the water, harming no one, ten remained floating on the water, nine were sunk, and two were towed to Corfu. In its report, Britain stated that the mines acquired on the sweep on November 13th were the same type of mines that sank the two British ships on October 22nd. It also stated that they appeared to be German-made. In anticipation of the claim that these could have been German mines left over from WWII, the British added that the mines appeared newer. They "were free from marine growth and that they still had grease on their mooring cables"[13]

THE MOOT COURT: *THE UNITED KINGDOM VS. THE PEOPLE'S REPUBLIC OF ALBANIA*

In January of 1947, the conflict between the British and Albanian governments was put on the agenda of the UN Security Council. On February 18th of that year, Britain went on record in the Security Council meeting, stating that "an unnotified minefield had [either] been laid in the Corfu Straits by the Albanian Government or with its connivance."[14] In response, the next day, a representative from Albania stated that the "Albanian Government had not laid, or known who had laid, the mines and that the British warships had violated Albanian sovereignty over its territorial waters with a view to provoking incidents."[15]

After being unable to settle the conflict between the parties, the UN Security Council passed a Resolution in April of 1947, voting to send the case to the International Court of Justice to be examined as the first contentious case before the court.

Initially, Albania declined this offer, stating that as a non-member to the United Nations and thus need not be bound to participate in a contentious case. However, the court rejected this objection, noting that Albania had reached out to the United Nations for advisement, and the case continued. For this moot court, the legal question posed is: *Was Albania in violation of its obligations under international law toward the British during the incidents in the Corfu Channel in 1947?*

NOTES

1. United Nations International Law Commission, "Draft Articles on Responsibility of States for Internationally Wrongful Acts," 2001. Available at: https://legal.un.org/ilc/texts/instruments/english/commentaries/9_6_2001.pdf.

2. United Nations, "Charter of the United Nations," October 24, 1945. Available at: https://unispal.un.org/DPA/DPR/unispal.nsf/0/7F0AF2BD897689B785256C3 30061D253.

3. "Burning Secrets of the Corfu Channel Incident." 2014a. Wilson Center. September 9, 2014. https://www.wilsoncenter.org/publication/ burning-secrets-the-corfu-channel-incident.

4. Ibid.

5. Ibid.

6. Ibid.

7. Ibid.

8. Ibid.

9. Ibid.

10. Ibid.

11. Ibid.

12. Ibid.

13. Munro, Hector A., "The Case of the Corfu Minefield," *Mod. L. Rev.* 10 (1947): 363.

14. Ibid.

15. Ibid.

Chapter 8

Dispute Resolution Mechanisms

Article 33 of the United Nations Charter requires all member-states to resolve any disputes with other states through peaceful means. Further, it and other treaties offer various dispute resolution mechanisms states can use to resolve disputes from two-party negotiations to third-party judgments issued by arbitration panels or judicial organs.

And yet, the international system is filled with examples of states engaging in military actions to gain an advantage over others. One of the areas of growing tension is the South China Sea. Though nine states with coasts bordering the South China Sea are members of the UN Convention on the Laws of the Sea and thus have a right to claim waters off their coast, China has laid claim to the entire sea to exclude the other eight states. When the Philippines attempted to take China to the Permanent Court of Arbitration in 2013, China refused to participate, leaving the court to hold proceedings with China in absentia.

This chapter will first examine the various dispute resolution mechanisms states can choose and determine why some states would want specific mechanisms over others. Next, the chapter will present the codified rights and obligations for coastal states as clarified in the United Nations Convention on the Laws of the Sea (1981). Finally, this chapter will review escalating tensions in the South China Sea as China asserts its claim over the competing claims of eight other states, including the Philippines. This chapter will conclude with the details surrounding the case before the Permanent Court of Arbitration.

TYPES OF DISPUTE RESOLUTION MECHANISMS

When one or more states feel that another state is not upholding its obligations under international law, there are several mechanisms in place that states can use to resolve disputes. According to Article 33 of the UN Charter, "parties to any dispute, the continuance of which is likely to endanger the maintenance of international peace and security, shall, first of all, seek a solution by negotiation . . . mediation, conciliation, arbitration, judicial settlement, resort to regional agencies or arrangements, or other peaceful means of their own choice." Below is a short discussion of all the dispute resolution mechanisms in place throughout international law. This section will end with a discussion of the specific mechanisms offered in the UN Convention on the Laws of the Sea (1982)[1] for maritime issues that may arise between states. As noted in the UN Charter article mentioned above, there are five dispute resolution mechanisms, and these can be organized from less formal (e.g., negotiations) to more formal (a judicial organ). Below are brief details of each procedure.

Negotiations

As mentioned above, negotiations are considered to be the least formal of the five dispute resolution mechanisms. When two or more states disagree as to whether a state(s) obligations under international law are being met, the first recourse is usually to engage in direct negotiations among lawyers and/or policymakers for each state.

In some cases, states will use a Track II negotiation strategy, in which states send only low-level officials to negotiate, even in high stakes cases. This is not because it is of little priority to the state. In direct contrast, states often feel limited in their ability to negotiate if high-level officials are meeting. In such cases, the media and advocacy groups put significant attention and pressure on negotiating an advantageous outcome for one state over the other. Instead, Track II negotiations often are done confidentially and with low-level officials so that more options can be discussed freely. Then these low-level officials bring certain options to their high-level officials. Thus, more often than not, when you see high-level officials coming to an agreement after negotiations, there are perhaps dozens of Track II negotiations that have taken place to achieve such a breakthrough.

Mediation

As in domestic legal matters, mediation is a less formal meeting between adversaries in which a neutral third-party attempts to facilitate dialogue.

Though not always neutral, the United States has attempted numerous third-party mediations between Israel and the Palestinians and Arab neighbors as well. Though neutrality has been key to effective negotiations in the past (e.g., Algeria mediated a settlement between Iran and the United States after the U.S. hostage crisis in the 1979 Iranian Revolution, known as the "Algiers Accords"), it is often difficult to find a truly neutral third party for such mediation.

Conciliation

Conciliation is similar to mediation, except the third party delivers a final non-binding recommendation to the parties. The International Centre for the Settlement of Investment Disputes (ICSID) offers a permanent center for conciliation between states and private and public investment issues.[2]

Arbitration

Unlike the previous three dispute resolutions, arbitration is a formal process for obtaining a binding decision regarding disputes between states (and can address disputes between states and private parties). Though not often the case, arbitration in international law can allow the parties to reach a settlement of a dispute that is considered positive-sum. In contrast, judicial organs in domestic law tend to make only zero-sum rulings (i.e., one winner and one loser). The oldest and most well-known example of an arbitration panel is the Permanent Court of Arbitration (PCA). This organization has been around since 1899 and is housed in the Peace Palace in the Hague. This dispute resolution mechanism was created after states met for the 1899 Peace Conference. Its creation was motivated by a desire to see disputes surrounding war settled peacefully through increased international arbitration.

The Permanent Court of Arbitration has a group of arbiters it can pull from when a case arises. These individuals are selected by their states for six-year renewable terms. However, states involved in arbitration can also choose their arbiters. In such cases, there is almost always an odd number of arbiters: an even number selected by one state, the same even number selected by another state, and then these arbiters select a final arbiter to serve as the odd neutral party.

Judicial Organs

The final dispute resolution mechanism is a formal judicial organ responsible for hearing cases between states and issuing binding legal decisions. As noted above, more often than not, these organs issue a ruling in which one state is victorious over the other. When such rulings are in favor of the applicant, they include specific reparations that must be paid to the applicant by the respondent.

The most well-known of these is the United Nations' judicial organ, the International Court of Justice (ICJ). It also is housed within the Peace Palace in the Hague. This court is empowered to hear two types of cases: contentious cases in which a dispute between states needs to be resolved and advisory opinions in which one or more states and/or international organization organs ask the court for advice on a confusing area of international law or how the law would apply to certain real-world events. In contentious cases, states must be members of the United Nations (this currently applies to all states in the international system). Both states in dispute must consent to be a part of the hearing for the case to continue. Judges for the International Court of Justice are chosen by the General Assembly and the Security Council (working together) based on the judges' "independence, character, and expertise."[3]

THE UN CONVENTION ON THE
LAWS OF THE SEA (UNCLOS)

Following the Corfu Channel incident, the International Court of Justice had to rely on customary maritime law. As we know from this case, there were lasting questions about whether or not the Corfu Channel was an international strait or territorial waters. This was not the only maritime issue among states. There had been disagreements over how far a state's territorial waters extended from its coast (some wanted three miles, while others, ahem the United States, argued for more than 200 miles). Further, there were questions about economic activity in areas outside one's territorial waters, including fishing and extracting oil from the sea bed. States began convening in 1960, and it would take twenty-two more years to nail down specific provisions for maritime law in a treaty: the UN Convention on the Laws of the Sea (UNCLOS).

The UNCLOS is an extraordinarily long and detailed document. This section will focus on three key issue areas. First, it will review how UNCLOS designates territorial waters. This part will explain how coastal states' territorial waters are determined and exceptions for states that have historical claims beyond their established boundaries. Next, this section will review UNCLOS's mechanisms for parties to resolve their disputes (e.g., overlapping claims). And finally, this section will explain the declarations (i.e., addenda that explain how a state will fulfill its obligations) and discuss how declarations to UNCLOS have significantly increased the issue of overlapping historical claims.

Designation of Waters under UNCLOS

Under Article 2 of the United Nations Convention on the Laws of the Sea, each state has twelve nautical miles of territorial waters extending off the outermost point (baseline) of its coast. For example, if waters between the two countries were at most 20 miles wide, each state would be entitled to ten nautical miles.

Article 15, however, includes exceptions to this rule. In cases in which either the median between states' baselines are less than twelve nautical miles apart, the states must divide the waterway equally between them unless they have an agreement stating otherwise. More controversially, this exception includes its own exception. Article 15 reads that this equal division of waters between states "does not apply, however, where it is necessary by reason of historic title or other special circumstances to delimit the territorial seas of the two States in a way which is at variance therewith." This provision has encouraged coastal states to claim historical titles far beyond the waterways denoted in Article 2.

The impact of such an agreement extends well beyond 12 nautical miles. Once territorial waters can be determined for each state, Article 33 allows 12 more nautical miles beyond as a state's contiguous zone (in which a state may extend certain rights of the territorial waters in specific circumstances in which a breach of domestic laws of a state may be imminent, such as drug smugglers).

In addition, beginning at a state's baseline, Article 55-75 further allows a state an Exclusive Economic Zone (EEZ) that extends 200 nautical miles out to sea. Within an EEZ, a state has the exclusive right to exploit, develop, manage, and conserve all resources (e.g., fish or oil) in the water or seabed. Further, suppose a state believes its continental shelf is shallow (under 200 meters) and extends beyond the 200 nautical miles from shore. In that case, the state may make a submission to the Commission on the Limits of the Continental Shelf (CLCS) to have its EEZ extended. This is especially important in seas rich with fossil fuels to be extracted.

Islands (e.g., Hawaii) may extend a state's territorial waters *if* they are composed of natural material. Article 121, Section 1, describes an island as a "natural area of land, surrounded by water, which is above water at high tide." An island must consist of materials such as rock, coral reef, and sand. Section 2 of the same article states that all-natural islands have territorial waters 12 miles around them. Still, Section 3 of Article 121 requires the natural island to "sustain human habitation or economic life of their own" to have an EEZ.[4] Though states are allowed to construct non-natural islands (i.e., artificial islands), Article 60 states that these islands do not have territorial waters or EEZs (Text Box 8.1).

TEXT BOX 8.1   UNITED NATIONS CONVENTION ON THE LAWS OF THE SEA (1982) [ARTICLES 2, 15, 33, 55, 121, 60]

Article 2. Territorial Waters

UNCLOS determines all states will recognize from their shore to 12 nautical miles off their coast as their territorial waters. Within those waters, States are free to enforce any law, regulate any use, and exploit any resources. They are not, however, able to prevent the "innocent passage" of other states' naval and merchant ships through those waters. States must also keep waters navigable for all ships and cannot tax ships moving through territorial waters.

Article 15

Delimitation of the territorial sea between States with opposite or adjacent coasts

Where the coasts of two States are opposite or adjacent to each other, neither of the two States is entitled, failing agreement between them to the contrary, to extend its territorial sea beyond the median line every point of which is equidistant from the nearest points on the baselines from which the breadth of the territorial seas of each of the two States is measured. The above provision does not apply, however, where it is necessary by reason of historic title or other special circumstances to delimit the territorial seas of the two States in a way which is at variance therewith.

Article 33

1. In a zone contiguous to its territorial sea, described as the contiguous zone, the coastal State may exercise the control necessary to: (a) prevent infringement of its customs, fiscal, immigration or sanitary laws and regulations within its territory or territorial sea; (b) punish infringement of the above laws and regulations committed within its territory or territorial sea.

2. The contiguous zone may not extend beyond 24 nautical miles from the baselines from which the breadth of the territorial sea is measured.

Article 55

The exclusive economic zone is an area beyond and adjacent to the territorial sea, subject to the specific legal regime established in this Part, under which the rights and jurisdiction of the coastal State and the rights and freedoms of other States are governed by the relevant provisions of this Convention [other articles omitted].

Article 60

1. In the exclusive economic zone, the coastal State shall have the exclusive right to construct and to authorize and regulate the construction, operation and use of . . . artificial islands.

   . . .

8. Artificial islands, installations and structures do not possess the status of islands. They have no territorial sea of their own, and their presence does not affect the delimitation of the territorial sea, the exclusive economic zone or the continental shelf.

Article 121

1. An island is a naturally formed area of land, surrounded by water, which is above water at high tide.
2. Except as provided for in paragraph 3, the territorial sea, the contiguous zone, the exclusive economic zone and the continental shelf of an island are determined in accordance with the provisions of this Convention applicable to other land territory.
3. Rocks which cannot sustain human habitation or economic life of their own shall have no exclusive economic zone or continental shelf.

UNCLOS' Dispute Resolution Mechanisms

In keeping with Article 33 of the UN Charter, Article 279 of UNCLOS requires states to settle all disputes through peaceful means. Article 287, Section 1 notes that states "shall be free to choose" among four options for a dispute resolution mechanism via a declaration added to the treaty: the International Court of Justice, a specialized tribunal for maritime disputes, and two arbitration options. If two states choose the same procedure, Section 2 of Article 287 binds those states to that procedure unless they agree on another option. If two states do not agree on the same procedure, however, Section 3 of Article 287 warns the dispute "may be submitted only to arbitration unless the parties otherwise agree" (Text Box 8.2).

TEXT BOX 8.2   UNITED NATIONS CONVENTION ON THE LAWS OF THE SEA (1982) [ARTICLES 279 AND 287]

Article 279

Obligation to settle disputes by peaceful means: States Parties shall settle any dispute between them concerning the interpretation or application of this Convention by peaceful means.

Article 287

1. When signing, ratifying or acceding to this Convention or at any time thereafter, a State shall be free to choose, by means of a written declaration, one or more of the following means for the settlement of disputes concerning the interpretation or application of this Convention:
   a. The International Court of Justice
   b. The International Tribunal for the Law of the Sea (a court established to issue binding legal decisions surrounding maritime disputes)
   c. An arbitration panel (agreed upon by the UN Secretary-General
   d. A special arbitral tribunal that focuses on specific (often scientific) issues
2. If the parties to a dispute have accepted the same procedure for the settlement of the dispute, it may be submitted only to that procedure, unless the parties otherwise agree.
3. If the parties to a dispute have not accepted the same procedure for the settlement of the dispute, it may be submitted only to arbitration unless the parties otherwise agree.

Reservations vs. Declarations in UNCLOS

During negotiations over treaties, states may agree to include two different types of statements as annexes to a treaty: reservations or declarations. Reservations are statements made by a state in which they can choose to opt-out of a certain provision of a treaty thoroughly. Imagine, in the example of my parent's curfew, I agreed to the obligations of returning home at 10 pm every night, except for Saturday nights. In such a case, if reservations are allowed in the treaty, then a state can include a reservation so long as it does so when ratifying, signing, or acceding to a treaty (and not after).

Unlike reservations, which allow states to completely opt-out of one or more provisions but still be an obligation under the rest of the treaty, declarations clarify how a state plans to fulfill all of its obligations under the treaty. If I were to explain I would be home before 10 pm without any friends, I would be explaining how I would meet my obligations in more detail. Article 309 UNCLOS forbids reservations, but Article 310 allows for declarations "provided that such declarations or statements do not purport to exclude or to modify the legal effect of the provisions of this Convention in their application to that State" (Text Box 8.3).[5]

TEXT BOX 8.3   UNITED NATIONS CONVENTION ON THE LAWS OF THE SEA (1982) [ARTICLES 309 AND 310]

Article 309

Reservations and exceptions No reservations or exceptions may be made to this Convention unless expressly permitted by other articles of this Convention.

Article 310

Declarations and statements Article 309 does not preclude a State, when signing, ratifying, or acceding to this Convention, from making declarations or statements, however, phrased or named, with a view, inter alia, to the harmonization of its laws and regulations with the provisions of this Convention, provided that such declarations or statements do not purport to exclude or to modify the legal effect of the provisions of this Convention in their application to that State.

Most confusingly (and the reason we are discussing this case) is that both China and the Philippines submitted declarations that directly contradict each other. Specifically, China declared that it had a historic claim to a large swath of the South China Sea, codified in a Chinese law from 1992, and more commonly called the "Nine-Dash Line." Meanwhile, the Philippines (as well as other South China Sea coastal states) offered their own competing historical claims to its territorial waters as a former colony of America (and thus inheriting American's claim to the waters from 1898).

States are "free to choose" any of the dispute resolution mechanisms offered in Article 287. Though the Philippines stated that it is willing to submit to a peaceful resolution, China declared that it would submit to no arbitration panel or judicial organ provided in the Convention. Instead it would only discuss "through consultations" (Textbox 8.4).[6]

TEXT BOX 8.4   UNITED NATIONS CONVENTION ON THE LAWS OF THE SEA (1982) [CHINA AND THE PHILIPPINES' DECLARATIONS]

China's Declarations
Archipelago and Islands from 1992 as Historical Exceptions

The People's Republic of China reaffirms its sovereignty over all its archipelagos and islands as listed in Article 2 of the Law of the People's Republic of China on the territorial sea and the contiguous zone, which was promulgated on February 25, 1992.

Negotiations

People's Republic of China will effect, through consultations, the delimitation of the boundary of the maritime jurisdiction with the States with coasts opposite or adjacent to China respectively on the basis of international law and in accordance with the principle of equitability.

No Arbitration or Judicial Organs

The Government of the People's Republic of China does not accept any of the procedures provided for the Convention with respect to all the categories of disputes referred.

The Philippines' Declarations
Historic Title

Such signing shall not in any manner affect the sovereign rights of the Republic of the Philippines as successor of the United States of America, under and arising out of the Treaty of Paris between Spain and the United States of America of December 10, 1898, and the Treaty of Washington between the United States of America and Great Britain of January 2, 1930;

Procedures

The agreement of the Republic of the Philippines to the submission for peaceful resolution, under any of the procedures provided in the Convention, of disputes under Article 298 shall not be considered as a derogation of Philippine sovereignty.

CHINA'S EXCLUSIVE CLAIM TO THE SOUTH CHINA SEA

The Fall and Rise of China

Much of the territory under China's control today was held by the last Chinese dynasty, the Qing dynasty, from 1644 to 1912. During this time, security for China meant the maintenance of strong armies with the capacity to overpower threats that might invade from the north or west. Nearly all strategic events in East Asia prior to 1840 occurred on the continent and involved amassing strong armies, maneuvering them across the land to meet potential enemies, and building layered defenses to secure the Chinese homeland. Qing leaders failed, however, to complete a similar arc of security on their southern and eastern maritime flanks, leaving China strategically vulnerable to European advances in sea power.

Though China had attempted to ban the importation of opium, Great Britain had been illegally importing it from India for China since the late eighteenth century, resulting in widespread addiction in China and causing serious social and economic disruption. By the 1820s, 77 percent of Indian opium exports were heading to China.

The Opium Wars arose from China's attempts to suppress the opium trade. In March 1839, the Chinese government confiscated and destroyed more than 20,000 chests of opium—some 1,400 tons of the drug—that were warehoused at Canton by British merchants, dumping them into the South China Sea. Two Opium Wars followed, one between Britain and China (1839 to 1842) and the other when Britain and France joined forces against China (1856 to 1860). In both wars, Great Britain's Royal Navy demonstrated to the Chinese that it was decades, if not a full century, ahead of naval capabilities. In essence, when Great Britain and China went to war, the largest naval power (assisted by the French) quickly destroyed much of the smaller Chinese wooden war junks.

By 1880, the Chinese were trounced by the French, and Vietnam was established as the French colony of Indochina. As part of its victory over China, France claimed the Paracel Islands off the coast of northern Vietnam as part of its colony in 1888. The Paracel Islands at the time (and still) consist of about thirty uninhabited islets and reefs. Though the French had no interest in inhabiting these islands, they did extract bat guano to be used in fertilizers. Vietnam continues to lay claim to the Paracel Islands using the customary principle in international law, known as *uti possidetis* (Latin for "as you possess"), which allows all post-colonial states to maintain the territory once controlled by their colonial powers.

The continued decline in the power of the Qing dynasty finally led to a revolt in 1912 that culminated in the removal of the dynasty to be replaced by a Nationalist government wishing to put in place a constitutional monarchy. However, there were other factions who wished to see other forms of government take root in China, including Mao Zedong and his fellow Communists.

In 1937, as Japan was expanding southward and China's nationalist government proved no match, the Chinese guerrillas led by China's Communist leader, Mao Zedong, continued to fight the Japanese in the newly conquered area. Though the United States tried to bolster the Republic of China's ability to fight the Japanese, they were no match for the imperial army and navy's modern techniques and weapons.

While facing an external threat from Japan, the Republic of China was battling the internal threat from the Communist guerrillas led by Mao Zedong. After the United States dropped the second atomic bomb over Nagasaki, August 9th, 1945, ending the war in the Pacific, Stalin chose to invade Manchuria, further weakening the Republic of China. In Manchuria, the Chinese communists, supported by the Soviet Union, gained victory over the nationalists. With its surrender, the Japanese conceded all the islands gained in the South China Sea (including the Paracel and Spratly Islands) through its expansion before and throughout the war.

Though too weak to enforce its claims, the Republic of China unilaterally asserts a massive claim to most of the South China Sea by publishing a map with an eleven-dash line. This map was neither confirmed nor challenged by the United States at the time. As one U.S. naval intelligence report noted during this period, "the Chinese maintained a navy without ships."[7] And the French, embroiled in the Second French Indochina War, did not object initially either.

In May of 1946, a French warship attempted to assert French control over these islands once again by landing on the Paracel Islands. And in June of 1946, after the Philippines gained its long-promised independence from the United States, the Philippines laid claim to the Spratly Islands.

Battles domestically between the ROC and Communist guerillas, however, quickly resumed. After it became clear that the United States would take no large interventionist steps to defend the ROC, it fled to the newly returned island of Taiwan in 1947, where it has existed in exile ever since.

The People's Republic of China and the Nine-Dash Line

By 1949, the Communists founded the People's Republic of China (PRC) on the mainland and elected Mao as the Communist Party leader. The United States recognized it as China's sole legitimate government, and it did not establish formal diplomatic ties with the PRC until 1979. In 1953, once the People's Republic of China government came to power, it adopted the ROC's eleven-dash line map.

At this point, however, North Vietnam had become Communist as well. As a result, the Communist government of China agreed to remove two of the dashes claiming the Gulf of Tonkin as a goodwill gesture to North Vietnam that it would share the gulf with its Communist neighbor. Thus the PRC maintains the South China Sea claims in its nine-dash line map. To this day, China invokes the nine-dash line as the historical basis for its territorial claims in the South China Sea. Within this claim lies Taiwan (the island that hosts the ROC in exile), the Paracels, and the Spratlys (as well as the much smaller Pescadores, Pratas, and the Scarborough Shoals).

Most interestingly, though the ROC is still in exile in Taiwan and tensions remain high between the PRC and ROC, both governments maintain that they have full control of those portions of the South China Sea within the nine- or eleven-dash line. Figure 8.1 shows the current state of overlapping claims in the South China Sea.[8]

Escalating Tensions in the South China Sea

Throughout the 1980s and 1990s, China had an astounding average growth rate of nine percent of its GDP. Its success was even more astonishing as it began competing with democratic states while failing to democratize openly, instead of remaining Communist in name. Further, many were astounded that capitalism could be so successful in a state-led economy and arguably more competitive because it was a state-led economy that could build large export sectors with few interventions from diverse private interests. As it continued to rise, China became more aggressive in the South China Sea, as did the other states seeking to check China's growing power.

After the United States agreed to withdraw from Vietnam, the Communist state began asserting its claim to the Spratlys based on French occupation of them in the 1930s. In response, PRC forces begin to occupy the western portion of the Paracel Islands (planting flags on several islands and building an airfield and artificial harbor on the largest island, Woody Island). Following the reunification of Vietnam, the newly formed Socialist Republic of Vietnam upholds the South's former claims to the Spratlys and the right

South China Sea Islands

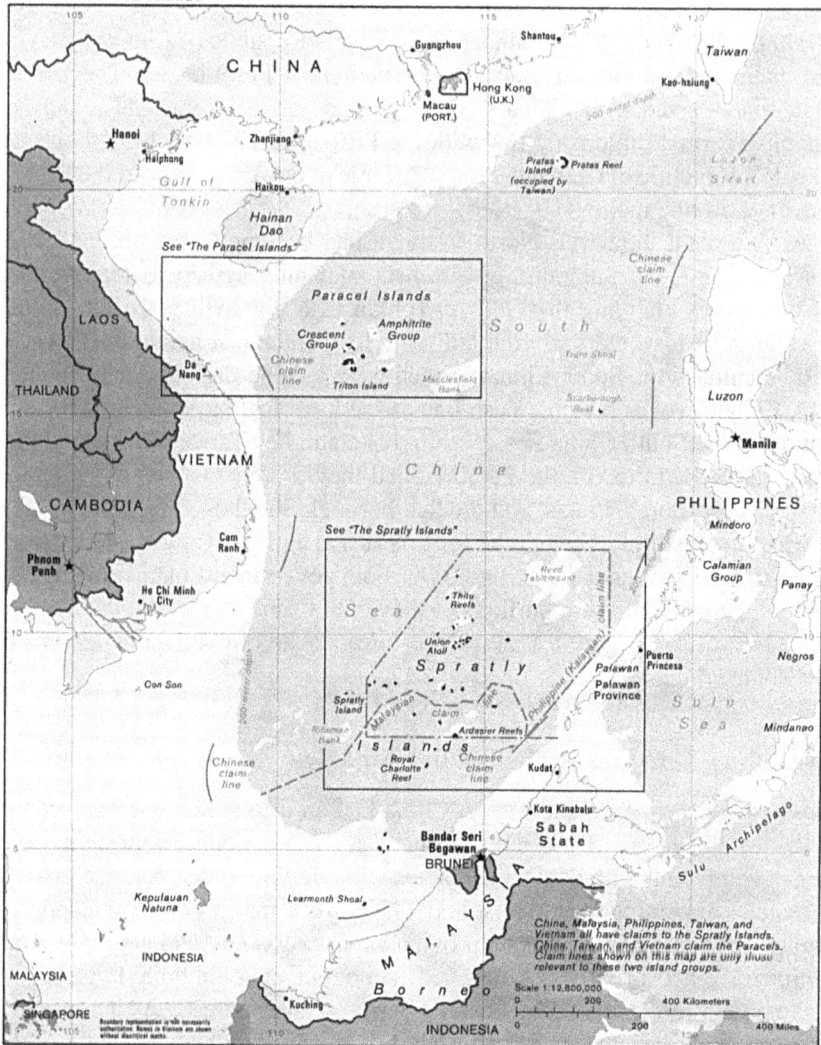

Figure 8.1   Map of Overlapping Claims in the South China Sea. *Source:* Courtesy of University of Texas Libraries.

to claim the Paracels. Moreover, Vietnam still occupies much of the Spratlys today.

After roughly a decade of relative calm in the South China Sea, in 1988, China and Vietnam began to show increased presence in the Spratly Islands once again. In 1987, Beijing (pursuing a more assertive stance in the area) established a physical presence on Fiery Cross Reef. A year later, the Chinese navy sank three Vietnamese vessels, killing seventy-four sailors in one of the most serious military confrontations in the South China Sea.

In 2010, Vietnam passed a maritime law asserting its jurisdiction over the disputed Spratly and Paracel Islands in respect of French colonial boundaries. In response, China announced a new city, named Sansha, to administer both the Paracels and Spratlys. Since then, relations between Hanoi and Beijing had been fluctuating. In the summer of 2011, Chinese surveillance ships cut the cables of oil and gas survey vessels operated by Vietnam's state-owned energy firm, PetroVietnam. In response, Hanoi began stepping up its defense budget since then and has remained an outspoken critic of Chin's further excursions into the sea. Though Vietnam has signed the Convention, it cites claims to both the Paracel and Spratlys island chains based on historic title.[9]

Malaysia began to increase its focus on the Spratlys in the 1970s when scientific reports estimated vast amounts of oil reserves in the seabed around the archipelago. In 1979, Malaysia unilaterally published a map, asserting its continental shelf (the shallow extension of a landmass under the water from a state's territory) to extend its jurisdiction into the South China Sea. Though Malaysia signed the Convention, it did not declare any historical claim. Instead, it asserted in its declaration that states should split EEZs as they do territorial waters (identically).

In 1998, China and the United States signed the Military Maritime Consultative Agreement, the first bilateral military agreement between the two countries following the Tiananmen Square protests. The Clinton administration works toward this agreement in response to China's navy shifting from being a mostly coastal defense force to operating a blue-water fleet beyond Chinese territorial waters. However, its efficacy was questioned in April 2001, when a Chinese F-8 interceptor and a U.S. Navy surveillance aircraft collided over the South China Sea, killing one Chinese pilot.

In 2010, the then-U.S. secretary of state Hillary Clinton reiterated Washington's neutrality on sovereignty in the South China Sea in a speech at an Asian regional security meeting in Hanoi and reaffirmed "open access to Asia's maritime commons" for all states. In late 2011, President Obama made a similar speech to the Australian parliament, announcing the United States will pivot its strategic attention to the Asia-Pacific, particularly the southern part of the region. The Obama administration announces pledges that reductions in defense spending would not come at the expense of commitments to the region.

The Philippines recorded at least five Chinese ships around the Spratly Islands between 2010 and 2011. In response to these skirmishes, the Philippine government begins referring to the South China Sea as the West Philippine Sea in all official communications. Soon after, the then-U.S.

secretary of state Hillary Clinton also began referring to the South China Sea as the West Philippine Sea.

THE MOOT COURT: *THE PHILIPPINES VS. THE PEOPLE'S REPUBLIC OF CHINA*

After a two-month standoff in the Spratlys beginning in April of 2012 between the Philippines and China, the Philippines initiated an international arbitration case at the Permanent Court of Arbitration. The case marks the first time a country has brought a claim against China under UNCLOS. Before the tribunal began, however, China repeatedly asserted its position to not participate in the proceedings. It justified this position by suggesting it declared under UNCLOS not to engage in any formal dispute resolution mechanisms mentioned within the Convention.

This moot court will offer a simulation of the real arbitration between the Philippines and China (although in the simulation, unlike the real scenario, China will be present). As in previous courts, the Justices (referred to in the Permanent Court of Arbitration as "Members of the Court") will decide on two distinct legal questions.

1. *Based on China's obligations under the UN Convention on the Laws of the Sea, does China have an obligation to be present for the arbitration?*
2. *Under the UN Convention on the Laws of the Sea, does China have the right to exclusive claim to the South China Sea based on historic title?*

NOTES

1. UN General Assembly. *Convention on the Law of the Sea*, December 10, 1982. Available at: https://www.un.org/depts/los/convention_agreements/texts/unclos/unclos_e.pdf.

2. International Center for Settlement of Investment Disputes, "Mediation & Conciliation," World Bank Group. Available at: https://icsid.worldbank.org/services/mediation-conciliation/conciliation/overview.

3. UN General Assembly, *Convention on the Law of the Sea*, December 10, 1982. Available at: https://www.un.org/depts/los/convention_agreements/texts/unclos/unclos_e.pdf.

4. UN General Assembly, *Convention on the Law of the Sea*, December 10, 1982. Available at: https://www.un.org/depts/los/convention_agreements/texts/unclos/unclos_e.pdf.

5. UN General Assembly, *Convention on the Law of the Sea*, December 10, 1982. Available at: https://www.un.org/depts/los/convention_agreements/texts/unclos/unclos_e.pdf.

6. Hayton, Bill, "Calm and Storm: The South China Sea after the Second World War," Asia Maritime Transparency Initiative, Center for Strategic and International Studies," August 13, 2015. Available at: https://amti.csis.org/calm-and-storm-the-south-china-sea-after-the-second-world-war/.

7. Dan Blumenthal, Michael Auslin, and Michael Mazza, "A South China Sea Strategy," American Enterprise Institute. Available at: https://www.aei.org/a-south-china-sea-strategy/.

8. UN General Assembly, *Convention on the Law of the Sea*, December 10, 1982. Available at: https://www.un.org/depts/los/convention_agreements/texts/unclos/unclos_e.pdf.

9. UN General Assembly, *Convention on the Law of the Se*a, December 10, 1982. Available at: https://www.un.org/depts/los/convention_agreements/texts/unclos/unclos_e.pdf.

Chapter 9

Territorial Claims

Certain territories are protected by international law from exclusive claims. These territories are protected under the principles of *terra nullius* ("land owned by no one") and *terra communis* ("land collectively owned by humanity"), and they include the high seas, Antarctica, and outer space.

The issue with each of these territories is that they are to be shared in a world without an enforcement mechanism. However, in some cases, states may wish to claim these areas exclusively, and other states may want to dominate the territories to keep them shared and open for all.

Outer space offers vast potential for exploration and scientific discovery for all of humanity, but it also provides extractive resources, commercial tourism potential, and the lure of military domination over the entire globe from above.

This chapter will first examine the principles of *terra nullius* and *terra communis* within the outer space law. Next, this chapter will examine the race to dominate space throughout the last century. Finally, this chapter will examine the newly formed fifth branch of the U.S. Department of Defense, U.S. Space Force, and discuss future hypothetical roles for its military presence in space.

TERRA NULLIUS AND *TERRA COMMUNIS*

Within international law, there are areas on the earth and space in which no one state lays claim (i.e., *terra nullius*, or "land owned by no one"). Thus all states can share (i.e., *terra communis*, or "land collectively owned by humanity"). Any area of the global waterways not designated as internal waters (e.g., lakes and rivers within the territory of a state), territorial waters, contiguous zones, EEZs, or international straits are considered to be part of the high seas. Article 87 and 90 of the UN Convention on the Laws of the Sea (UNCLOS) designates the high seas as waters in which all states (whether "coastal or land-locked") can enjoy the freedom to navigate these water as well as engage in various activities (e.g., lay submarine cables and pipelines, fish, and conduct scientific research). To enjoy this right, Article 88 of UNCLOS requires states to use the high seas only for peaceful purposes, and Article 89 states no state may "subject any part of the high seas to its sovereignty."[1]

Antarctica is another example of territory that is both terra nullius and terra communis. The Antarctic Treaty (1961) formally enshrines the continent as a terra nullius as it forbids any state to lay claim to the continent (Article IV) and requires that the territory only be used for peaceful purposes (Article I). Articles II and III of the treaty also designate the territory as terra communis by allowing all states the right to conduct scientific investigations on the continent so long as they freely exchange information related to any discoveries they make.

A third and final area designated using these two principles is outer space. Beginning in the 1950s and at the height of Cold War tensions, the international community began to be concerned that technological advancements and evolution of weapon systems would lead to the weaponization of space. Thus, with the space race taking off (pun intended), the United States supported and encouraged the United Nations to draft international law directly related to how outer space would be regulated. Specifically, in his address to the UN General Assembly on September 22, 1960, President Eisenhower proposed that the principles of terra nullius and terra communis applied to the high seas and Antarctica be used to regulate space. The international community has subsequently codified five treaties on outer space: one broad document and four smaller ones that focus on aspects first mentioned in the first treaty.

The Outer Space Treaty (1967)

The main treaty on outer space is formally called the Treaty on Principles Governing the Activities of States in the Exploration and Use of Outer Space, including the Moon and Other Celestial Bodies (1967), often referred to simply as the Outer Space Treaty. As noted in detail below, the Outer Space Treaty identifies outer space as terra nullius (i.e., Article II forbids any national appropriation of space, including the "Moon and other celestial bodies." And most of the rest of the treaty identified space as terra communis to be used for peaceful purposes (Article IV) and explored by all "without discrimination of any kind" (Article I) (Text Box 9.1).

TEXT BOX 9.1   TREATY ON PRINCIPLES GOVERNING THE ACTIVITIES OF STATES IN THE EXPLORATION AND USE OF OUTER SPACE, INCLUDING THE MOON AND OTHER CELESTIAL BODIES 1967 (THE OUTER SPACE TREATY)

Article I

The exploration and use of outer space, including the Moon and other celestial bodies, shall be carried out for the benefit and in the interests of all countries, irrespective of their degree of economic or scientific development, and shall be the province of all mankind. Outer space, including the Moon and other celestial bodies, shall be free for exploration and use by all States without discrimination of any kind, on a basis of equality and in accordance with international law, and there shall be free access to all areas of celestial bodies. There shall be freedom of scientific investigation in outer space, including the Moon and other celestial bodies, and States shall facilitate and encourage international cooperation in such investigation.

Article II

Outer space, including the Moon and other celestial bodies, is not subject to national appropriation by claim of sovereignty, by means of use or occupation, or by any other means.

Article III

States Parties to the Treaty shall carry on activities in the exploration and use of outer space, including the Moon and other celestial bodies, in accordance with international law, including the Charter of the United Nations, in the interest of maintaining international peace and security and promoting international cooperation and understanding.

Article IV

States Parties to the Treaty undertake not to place in orbit around the Earth any objects carrying nuclear weapons or any other kinds of weapons of mass destruction, install such weapons on celestial bodies, or station such weapons in outer space in any other manner.

The Moon and other celestial bodies shall be used by all States Parties to the Treaty exclusively for peaceful purposes. The establishment of military bases, installations and fortifications, the testing of any type of weapons and the conduct of military manoeuvres [sic] on celestial bodies shall be forbidden.

The use of military personnel for scientific research or for any other peaceful purposes shall not be prohibited. The use of any equipment or facility necessary for peaceful exploration of the Moon and other celestial bodies shall also not be prohibited.

Article V

States Parties to the Treaty shall regard astronauts as envoys of mankind in outer space and shall render to them all possible assistance in the event of accident, distress, or emergency landing on the territory of another State Party or on the high seas. When astronauts make such a landing, they shall be safely and promptly returned to the State of registry of their space vehicle.

In carrying on activities in outer space and on celestial bodies, the astronauts of one State Party shall render all possible assistance to the astronauts of other States Parties. States Parties to the Treaty shall immediately inform the other States Parties to the Treaty or the Secretary-General of the United Nations of any phenomena they discover in outer space, including the Moon and other celestial bodies, which could constitute a danger to the life or health of astronauts.

Article VI

States Parties to the Treaty shall bear international responsibility for national activities in outer space, including the Moon and other celestial bodies, whether such activities are carried on by governmental agencies or by non-governmental entities, and for assuring that national activities are carried out in conformity with the provisions set forth in the present Treaty.

The activities of nongovernmental entities in outer space, including the Moon and other celestial bodies, shall require authorization and continuing supervision by the appropriate State Party to the Treaty. When activities are carried on in outer space, including the Moon and other celestial bodies, by an international organization, responsibility for compliance with this Treaty shall be borne both by the international organization and by the States Parties to the Treaty participating in such organization.

Article VII

Each State Party to the Treaty that launches or procures the launching of an object into outer space, including the Moon and other celestial bodies, and each State Party from whose territory or facility an object is launched, is internationally liable for damage to another State Party to the Treaty or to its natural or juridical persons by such object or its component parts on the Earth, in air space or in outer space, including the Moon and other celestial bodies.

Article VIII

A State Party to the Treaty on whose registry an object launched into outer space is carried shall retain jurisdiction and control over such object, and over any personnel thereof, while in outer space or on a celestial body. Ownership of objects launched into outer space, including objects landed or constructed on a celestial body, and of their component parts, is not affected by their presence in outer space or on a celestial body or by their return to the Earth. Such objects or component parts found beyond the limits of the State Party to the Treaty on whose registry they are carried shall be returned to that State Party, which shall, upon request, furnish identifying data prior to their return.

Article IX

In the exploration and use of outer space, including the Moon and other celestial bodies, States Parties to the Treaty shall be guided by the principle of cooperation and mutual assistance and shall conduct all their activities in outer space, including the Moon and other celestial bodies, with due regard to the corresponding interests of all other States Parties to the Treaty. States Parties to the Treaty shall pursue studies of outer space, including the Moon and other celestial bodies, and conduct exploration of them so as to avoid their harmful contamination and also adverse changes in the environment of the Earth resulting from the introduction of extraterrestrial matter and, where necessary, shall adopt appropriate measures for this purpose.

If a State Party to the Treaty has reason to believe that an activity or experiment planned by it or its nationals in outer space, including the Moon and other celestial bodies, would cause potentially harmful interference with activities of other States Parties in the peaceful exploration and use of outer space, including the Moon and other celestial bodies, it shall undertake appropriate international consultations before proceeding with any such activity or experiment.

A State Party to the Treaty which has reason to believe that an activity or experiment planned by another State Party in outer space, including the Moon and other celestial bodies, would cause potentially harmful interference with activities in the peaceful exploration and use of outer space, including the Moon and other celestial bodies, may request consultation concerning the activity or experiment.

Article X

In order to promote international cooperation in the exploration and use of outer space, including the Moon and other celestial bodies, in conformity with the purposes of this Treaty, the States Parties to the Treaty shall consider on a basis of equality any requests by other States Parties to the Treaty to be afforded an opportunity to observe the flight of space objects launched by those States. The nature of such an opportunity for observation and the conditions under which it could be afforded shall be determined by agreement between the States concerned.

Article XI

In order to promote international cooperation in the peaceful exploration and use of outer space, States Parties to the Treaty conducting activities in outer space, including the Moon and other celestial bodies, agree to inform the Secretary-General of the United Nations as well as the public and the international scientific community, to the greatest extent feasible and practicable, of the nature, conduct, locations and results of such activities. On receiving the said information, the Secretary-General of the United Nations should be prepared to disseminate it immediately and effectively.

Article XII

All stations, installations, equipment, and space vehicles on the Moon and other celestial bodies shall be open to representatives of other States Parties to the Treaty on a basis of reciprocity. Such representatives shall give reasonable advance notice of a projected visit, in order that appropriate consultations may be held and that maximum precautions may be taken to assure safety and to avoid interference with normal operations in the facility to be visited.

THE DOMINION OF SPACE

Cold War Space Race

This book has covered territories exclusively controlled by states and those shared by all (e.g., the high seas). Another area in which the international community has passed international law to share freely "without discrimination of any kind" is space. Below includes the history behind space exploration as well as the details surrounding the main outer space treaty ("Treaty on Principles Governing the Activities of States in the Exploration and Use of Outer Space, Including the Moon and Other Celestial Bodies") and the four subsequent treaties which elaborated on articles presented in the first.

Nazi Technology

The early speculative study of space travel was international in focus. In 1904, a Russian named Tsiolkovsky published a detailed look at the mathematical requirements to propel a rocket into space. From there, U.S. rocket scientist Robert H. Goddard was the first to propose that rockets could be used to travel to the moon using liquid fuels (instead of more basic solid-fuel, or gunpowder rockets, used as early as the thirteenth century). His work was funded by the Smithsonian Institute, Charles Lindbergh, and later the Guggenheim Fund. Though largely ridiculed in the United States for his ideas, German scientists and mathematicians took notice.

Though earlier studies focused on space exploration's plausibility, the first rockets to be built were in Germany during the early 1930s by a rocket club trying to experiment with actualizing these early conceptions. By the mid-1930s, the German military began a facility for space research on the Baltic Sea. There they developed the original ballistic missile (the V2 or "Vengeance Weapon 2"), considered the prototype for the first space rocket.

Toward the end of WWII, just a few months before Germany surrendered to the Allied forces in Europe, many of the scientists working on the Nazi rocket program surrendered to the United States, believing they would be able to levy their expertise for clemency. Their plan worked, and the plans and knowledge of the V2 that they brought to the United States were instrumental in the U.S. space program.

The Soviet Union established a military facility devoted to rocket research as early as 1921. By 1933, two aeronautical engineers, Valentin Glushko and Sergey Korolyov, launched the first Soviet liquid-fuel rocket. Though the Soviets visited Germany's rocket facility after WWII, they did not benefit from German scientists' immigration as the United States did.

Satellites for Spying

Though the technology had been pursued for decades, the first rockets were not intended to be used as weapons. Instead, both the Soviet Union and U.S. rocket programs' focus was to launch satellites into space with sophisticated cameras attached that could be used to spy on one another. Interestingly, this effort was chosen as a means to be in adherence to international law. By

1944, two treaties (the Paris Convention of 1919 Relating to the Regulation of Aerial Navigation and the Chicago Convention on International Aviation) prohibited states from entering the airspace over a state's territory (from the ground to about 3.4 miles above the earth's surface) without permission.[2] As a result, both the United States and the USSR sought spying capabilities outside the other's airspace in the area known as aerospace, or the outermost layer of the earth's surface and outer space.

In October 1957, the USSR launched the first aerospace satellite, Sputnik (Russian for "satellite"), via a ballistic missile.[3] The U.S. military doubted that the USSR had the technological prowess to launch a satellite (as the ballistic missile testing had been kept secret until August of that same year). It looks like they needed those satellites for spying after all. In 1957 and 1958, the Soviets launched two larger satellites into space. The second satellite had a dog named Laika on board so the Soviets could show they could launch life into space. The dog, sadly, did not make it. The third satellite took measurements of the earth's atmosphere. In 1960, Sputnik 5 took two dogs into space. Both survived.

One year after the orbit of Sputnik 2 (the first one with the dog) in 1957, the UN General Assembly adopted Resolution 1348, calling for the establishment of a Committee on the Peaceful Uses of Outer Space (COPUOS). In the Resolution, the General Assembly recognizes the "common interest of mankind in outer space" and that space should be "used for peaceful purposes only." It further explicitly noted that the formation of COPUOS was to avoid "the extension of present national rivalries into [space]." In 1959, COPUOS became a permanent committee with twenty-four members. Today it has eighty-four members.

Initially, Eisenhower dismissed the Soviets' success, calling the satellite "one small ball in the air." In actuality, he welcomed the presence of the satellite as precedence for establishing the U.S. presence in space as well. U.S. public opinion, however, saw that science fiction was becoming a reality, and it was the Soviets who were making this happen. There was, as one historical record describes it, a "crisis of confidence" in the American public as it viewed the exploration into space as part of "America's destiny." Instead, one scholar writes that "the American response to the accomplishment of the Soviet Union was comparable to the reaction I could remember to Lindbergh's landing in France, the Japanese bombing of Pearl Harbor, and Franklin D. Roosevelt's death."

The result of this public reaction was for the Eisenhower administration to devote considerable funding and attention to scientific research. By the beginning of 1958, the U.S. (with the help of Dr. Wernher Von Braun, one of the key German emigres) launched their first satellite. To ensure the satellite was completed as soon as possible, Eisenhower ordered the army, navy, and air force to compete for the project (NASA was not created until July 1958). During the first attempt at a launch, Braun's team used one of their ballistic launcher prototypes to get their satellite to space in January of 1958.

The National Air & Space Agency (NASA) was publicly established by Eisenhower months after the launch of the first U.S. satellite in the National Aeronautics and Space Act of 1958. The president's first inclination was to have all U.S. space efforts, including those of a civilian character, managed by the Department of Defense. He was convinced, however, that it made more sense to create a separate civilian space agency to carry out an open program of scientific activities and to engage in international cooperation.

Meanwhile, a second organization called the National Reconnaissance Organization (NRO) was created to use the same technological advancements to spy on the Soviet Union. Though this program was created in 1958, the details of this program did not become public knowledge until 1992. The Corona program produced spy satellites that would originally take pictures—with rolls of film having to be dropped, recovered by plane, and then manually developed—and eventually used radar and electronic-signaling to gather intelligence.

Discussions of Outer Space Law

With the space race taking off (pun intended) in the late 1950s and early 1960s, western powers became concerned about the possibility that space could be militarized. As a result, the United States led several United Nations pushes to regulate space under international law, even calling for all-out disarmament. Addressing the General Assembly on September 22, 1960, President Eisenhower proposed that the principles of a treaty that focused on the Antarctic be applied to outer space and celestial bodies. Like Antarctica, he argued that no one state could make territorial claims (Article IV), it should be used for peaceful purposes only (Article I), there should be the freedom of scientific investigation (Article II), and information about discoveries should be freely exchanged (Article III).[4]

The Soviet Union, however, was leading the space race and did not want to curb its advantage in space. As a result, it offered to consider space disarmament if the United States agreed to disarm some of its short- and medium-distance ballistic missile bases on Earth (where the USSR was at a relative disadvantage). The United States denied the deal.

To move forward on regulating, and ideally stopping, the weaponization of space, the UN General Assembly passed Resolution 1721 in December of 1961. The Resolution reinforced that "Outer space and celestial bodies . . . are not subject to national appropriation" and requests all member-states participating in space launches to register their "space objects" to the United Nations for cataloging in a public registry.[5]

In addition to being the first to put a satellite in orbit, the Soviets were also the first to put a person in space. On April 12, 1961, Russian Lt. Yuri Gagarin became the first human to orbit Earth. Just one month later, Alan Shepard became the first American to fly into space, and in February of 1962, John Glenn was the first American to orbit Earth (i.e., the Mercury program).

Following the Soviets' successful launch of the first man into space (Yuri Gagarin) in April of 1961, President Kennedy tasked NASA with the goal of putting a man on the moon by the end of the decade. After receiving this mandate, NASA's budget increased 89 percent in 1961 and then 101 percent more from 1961 numbers in 1962. It soon became a 34,000-person agency located in D.C. as well as ten other facilities around the country managed by various universities and industrial contractors.

Though Kennedy's legacy includes the very public push to send Americans to the moon, NASA documents privately revealed that he was concerned about space as a second battlefield on which Cold War tensions could reach their peak. A month after his call to reach the moon, Kennedy approached the Soviet leader, Kruschev, with the idea of cooperating on a moon landing. Khrushchev agreed if larger nuclear disarmament could be reached first.

Kennedy declined this agreement, though he returned to his original proposal in September 1963 after successfully negotiating with Kruschev to abandon their missiles in Cuba the previous fall. He died just two months after suggesting new cooperation. It is believed, however, that Kruschev would have declined either way as the Soviets were attempting to launch their moon program for the fiftieth anniversary of the Bolshevik Revolution. This was not achieved due to financial setbacks and infighting.

Though the USSR had been against a treaty that regulated weapons in space, its outlook on this and other weapons issues changed after the Cuban Missile Crisis when the United States and USSR came to the brink of war. Moreover, scientific advancements confirmed that the radioactive fallout from a nuclear weapon was more severe, longer-lasting, and more widespread than initially believed.

In August of 1963, the Nuclear Limited Test Ban Treaty was signed, prohibiting the testing of nuclear weapons in the atmosphere, underwater, and in outer space (leaving underground testing as the only possible option). After this, on September 19, 1963, the Soviet Foreign Minister told the General Assembly that the Soviet Union wished to conclude an agreement banning the orbiting of objects carrying nuclear weapons. The U.S. ambassador replied that the United States had no intention of orbiting weapons of mass destruction, installing them on celestial bodies, or stationing them in outer space. The General Assembly unanimously adopted a resolution on October

17, 1963, welcoming the Soviet and U.S. statements and calling upon all states to refrain from introducing weapons of mass destruction into outer space. Seeking to sustain the momentum for arms control agreements, the United States pressed for a treaty that would give further substance to the UN resolution. An agreement was reached on January 27, 1967. On April 25, the Senate voted unanimously to ratification, and it entered into force on October 10, 1967.

In the process of debating the Outer Space Treaty, there were issues about the obligations of states to rescue both astronauts and spacecraft when missions go awry. Specifically, there was concern that when a mission returned to Earth, it may not land in the high seas as anticipated. In such cases, there was concern by both the United States and USSR that the technological advancements and the astronauts themselves could be held captive by the other party. Though this agreement is in keeping with the Outer Space Treaty, this led a separate discussion to unfold concerning the rescuing of both persons and objects, of which the United States and USSR were on opposing sides.

For the United States, the concern was ensuring that any state that became aware of the danger to personnel or craft would be responsible for attempting to assist in rescuing and returning the personnel and/or craft to the state to which they belonged. The Soviets agreed to the obligation to assist in rescue and to return personnel to the launching state after a Soviet astronaut was killed. This astronaut had difficulty with his poorly designed rocket. After orbiting the earth nineteen times and waiting for the right conditions to land on or near the Soviet Union, he ultimately attempted a night landing. During the landing, his parachute failed to deploy on reentry and crashed into the Soviet steppe. Soviet officials agreed to the agreement as they reasoned that, were the agreement to have been in place, they could have had the option of attempting his landing outside of the Soviet Union's jurisdiction. This agreement is seen as an elaboration on Article V of the Outer Space Treaty, which designates "astronauts as the envoys of mankind."

As a result, a second treaty specifically addressed the Rescue and Return of Astronauts. Under this treaty, states are required to immediately notify the launching state and the United Nations in cases where an accident, distress, an unintended landing, and so on. Moreover, this treaty requires that all efforts must be taken to assist in rescuing and returning the astronaut and all of the space objects to the launching state.

Landing on the Moon

In the United States, Apollo moved forward as a high-priority program. After the assassination of President Kennedy in November 1963, it became seen as a memorial to the fallen young president. Johnson, however, had no vision for what would become of NASA once this goal was accomplished and made no efforts to fund new programs.

This effort was not as politically captivating as it once was. Though astronauts became real-world heroes, the U.S. government rested on laurels. Moreover, the Soviets made four failed attempts to launch a lunar landing craft between 1969 and 1972, including a launch-pad explosion in July of 1969. As a result, the U.S. public felt they had "won" the space race, and attention turned elsewhere.

It was under Nixon that NASA officially landed on the moon on July 20th, 1969. After the moon landing, Nixon agreed to fund the development of both a space shuttle (a larger reusable rocket) and a staffed space station program. Nixon seemed most interested in the idea of NASA developing space shuttles capable of disposing of nuclear waste into space. He did so rhetorically, however. Soon after making the public declaration for both programs, he proceeded to decrease NASA's budget by 75 percent. NASA decided to focus its efforts on a space station.

The 1970s: Detente in Space

As early as 1969, the Soviets began to shift their emphasis from human spaceflight to the development of stations that would orbit the Earth and carry out extended observations. The first Soviet space station, called Salyut 1, was launched on April 19, 1971. Using some remaining hardware from the soon-to-be-canceled Apollo program, NASA developed Skylab, which launched in May of 1972. Skylab remained in orbit for six years, and experiments conducted aboard the craft obtained vast amounts of scientific data and demonstrated that humans could live and work productively in space for months at a time.

President Ford (an avid space fan) resurrected NASA's prominence in three different ways. In 1975, amidst a detente in Cold War tensions, an Apollo space shuttle rendezvoused and docked with a Soviet space shuttle to test landing and docking capacities among ships. A year later, Ford funded crewless missions (e.g., Galileo to Jupiter) and the Hubble Space Telescope to increase observations beyond Earth's orbit.

By the end of the 1970s, however, (due to an economic recession) the Skylab program lost all its funding and had to be discontinued. The Soviets, however, continued to send five additional stations into orbit throughout the decade. At least one of these space stations, the Salyut 3, included an aircraft cannon aboard, which was considered capable of destroying a satellite. Though the Salyut 3 tracked American space endeavors, no attack ever occurred.

Strategic Defense Initiative ("Star Wars")

Though Carter spoke highly of the space program (he once noted that "the challenge of space takes us very close to the heart of things"), in practice, there was little evolution in the program during his administration. In contrast, Reagan was among the most ardent presidential supporters of the space program. After a six-year hiatus in his first year in office, the first space shuttle, Columbia, launched its first mission. Between the launch of Columbia in 1981 and the Challenger, there were twenty-four space shuttle flights. For many, Reagan was present. As one author notes, "Reagan was thrilled, and he loved seeing NASA scientists and technicians at Houston Control waving small American flags when the launch was declared a success."

Both his love of space and his desire to beat the Soviets in the arms race led Reagan to make two key military decisions related to space. In 1982 his Administration created a Space Command as part of the Air Force. And on March 23, 1983, he gave a speech calling for a nuclear weapons defense system in space. He named the program that he introduced the "Strategic Defense Initiative" or SDI. In theory, this program would use surveillance satellites to detect a nuclear missile from the USSR and then use space-based lasers and subatomic particle beams to explode the missile in space before it reached the atmosphere above the United States.

In reality, this technology was (and is) far from being realized. By the end of the century, the United States had spent $60 billion on the SDI and faced much condemnation by its opponents. It was Democratic Senator Ted Kennedy that gave SDI the nickname "Star Wars." Though there was much debate over SDI's cost, its political implications, and its technical feasibility, many argue that the projection of power inherent in this program was one of the key factors that led the USSR to give up on its Cold War stance.

In 1984, the president overruled most of his advisers and gave NASA his approval to develop a permanent space station. NASA sought that approval fifteen years earlier and was forced to wait until the space shuttle was regularly flying. Reagan announced his approval in the most public way possible, during his January 25, 1984 State of the Union address. "A space station will permit quantum leaps in our research in science, communications, in metals, and in lifesaving medicines which could be manufactured only in space," Reagan said. He also indicated the United States would invite its allies to participate in the space station program in the same speech.

The End of the Space Race

Though the Reagan Administration considered exploring private partnerships or commercial activities in space and NASA went so far as to create an Office of Commercial Programs, the explosion of the Challenger in 1986 (which included aboard it a school teacher) led the Administration to decide to pro-hibit the use of space shuttles to help launch commercial activities in space.

During the Bush and Clinton years, the call in the United States was for a U.S.-led space station. Whereas the Bush administration advocated calling it Space Station Freedom, Clinton renamed the project the International Space Station to get Russia to cooperate in its design and construction. Though Clinton was less interested in NASA, agreeing to cut its budget throughout his tenure, he saw the space station as a means by which to get Russia to agree to other positive political and non-proliferation agreements. By 1993, Russia joined the project, along with Japan, Canada, and several European countries. In 1994, Clinton noted in his State of the Union address that "instead of build-ing weapons in space, Russian scientists will help us build the International Space Station."[66]

In 2003, the Columbia shuttle was the second shuttle to break up while returning home from its mission. The tragedy led the Bush Administration to permanently ground the remaining fleet (i.e., no flight after 2010) and lean on the Russian space shuttles to keep the International Space Station supplied until the United States could have different vehicles to safely help people to orbit and eventually to the moon.

Elected during the unfolding of the financial crisis of 2009, President Obama decided not to pursue any new programs for NASA that would result in space travel. Instead, the agency focused on building vehicles' capacity to travel in space while testing these vehicles only on Earth. In protest, Neil Armstrong and other astronauts sent an open letter condemning these cuts. In response, Obama promised that the United States would use these innova-tions to trip to Mars by 2030.

The use of satellites, originally made for public and military purposes, is the best example to elaborate on space commercialization development. There are three main forms of satellite use. The earliest form was remote sensing, used mainly for spying on other states via a high-powered camera lens. By the mid-1960s, however, the technology has advanced to produce telecommunications satellites, or satellites able to transmit a signal using electromagnetic waves to direct (and amplify) information from one point on Earth to a second point where there is a receiver. The first "telecom-munications" satellite was a large balloon (i.e., Echo 1) launched in 1960 to bounce radio waves back to earth. The next commercial satellite was launched by AT&T in 1962. There are currently around 2,000 commercial telecommunications satellites around Earth, by non-governmental organiza-tions, international organizations, and governments. A third and more recent satellite type is navigation. Companies, like GPS, will use their satellites to track navigational courses.

In the United States, there are two major companies hoping to perform asteroid mining in the coming years: Deep Space Industries and Planetary Resources. To assist these companies in beginning their quest for minerals in space, the United States passed a law allowing U.S. citizens to extract minerals from mineral-rich asteroids, so long as they did not claim the asteroid.

With the retirement of space shuttles by NASA under the Obama Administration (as they focused instead on uncrewed vehicles), President Obama also directed NASA to create a program that awarded grants to private companies so they could develop spacecraft to fill this void, so as not to require American astronauts to be dependent on other states for a lift to space. With the successful rocket recycle experiment conducted by SpaceX in December 2015 and its latest success in 2018, when it successfully launched an orbiting rocket, the company planned to launch its first manned aircraft in 2019. Yusaku Maezawa, a Japanese billionaire, will be the first commercial passenger to attempt an orbit around the Moon.

SPACE FORCE

On June 11th, 2018, President Trump made a speech in which he stated: "When it comes to defending America, it is not enough to merely have an American presence in space. We must have American dominance in space."[7] Established on December 20, 2019, the U.S. Space Force (USSF) is a new branch of the Armed Forces and thus under the guidance and direction of the Secretary of Defense. According to the USSF, its mission is to organize, train, and equip space forces in order to "protect U.S. and allied interests in space and to provide space capabilities to the joint force."[8]

Prior to Space Force, there was a Space Command within the Air Force branch of the Department of Defense. This command was only allowed to assist peaceful exploration of space and rescue astronauts in danger and thus, though part of the defense apparatus, held no defense role. In contrast, Trump's Space Force is tasked with: (1) acquiring military space systems, (2) maturing the military doctrine for space power, and (3) organizing space forces to present to our Combatant Commands. Substantively, Space Force could extend the U.S.' national security to space.

THE MOOT COURT: *RUSSIA VS. THE UNITED STATES*

As both a nuclear power and an early explorer of space, Russia will be the state to argue that the United States' Space Force violates Outer Space Law in this fictional case. As Space Force's future remains unclear, this case will present three hypothetical scenarios in which the United States would increase its military presence in outer space. The legal questions posed before the International Court of Justice is:

> *Would any one of these possible military actions in space by the United States violate international space law:*
> 1. *Equipping orbiting space objects with anti-projectile (e.g., asteroid) capability?*
> 2. *Equipping orbiting space objects with anti-missile capability?*
> 3. *Stationing soldiers on a permanent outpost on the moon?*

NOTES

1. UN General Assembly, *Convention on the Law of the Sea*, December 10, 1982. Available at: https://www.un.org/depts/los/convention_agreements/texts/unclos/unclos_e.pdf.

2. "Convention on International Civil Aviation—Doc 7300," n.d. Accessed February 2, 2020. Available at: https://www.icao.int/publications/pages/doc7300.aspx.

3. Contributor, Posts By This. n.d. "Sputnik's Impact on America," Accessed February 2, 2020. Available at: https://www.pbs.org/wgbh/nova/article/sputnik-impact-on-america/.

4. United Nations, *Antarctic Treaty*, Treaty No. 5778, June 23, 1961. Available at: https://treaties.un.org/pages/showDetails.aspx?objid=0800000280136dbc.

5. Wickramatunga, Robert. n.d. "General Assembly Resolution 1721 (XVI)," Accessed February 2, 2020a. Available at: https://www.unoosa.org/oosa/en/ourwork/spacelaw/treaties/resolutions/res_16_1721.html.

6. Clinton, William, "State of the Union Address," January 25, 1994. Available at: https://clinton.presidentiallibraries.us/items/show/16126.

7. Trump, Donald J. "Remarks by President Trump at a Meeting with the National Space Council and Signing of Space Policy Directive-3," *The White House*, The United States Government, June 11, 2018. Available at: https://www.whitehouse.gov/briefings-statements/remarks-president-trump-meeting-national-space-council-signing-space-policy-directive-3/.

8. United States Space Force, "About the Space Force," Available at: https://www.spaceforce.mil/About-Us/About-Space-Force/.

Chapter 10

The Use of Force

Article 2(4) of the United Nations Charter obligates states to refrain from "the threat or use of force against the territorial integrity or political independence of any state."[1] Article 51 of the same document, however, states that nothing "in the present Charter shall impair the inherent right of individual or collective self-defense if an armed attack occurs against a Member of the United Nations, until the Security Council has taken measures necessary to maintain international peace and security."[2]

In the 1990s, the dissolution of the Socialist Federal Republic of Yugoslavia resulted in a series of interethnic conflicts over new borders, control within a new power vacuum, and deep-seated animosity and hatred, which led to the death of more than 130,000 people. The last of the bloody wars was one within Kosovo, a disputed autonomous region. Though Kosovo had once been a part of the Kingdom of Serbia, ethnic Albanians within the region wished to succeed from Serbia and join Albania.

After a divided UN Security Council (UNSC) failed to impose peace throughout the earlier conflicts, in 1998, the NATO Council voted to take action against the Serbian army to end its attacks on the Kosovar Albanians within this region. Though praised by some as a humanitarian intervention based on the burgeoning norm of the responsibility to protect all individuals from harm, others determined the NATO members to be in direct violation of their obligation to refrain from the threat or use of force unless attacked. This chapter will explore the right to go to war, known as *jus ad bellum* ("laws before war"). Next, it will explore the political and ethnic factors that lead to the Yugoslav Wars. Finally, it will focus on both the UNSC's inability to take action and the decision of NATO to act in Kosovo.

INTERNATIONAL LAW ON THE USE
OF FORCE (JUS AD BELLUM)

The right to self-defense is codified in the UN Charter. Article 2(4) of the UN Charter articulates that all "states should refrain in their international relations from the threat or use of force."[3] Further in the Charter, however, it revises this statement with Article 51's assertion that "Nothing in the present Charter shall impair the inherent right of individual or collective self-defense if an armed attack occurs against a Member of the United Nations until the Security Council has taken measures necessary to maintain international peace and security." This statement formally codified a custom that had been recognized for centuries in international law of the inherent right to self-defense. Though the UN Charter presents self-defense as only being operationalized once an "armed attack occurs," customary law has noted that a state need not actually be hit to defend itself, so long as there is the "existence of an imminent threat."

Article 24, Section 1 of the UN Charter gives the UNSC the "primary responsibility for the maintenance of international peace and security."[4] In fulfilling this responsibility, the UNSC may adopt a range of measures, including the establishment of UN peacekeeping operations. The Security Council may make recommendations (Article 39) or call upon the parties concerned to comply with provisional measures (Article 40). If armed forces are to be deployed, Article 41 notes they are first used to provide a deterrence to further conflict. If this proves inadequate, then Article 42 allows the Security Council "to take such action by air, sea, or land forces as may be necessary to maintain or restore international peace and security."

Though the Security Council is granted primary responsibility for maintaining international peace and security, Article 53 of the UN Charter states that the Security Council may utilize such collective security organizations "for enforcement action under its authority." It makes clear, however, that there should be no action taken by these organizations "without the authorization of the Security Council, with the exception of measures against any enemy state." Within the UN Charter, the term enemy state applies to "any state that was an enemy to one of the signatories of this Charter in WWII." At the time the Charter went into force, these states included the former Axis powers of Bulgaria, Finland, Germany, Hungary, Italy, Japan, and Romania (Text Box 10.1).[5]

TEXT BOX 10.1 CHARTER OF THE UNITED NATIONS (1945) [ARTICLES 2(4), 24, 51, AND 53]

Article 2 (4)

All Members shall refrain in their international relations from the threat or use of force against the territorial integrity or political independence of any state, or in any other manner inconsistent with the Purposes of the United Nations.

Article 24

In order to ensure prompt and effective action by the United Nations, its Members confer on the Security Council primary responsibility for the maintenance of international peace and security, and agree that in carrying out its duties under this responsibility the Security Council acts on their behalf.

Article 51

Nothing in the present Charter shall impair the inherent right of individual or collective self-defense if an armed attack occurs against a Member of the United Nations, until the Security Council has taken measures necessary to maintain international peace and security. Measures taken by Members in the exercise of this right of self-defense shall be immediately reported to the Security Council and shall not in any way affect the authority and responsibility of the Security Council under the present Charter to take at any time such action as it deems necessary in order to maintain or restore international peace and security.

Article 53

1. The Security Council shall, where appropriate, utilize such regional arrangements or agencies for enforcement action under its authority. But no enforcement action shall be taken under regional arrangements or by regional agencies without the authorization of the Security Council, with the exception of measures against any enemy state, as defined in paragraph 2 of this Article, provided for pursuant to Article 107 or in regional arrangements directed against renewal of aggressive policy on the part of any such state, until such time as the Organization may, on request of the Governments concerned, be charged with the responsibility for preventing further aggression by such a state.
2. The term enemy state as used in paragraph 1 of this Article applies to any state which during the Second World War has been an enemy of any signatory of the present Charter.

The North Atlantic Treaty Organization (NATO) is a collective security organization. In its founding treaty, the NATO Charter, the preamble states that the organization's purpose is to "reaffirm . . . . the purposes and principles of the Charter of the United Nations." In keeping with the right to self-defense within the Charter, Article 5 determines that the organization will act collectively in response to "an armed attack against one or more" of its members only and thus is within the obligations under the UN Charter to be used only in situations of self-defense (Text Box 10.2).

TEXT BOX 10.2   THE NORTH ATLANTIC TREATY (1949) [PREAMBLE AND ARTICLE 5]

Preamble

The Parties to this Treaty reaffirm their faith in the purposes and principles of the Charter of the United Nations and their desire to live in peace with all peoples and all governments.

Article 5

An armed attack against one or more of them in Europe or North America shall be considered an attack against them all and consequently, they agree that, if such an armed attack occurs, each of them, in exercise of the right of individual or collective self-defense recognized by Article 51 of the Charter of the United Nations, will assist the Party or Parties so attacked by taking forthwith, individually and in concert with the other Parties, such action as it deems necessary, including the use of armed force, to restore and maintain the security of the North Atlantic area.

Beyond these sources of international law is the norm posited by the General Assembly in a resolution that claims the international community has a Responsibility to Protect (R2P) and should consider this norm more fully.[6] The concept acknowledges that states are the primary entities responsible for the welfare of their people. If, however, they fail to protect their people or target them directly, then it is the responsibility of the international community to intervene on behalf of those being targeted. This type of intervention is known as humanitarian intervention. Currently, the UNSC is the only international body legally allowed to authorize force for the "purposes of international peace and security" rather than self-defense, which is a right of all states. As a result, any humanitarian intervention would have to be authorized by the UNSC and would have to be the last option.

THE YUGOSLAV WARS (1991 TO 2001)

"Greater Serbia"

The Balkans is a mountainous region in southeastern Europe at the center of overlapping political and religious claims. In the third century, the expanding Roman Empire became too vast to be controlled, and Emperor Diocletian divided it into halves. The Western Empire would be governed by Rome, while the Eastern Empire would be ruled by a Christian convert, Constantine, from the city of Byzantium, which he renamed Constantinople and is present-day Istanbul. Over the centuries, the Byzantine Empire would consolidate control over the Balkans, spreading Eastern Orthodox Christianity (a divergent view of Catholicism that burgeoned into a different theological foundation in the Great Schism of the 11th century).

With the Balkan region were a myriad of ethnic groups, including the early Greeks (Macedonians), Croats, Slovenes, Bosniaks, Albanians, Montenegrins, and Serbs. The Serbs were ethnic Slavs (originally from present-day) Russia who migrated into the region in the third century (about the time Byzantine Empire was established).

Though the Serbs originally fought as mercenaries against the Byzantine Empire, in the tenth century, Byzantine Emperor Michael III commissioned a missionary named Cyril to translate the Bible into a written form of the spoken Slavic for the purposes of evangelizing the Serbs. This written language would be called the Cyrillic alphabet. The Byzantines were successful in converting the Serbs within their empire to Orthodox Christianity. However, offering them a way to practice through their own language did not make the Serbs any more loyal to the Empire.

When in the thirteenth century, the Byzantines were fighting off Muslim invaders in the Crusades, the Serbs formed the Kingdom of Serbia out of vast Byzantine territory. Though the Byzantines tried multiple times to regain the territory, they were unsuccessful. By the fourteenth century, the Serbian King recast his role as "Emperor of the Serbs, Greeks, Bulgarians, and Albanians" and proceeded to launch a military expansion across the region.

The Battle of Kosovo and "Turkish Night"

The success of the Serbs ended, however, with the invasions of the Ottomans into the Balkan region in the fifteenth century. While other ethnic groups throughout the region (e.g., the Bosniaks) did not struggle against the Ottoman rule, the Serbs were consolidated as a powerful Christian kingdom against a Muslim conqueror. As a result, the Serbs battled brutally against the Ottomans until they lost in the Battle of Kosovo, named after a small region under Serbian control, in 1389. Within this defeat, Kosovo became a symbol of the loss of a "Greater Serbia."

For the next five centuries, until its independence from the Ottomans in 1878, Serbs fought against the Muslim rule. Described by Serbians as the "Turkish night," the period of Ottoman rule shaped a Serbian nationalism built on pride and a sense of deep nostalgia.

In 1690, the Serbs chose to align with the Austrians against the Ottomans. When the Austrians were unsuccessful, tens of thousands of Serbs migrated out of Old Serbia (the territory originally under the Kingdom of Serbia) and toward the Austro-Hungarian Empire. Initially, most resettled in a grey zone between the Empires (which is present-day Croatia and Bosnia-Herzegovina) and later moved even further into the Austro-Hungarian Empire.

This Serbian diaspora served an important role in stoking Serbian nationalism as they were free of Ottoman rule and able to rise higher into the middle class than their counterparts under Ottoman feudalism. Interestingly, in much of the territory that Serbs abandoned, new ethnic groups moved in. Kosovo, for example, saw an increase in Albanians once Serbs fled.

Independence and the Rise of the Yugoslav Federation

By the nineteenth century, the Ottoman Empire was widely considered to be the "sick man of Europe."[7] Russia and Austria noticed. Russia assisted the Serbians, Montenegrins, and Bulgarians in gaining independence in 1878. Meanwhile, Austria was expanding its empire along the Dalmatian coast into Croat and Slovenian territories once held by the Ottomans.

Before Serbia would be fully able to concentrate on Austria, it needed to rid the First Balkan War against the Ottomans. Though the Balkan states proved victorious, they soon began to disagree, however, over how to divide the spoils of war, leading to the Second Balkan War among the Balkan states.

It was in these wars that Serbia gained parts of Macedonia and Kosovo. By the time the Serbs regained Kosovo, the territory was mostly occupied by Albanians who had migrated there when the Serbs left during Ottoman rule. These Albanians, though in Serbian territory, remained ethnically distinct from Serbs and practiced Islam and thus had little interest in being controlled by Serbia. As Serbia's dominance in the Balkans congealed, tensions between it and Austria increased. When the Austrians pushed for larger borders for Albania that bled into Serbian territory (including seizing the beloved symbol of an old Serbia, Kosovo), the rivalry between the two states reached a break-ing point. On June 28, 1914, a member of a Serbian nationalist group called the "Black Hand" assassinated Austrian Archduke Franz Ferdinand, igniting World War I.

When the war ended, the issue over what would happen to the Balkans con-cluded in the Kingdom of Yugoslavia. The Triple Entente (i.e., Great Britain, France, and Russia) agreed that the Kingdom would be a constitutional monarchy with a representative government based on ethnic representation. The stability of this regime was short-lived, however, as the Serbs tended to dominate demographically and thus controlled government. When the government became so unstable as to have parliamentarians murdering other parliamentarians in the parliament building, the king dissolved the constitu-tional government completely.

At the onset of WWII, the Germans and Italians invaded Yugoslavia in early April of 1941, carving up the territory. Hungry would get the Banat region (with ethnic Hungarians), Albania would be used to launch invasions into Greece, and Italy would gain the Croatian and Bosnian territories along the Adriatic since Croatia was dabbling in fascism before World War II. The Ustasha Movement was a revolutionary group formed in the late 1920s that sought a greater Croatia and promoted the genocide of Serbs, Romani people, and Jews. The Nazis thus saw an ally in the Ustasha and allowed Croatia to remain "independent" of Nazi or Italian occupation, so long as the Ustasha were in charge.

Amid the fascist occupation, a resistance movement began to grow. From the beginning, this resistance movement was organized by Josip Broz, though people knew him mostly by his code name, Tito. Born from a Croatian father and Serbian mother, Tito had participated in the Bolshevik Revolution in 1917 before returning home to Yugoslavia and joining the Communist Party.

Though the Federal People's Republic of Yugoslavia enacted many Communist reforms (e.g., nationalizing the means of production and set-ting up a central planning office), Tito was never comfortable being a pup-pet of Stalin. As a result, he rebelled against the Soviet Union to the point Yugoslavia was expelled from the Soviets' sphere of influence.

Either because he was ousted from the Communist club or other factors, Tito began to ease away from a rigid form of Communism in Yugoslavia. By 1965, he allowed capital-rich enterprises such as commercial banks to be established and was considerably popular, even within a divided nation.

Yugoslav Wars: The Revival of a "Greater Serbia"

Many suggest (myself included) that Tito was the tie that bound these differ-ent states together into one federation and quieted the tension among ethnic groups throughout the Balkans. After Tito died in 1980, old ethnic tensions were revived once again.

The next leader of Yugoslavia was a Serbian politician named Slobodan Milošević. Milošević rose to power by pushing forth Serbian nationalist rhetoric, promising to protect ethnic Serbs across Yugoslavia (e.g., in the other five states) against persecution and use the institutions of the Federation for the benefit of the Serbian people.

This was a threat enough for Slovenia, Croatia, Macedonia, and Bosnia and Herzegovina to form independence parties and call for secession from Yugoslavia in June 1991. Thus, in April of 1992, a new Federal Republic of Yugoslavia was inaugurated, comprising only Serbia and Montenegro.

Croatian War (1991 to 1992)

Serbian minorities within Croatia began to be uneasy as Croatia moved toward independence. Their uneasiness stemmed from the realities of World War II, when the fascist Ustasha had targeted Serbs. In preparation for potential ethnic persecution, the Serbs in Croatia (around twelve percent of the total population) began to form militias against the Croatian state.

Thus, the Serbian army focused their forces against the Croatians, leaving Slovenia and Macedonia free to declare independence without incident. In June of 1991, the predominantly Serbian Yugoslav army went into Croatia to assist these militias with the extended purpose of retaining territory in which Serbs were concentrated for the Serbian state. Yugoslav forces shelled Dubrovnik and other Dalmatian cities and occupied about one-third of Croatian territory.

In the ensuing war, both the Croats and Serbs massacred civilians. As the Yugoslavian (Serbian) Army moved into Croatia in autumn of 1991, it began to expel Croat populations from their homes, forced these civilians into concentration camps, shelled entire cities, and summarily executed ethnic Croats in the streets.

By the end of 1991, more than one-third of Croatia was under Serbian control (and there were 318,000 refugees fleeing Croatia for Slovenia, Austria, and Macedonia among other places).

During the Croatian War, the UNSC passed four Resolutions.[8] The first Resolution (713) called for a ceasefire agreement, but this was ignored by both the Croats and Serbs. In November of 1991, the Security Council passed a second Resolution (721) unanimously voting to send peacekeepers agreement once a ceasefire agreement was reached. Though both sides called for a peacekeeping force, neither could agree on boundaries to enact a ceasefire. Thus the third Resolution a month later (724) simply stating that the "conditions for establishing a peacekeeping operation in Yugoslavia still do not exist."

As the fighting intensified into 1992 and the General Assembly voted to allow Croatia, Slovenia, and Montenegro recognition of statehood and membership status to the organization (UNGA Resolutions 236 to 238), the Security Council passed its fourth and final Resolution (749), agreeing to send peacekeepers to patrol the boundaries between Croatia and Serbia and calling on both parties to not "resort to violence, particularly in any area where the Force is based or deployed."[9] By 1994, both sides were exhausted, and the conflict halted without any peace agreement reached.

Bosnian War (1992 to 1995)

Before the Croatian war ended, the Bosnian War began between ethnic Bosniak Muslims and the Serbian-dominated Yusoglav Army. When the Bosnians voted for independence from Yugoslavia, this angered the Serbs within Bosnia and Herzegovina, who comprised one-third of the population. The Serbs within Bosnia responded by forming a militia and laying siege to the capital, Sarajevo, from 1992 to the end of 1995.

Throughout the war, Bosnian Serbs, assisted by the Yugoslav Army, successfully gained control of nearly three-quarters of the country and began "ethnically cleaning" the territory of non-Serbs. Ethnic cleansing is a Serbian term (*ciscenje terena*) for genocide by creating an ethnically homogenous area by forcibly expelling, or killing, a particular ethnic group.

The UN moved more quickly in response to the conflict in Bosnia than it had in Croatia, calling on states to respect a ceasefire (Res. 752), enacting a full embargo on all goods to Yugoslavia except humanitarian aid (757 and 760), expanding the peacekeepers mandate to Bosnia (758 and 761), labeling some of the acts as being in violation of the Geneva Conventions (780), suspending the membership status of Yugoslavia (777) among others, and issuing a no-fly zone (816).

By the beginning of 1993, the UN felt it was clear it needed to do more. In February, the UNSC passed Resolution 808, establishing "an international tribunal shall be established for the prosecution of persons responsible for serious violations of international humanitarian law committed in the territory of the former Yugoslavia since 1991."[10]

The assaults, however, continued. To protect both civilians and peacekeepers from the onslaught, the Security Council designated safe zones throughout Bosnia in May of 1993 (Resolution 824). One such safe zone was the town of Srebrenica, bordering Serbia. In July 1995, however, one of the greatest modern atrocities was committed in that town, when the Serbs broke through a small UN peacekeeping force into the town, expelled more than 20,000 civilians, and then executed more than 7,000 Bosniak boys and men. This attack was the worst mass murder on European soil since World War II."[11]

In the first year of the Bosnian War, NATO offered the UNSC support monitoring compliance with its Resolutions (e.g., inspect cargo ships to ensure compliance with the embargo). Beginning in 1993, however, that role expanded as it was given the power to enforce a no-fly-zone under UNSC Resolution 816. This role became a combat one in February of 1994 when NATO forces shot down Serbian fighter jets bombing a factory in northern Bosnia.

After the attack in Srebrenica, NATO began airstrikes directed against Serbian military targets within and around Sarajevo, until they were forced to withdraw. When the Serbs decided to enter peace negotiations in November, NATO argued that it played a key role in the outcome, while others argued that NATO intervention moved beyond the spirit of the NATO Charter.

Kosovo War (1998 to 1999)

After centuries of being conquered (by Ottomans, then Austrians, and later Serbs), the region of Kosovo, composed predominantly of ethnic Albanians, called for independence from Yugoslavia and declared independence in July of 1990. As the Kosovar witnessed the bloody conflicts in Croatia and Bosnia in 1991 and 1992, they determined that the Serbian government would will-ingly use military force against them.

Though initially, the Kosovar Albanians tried nonviolent tactics, in 1996, a guerilla group named the Kosovo Liberation Army (KLA) began to attack Serbian officials and law enforcement throughout Kosovo using arms pro-vided to them by Albania. Once the KLA stepped up its tactics in 1997, the Yugoslav military entered Kosovo and launched a military offensive in the heart of Kosovo in Drenica in early 1998.

As one Human Rights Watch report indicates, "the Serbian police and Yugoslav Army committed summary executions [including murdering children with an ax], indiscriminately attacked civilians [including dismem-berment], and systematically destroyed civilian property [e.g., intentional contamination of wells and livestock have been shot]."[12]

The brutality of this campaign drove hundreds of recruits into the KLA's ranks. Yugoslav military tactics also drove thousands of ethnic Albanian vil-lagers from their homes. By late summer, the plight of these refugees pouring into Albania and Macedonia had become a source of serious international concern. Toward the end of September of 1998, the UN Commission for Refugees estimated that more than one-quarter of all homes in the conflict areas within Kosovo were completely destroyed.[13]

As the violence erupted in yet a third Balkan area against ethnic minorities, the UNSC called for a no-fly zone (Res 1203) and the continued access for civilians to humanitarian relief (1239). Feeling the United Nations was again slow to act, the NATO Council met on October 13th, 1998, and agreed to authorize an ultimatum for Serbia to withdraw from Kosovo or face NATO airstrikes. Initially, Milošević seemed agreeable, even discussing possible peace agreements for the region, but the slated presence of 30,000 NATO troops to maintain order within the region was untenable for the Serbian leader.

Immediately after this agreement fell through, Serbian military and police forces stepped up the intensity of their operations against the ethnic Albanians in Kosovo. By March 1999, NATO "Operation Allied Forces" was launched with the stated purposes of ending all military action in Kosovo, pushing all Serbian forces from the region, and negotiating both a return of refugees and a stable political agreement for the future of the region.

After almost three months and hundreds of airstrikes, Milošević agreed to withdraw his forces from Kosovo. In June of 1999, the UNSC passed its final Resolution in the Balkan Wars (Res 1244), establishing a NATO-led peace-keeping mission into Kosovo.[14] Before the end of the war, the International Criminal Tribunal for the Former Yugoslavia issued an arrest warrant for Milošević. Though proceedings began against him, he died in prison before the Justices could issue their final judgment.[15]

THE MOOT COURT: *THE RUSSIAN FEDERATION VS. NATO MEMBERS*

On March 25th, 1999, Russia, Belarus, and India drafted a resolution condemning the NATO airstrikes. The Resolution, which failed to garner nine votes, stated that it was "deeply concerned" with NATO's use of military force against the Federal Republic of Yugoslavia "without the authorization by the Council." The draft resolution went on to affirm "that such unilateral use of force constitutes a flagrant violation of the United Nations Charter" and determined that the "use of force by NATO against the Federal Republic of Yugoslavia constitutes a threat to international peace and security." After the full withdrawal of Yugoslav forces from Kosovo, NATO suspended its air operations in 1999.

In this fictional moot court, Russia has chosen to continue its protest of NATO actions before the International Court of Justice. For this moot court, the legal question posed before the International Court of Justice is: Were the NATO members in violation of their obligations under *jus ad bellum* for their decision to intervene in Kosovo in 1998?

NOTES

1. United Nations, "Charter of the United Nations," October 24, 1945. Available at: https://unispal.un.org/DPA/DPR/unispal.nsf/0/7F0AF2BD897689B785256C3 30061D253.

2. United Nations, "Charter of the United Nations," October 24, 1945. Available at: https://unispal.un.org/DPA/DPR/unispal.nsf/0/7F0AF2BD897689B785256C3 30061D253.

3. United Nations, "Charter of the United Nations," October 24, 1945. Available at: https://unispal.un.org/DPA/DPR/unispal.nsf/0/7F0AF2BD897689B785256C3 30061D253.

4. United Nations, "Charter of the United Nations," October 24, 1945. Available at: https://unispal.un.org/DPA/DPR/unispal.nsf/0/7F0AF2BD897689B785256C3 30061D253.

5. United Nations, "Charter of the United Nations," October 24, 1945. Available at: https://unispal.un.org/DPA/DPR/unispal.nsf/0/7F0AF2BD897689B785256C3 30061D253.

6. General Assembly Resolution 63/308, *The Responsibility to Protect*, A/RES/67/97 (September 14, 2009). Available at: https://www.un.org/en/ga/63/resolutions.shtml.

7. Livanios, Dimitris, "The 'Sick Man' Paradox: History, Rhetoric and the 'European Character' of Turkey," *Journal of Southern Europe and the Balkans* 8, no. 3 (2006): 299–311.

8. United Nations Security Council, "Resolutions," Available at: https://www.un.org/securitycouncil/content/resolutions-0.

9. United Nations Security Council, "Resolutions," Available at: https://www.un.org/securitycouncil/content/resolutions-0.

10. United Nations Security Council, "Resolutions," Available at: https://www.un.org/securitycouncil/content/resolutions-0.

11. "The Fall of Srebrenica and the Failure of UN Peacekeeping | Bosnia and Herzegovina," *Human Rights Watch*, October 15, 1995. Available at: https://www.hrw.org/report/1995/10/15/fall-srebrenica-and-failure-un-peacekeeping/bosnia-and-herzegovina.

12. "Humanitarian Law Violations in Kosovo," *Human Rights Watch*, October 1, 1998. Available at: https://www.hrw.org/report/1998/10/01/humanitarian-law-violations-kosovo.

13. "A Week of Terror in Drenica," *Human Rights Watch*, 1999. Available at: https://www.hrw.org/reports/1999/kosovo/.

14. United Nations Security Council, "Resolutions," Available at: https://www.un.org/securitycouncil/content/resolutions-0.

15. United Nations International Criminal Tribunal for the former Yugoslavia, Slobodan Milošević Trial—The Prosecution's Case," Available at: https://www.icty.org/en/content/slobodan-milo%C5%A1evi%C4%87-trial-prosecutions-cas.

Chapter 11

International Humanitarian Law

One of the most foundational successes of international law has been the formal codification of international humanitarian law within the Geneva Conventions. These Conventions and their common article and the additional protocols are collectively known as *jus in bello* (or "the laws of war"). The four Conventions have been signed and ratified by every state in the world,[1] and they guarantee protections to humanitarian aid workers, prisoners of war, and civilians within an armed conflict. However, there is debate among scholars and policymakers as to whether these laws of war can be applied to individuals associated with terrorist organizations, like Al-Qaeda.

This chapter will first examine the evolution of international humanitarian law, discussing each of the main components of the Geneva Conventions. Next, this chapter will examine the actions taken by the United States following the September 11th attacks, including creating a category outside of the protections of the Geneva Conventions, known as "unlawful combatant." Finally, this chapter will examine the grey legal status of individuals labeled "unlawful combatants" who are currently detained at a U.S. naval base turned detention center on Guantánamo Bay in Cuba.

INTERNATIONAL HUMANITARIAN LAW (IHL)

Though humans are the essential creators of international law and its subjects, rarely is the individual the focus of international law. Instead, most international law focuses on the rights and obligations of states vis-a-vis other states. There are two regimes (or subject areas) within international law in which the human is central: international human rights law and international humanitarian law.

Whereas human rights are afforded to all people at all times, international humanitarian law focuses on the right afforded to individuals within an armed conflict. It is for this reason that humanitarian law is also known as the "laws of war." The clearest, most well-defined, and binding documents that address humanitarian law are the Geneva Conventions.

The Geneva Conventions (1948)

Though international humanitarian law existed for centuries in customary law, WWII showed the world that these laws were not forceful enough in the face of rising nationalism, raw expansionism, the destructive power of new military and naval technologies, and war across five of seven continents. Following WWII, when the death toll estimates reached as high as 25 million for soldiers and another 25 million for civilians from conflict alone (not including those that died from indirect factors of war such as famine and disease), the International Red Cross called for a push toward more robust international humanitarian laws.

Following World War II, the International Red Cross hosted a Convention in Geneva, Switzerland, to discuss updating and codifying the laws of war.[2] This meeting culminated in four Geneva Conventions.

The First and Second Geneva Conventions

The first of the four Geneva Conventions is the Convention on the Wounded and Sick in Armed Forces in the Field. This treaty determined how individuals would be protected from attack if no longer healthy or able to fight because of bodily wounds. In addition, it also protected those medical and religious personnel on or near the battlefield from attack as well. In this First Convention, the symbol of the Red Cross was noted as the internationally recognized symbol to distinguish these individuals within a conflict. The second Geneva Convention, known formally as the Convention on the Wounded, Sick, & Shipwrecked in Armed Forces at Sea, closely follows the provisions of the First Convention but applies these protections to maritime conflicts.

The Third Geneva Convention

Though the third Geneva Convention, known formally as the Convention Relative to the Treatment of Prisoners of War, distinguishes which individuals during a conflict may be protected under the prisoner of war status and what rights are afforded to them. Most broadly, prisoner of war status applies in conditions in which enemy forces have captured an individual.

In addition to members of armed forces, Article Four of the Third Geneva Convention allows members of other armed groups to be granted prisoner of war status as well. Both members of militias and volunteer corps (including those of "organized resistance movements") may be granted prisoner of war status, so long as they: have some chain of command, wear a "distinctive sign" that can be easily recognized, carry their arms openly, and "act in accordance with the laws and customs of war."[3]

As for the voluntary nature of the "voluntary corp," the convention allows for situations in which at the "approach of the enemy," individuals "spontaneously take up arms to resist the invading forces without having had time to form themselves into regular armed units, provided they carry arms openly and respect the laws and customs of war."[4]

Article Four also protects civilians who are accompanying the armed forces (e.g., aircraft crew members and journalists) and/or crewmembers of merchant vessels participating in the conflict. The rights and protections of combatants can be afforded to these individuals, "provided that they have received authorization from the armed forces which they accompany."[5] If in cases in which the status of a prisoner of war cannot be determined at the time of capture, Article Five requires the enemy forces to treat individuals as if they are prisoners of war until their status can be determined by a "competent tribunal" (Text Box 11.1).[6]

TEXT BOX 11.1   CONVENTION RELATIVE TO THE TREATMENT OF PRISONERS OF WAR, THIRD GENEVA CONVENTION (1948) [ARTICLES 4 AND 5]

Article 4

A. Prisoners of war, in the sense of the present Convention, are persons belonging to one of the following categories, who have fallen into the power of the enemy:

1. Members of the armed forces of a Party to the conflict as well as members of militias or volunteer corps forming part of such armed forces.
2. Members of other militias and members of other volunteer corps, including those of organized resistance movements, belonging to a Party to the conflict and operating in or outside their own territory, even if this territory is occupied, provided that such militias or volunteer corps, including such organized resistance movements, fulfill the following conditions:
   a. that of being commanded by a person responsible for his subordinates;
   b. that of having a fixed distinctive sign recognizable at a distance;
   c. that of carrying arms openly;

   d. that of conducting their operations in accordance with the laws and customs of war.

   . . .

4. Persons who accompany the armed forces without actually being members thereof, such as civilian members of military aircraft crews, war correspondents, supply contractors, members of labor units or of services responsible for the welfare of the armed forces, provided that they have received authorization from the armed forces which they accompany.

   . . .

6. Inhabitants of a non-occupied territory who, on the approach of the enemy, spontaneously take up arms to resist the invading forces, without having had time to form themselves into regular armed units, provided they carry arms openly and respect the laws and customs of war.

Article 5

The present Convention shall apply to the persons referred to in Article 4 from the time they fall into the power of the enemy and until their final release and repatriation. Should any doubt arise as to whether persons having committed a belligerent act and having fallen into the hands of the enemy belong to any of the categories enumerated in Article 4, such persons shall enjoy the protection of the present Convention until such time as their status has been determined by a competent tribunal.

The Fourth Geneva Convention

The final of these Conventions is known formally as the Convention Relative to the Protection of Civilian Persons During Times of War. This convention directly explains the rights afforded to civilians during a conflict. Article 13 protects the equality of all civilians "without any adverse distinction based, in particular, on race, nationality, religion or political opinion."[7]

   The Convention obligates states to provide protection for civilians. Specifically, Article 32 forbids states from "taking any measure of such a character as to cause the physical suffering or extermination of protected persons in their hands . . . whether applied by civilian or military agents" of the state. Article 33 prohibits any person from being "punished for an offense he or she has not personally committed." Article 34 prohibits taking civilians hostage, though Article 78 does allow for an occupying power to intern non-combatants or assign them residencies "for imperative reasons of security" (Text Box 11.2).[8]

TEXT BOX 11.2   CONVENTION RELATIVE TO THE PROTECTION OF CIVILIAN PERSONS DURING TIMES OF WAR FOURTH GENEVA CONVENTION (1948) [ARTICLES 13, 32-34, AND 78]

Article 13

[These] provisions . . . cover the whole of the populations of the countries in conflict, without any adverse distinction based, in particular, on race, nationality, religion or political opinion, and are intended to alleviate the sufferings caused by war.

Article 32

The High Contracting Parties specifically agree that each of them is prohibited from taking any measure of such a character as to cause the physical suffering or extermination of protected persons in their hands. This prohibition applies not only to murder, torture, corporal punishment, mutilation and medical or scientific experiments not necessitated by the medical treatment of a protected person, but also to any other measures of brutality whether applied by civilian or military agents.

Article 33

No protected person may be punished for an offense he or she has not personally committed. Collective penalties and likewise all measures of intimidation or of terrorism are prohibited. Pillage is prohibited. Reprisals against protected persons and their property are prohibited.

Article 34

The taking of hostages is prohibited.

Article 78

If the Occupying Power considers it necessary, for imperative reasons of security, to take safety measures concerning protected persons, it may, at the most, subject them to assigned residence or to internment. Decisions regarding such assigned residence or internment shall be made accord-ing to a regular procedure to be prescribed by the Occupying Power in accordance with the provisions of the present Convention. This procedure shall include the right of appeal for the parties concerned. Appeals shall be decided with the least possible delay. In the event of the decision being upheld, it shall be subject to periodical review, if possible every six months, by a competent body set up by the said Power. Protected persons made subject to assigned residence and thus required to leave their homes.

Common Article Three and Additional Protocols

Each of the four Geneva Conventions was signed by every state in the world. That said, there was much debate over whether or not the four conventions should be extended to civil, or intrastate, conflicts as well as interstate ones. In the end, the four conventions only apply to interstate conflicts, and a common article was drafted that extends much of the protections within the original conventions to civil wars. The United States did not sign this Common Article Three.

After the Conventions and Common Article were concluded, there were debates as to whether the Third Convention afforded protection to individuals fighting within an insurgent group against a colonial power or fighting. Additional Protocol I chose to expand the nature of the conflicts to struggles against colonial powers (i.e., Article 1) and to extend the protection of individuals as prisoners of war to armed combatants who "cannot so distinguish himself while he is engaged in a military deployment preceding the launching of an attack in which he is to participate" (i.e., Article 44).[9]

President Reagan soundly rejected Additional Protocol I based on the two articles noted above. First, in response to Article 1, he suggested that it "elevates the international legal status of self-described 'national liberation' [who may] make a practice of terrorism." Secondly, he claimed that Article 44 "sweeps away years of law by 'recognizing' that an armed irregular, 'cannot' always distinguish himself from non-combatants."[10] Reagan argued that allowing combatants to hide their visible distinctions would obliterate the "distinction between combatants and non-combatants."

The United States did, however, sign both Additional Protocols II and III. The second additional protocol allowed for the extended protection of civilians and medical personnel during an intrastate armed conflict, which Reagan was more comfortable with, suggesting that it "would mitigate many of the worst human tragedies of the type that have occurred in internal conflicts of the present and recent past."[11] The Senate did not act to ratify the Protocol, as it viewed the legal distinction between combatant and civilian to remain ambiguous. Though Clinton tried to submit it for ratification again in 1999, he was unsuccessful as well. Additional Protocol III, however, passed ratification. This protocol extended the symbols of protection for medical and religious personnel beyond the cross and crescent moon (which has been added subsequently) to include a red diamond as well.

As a result, the United States is explicitly bound to the first four Geneva Conventions, which apply to interstate conflict. Though it extends these protections to civilian and medical personnel involved in intrastate conflicts, it did not adopt the Common Article Three or Additional Protocol II. As a result, the United States neither applies the existing definition of prisoner of war to intrastate conflicts (as Common Article Three does), nor does it allow for the category of fighter afforded prisoner of action to be expanded (as Additional Protocol II would have done).

THE UNITED STATES' USE OF THE TERM "UNLAWFUL COMBATANT"

On September 11th, the United States was attacked by the terrorist group, Al-Qaeda. There were four coordinated attacks that day, as Al-Qaeda operatives four commercial passenger airplanes departing from northeastern airports were hijacked. Terrorists flew two planes into the World Trade Centers' Twin Towers, a third plane crashed into the Pentagon, and a fourth was destined for D.C. before passengers aboard thwarted the hijackers; that plane crashed into a field in Shanksville, Pennsylvania. The day after these attacks, President Bush declared that the United States would respond with a global "war on terror."

Less than a month after the attacks, the United States launched a military campaign against Afghanistan as part of this "war on terror." Specifically, the United States chose to engage in Afghanistan for two purposes: (1) finding members of Al-Qaeda—the terrorist organization that orchestrated the attacks, and (2) toppling the Taliban—the government of Afghanistan that had allowed Al-Qaeda a safe haven within its territory.

The Third Geneva Conventions explains that all persons deemed to be combatants during war are granted the protections of a prisoner of war if captured by the enemy. The Fourth Geneva Conventions explains that all persons who did not pick up arms were deemed to be civilians and thus afforded protection under the Fourth Convention against being attacked or captured.

After September 11th, the Bush Administration articulated a legal lacuna that existed between these two conventions. That is, the Administration argued that there are people who act like combatants (and thus are not solely civilians) but who also do not meet the criteria of combatants in the Third Convention.

The Administration responded to this perceived gap by calling combatants who did not meet the criteria mentioned in the Third Convention to be "unlawful combatants." The term "unlawful combatant" was first used in *Ex parte Quirin, 317 U.S. 1 (1942)*, a case against Nazi spies (one of whom was a U.S. citizen) that were tried by a military commission and executed during WWII. Within this case, the term was defined to mean persons "without uniform [who] come secretly through the lines for the purpose of waging war."[12]

"UNLAWFUL COMBATANTS" DETAINED AT GUANTÁNAMO BAY

This section will first examine how the United States acquired the base at Guantánamo Bay and the various ways in which it has been used before housing "unlawful combatants" captured in the War in Afghanistan. Next, this section will examine the specific situation of one of the Guantánamo detainees determined to be an "unlawful combatant," Uthman Abdul Rahim Mohammed Uthman, before discussing the status of Guantánamo detainees today.

History of the U.S. Presence at Guantánamo Bay

The U.S. naval base at Guantánamo Bay was established in 1898, following the Spanish-American War, in which the United States assisted Cuba in their fight for independence from Spain. It is the United States' oldest naval base, and the agreement between Cuba and the United States allowed the right to "lease on areas of land and water for the establishment of naval or coaling stations in Guantánamo and Bahia Honda" in exchange for an "annual sum of two thousand dollars . . . [for] as long as the former shall occupy and use said areas of land by virtue of said Agreement" (Article I).[13]

During the Cuban Revolution in the 1950s, the continued presence of the United States in Guantánamo Bay was rejected by Castro, claiming "the U.S. occupation of Guantánamo is illegal because imposed by force and a vestige of colonialism."[14] Since 1960, Cuba has not cashed the checks in the amount of U.S. $2,000 (raised to $4,085 since 1974) tendered by the United States as rent for the use of the territory, and the United States severed diplomatic relations between the two states in January of 1961. Fidel Castro threatened to kick the United States out of Guantánamo several times but was unable to do so due to military inferiority. When Castro ordered the water supply to be cut to the base in 1964, the U.S. Navy replied by building its own water and power plants. During the late twentieth century, the camp was used as a detention center for Haitian and Cuban refugees after attempting to reach the United States.

On January 11th, 2001, the Bush Administration began relocating 156 detainees to Guantánamo Bay, thus shifting its purpose from classifying and reviewing refugee status to detaining prisoners. The Freedom of Information

Act was used in a lawsuit by the Associated Press in 2006 to obtain more information about the prisoners of Guantánamo. The Pentagon proceeded to release an extensive list of detainees, including their names and nationalities. Less than one month later, the Department of Defense added 201 names to the list, stating that the revised list included every prisoner held at Guantánamo Bay since 2001. This list includes 759 people from 48 countries, all men. Of these men, 220 (or almost 30 percent) are from Afghanistan, 125 (around 17 percent) are from Saudi Arabia, 115 (15 percent) are from Yemen, 72 (around 9 percent) are from Pakistan. The other 29 percent originate from more than three dozen other countries.

Legal Challenges and Status of Guantánamo Today

There have been legal challenges to the detainment of individuals as "unlawful combatants" as violating the U.S. Constitution. The first U.S. Supreme Court case, *Rasul v. Bush* (2004),[15] challenged the constitutionality of holding detainees without presenting them with charges (e.g., habeas corpus) or granting them due process. Though a previous case, *Johnson v. Eisentrager* (1950),[16]argued that non-citizens are not afforded these rights during a time of war, *Rasul v. Bush* overturned this decision.

A second case before the Supreme Court, *Hamdi v. Rumsfeld, 542 U.S. 507 (2004)*,[17] attempted to claim that Yaser Esam Hamdi, a United States citizen who had joined Al-Qaeda, should be afforded *both* the protection of the U.S. Constitution and the protection of the Third Geneva Convention. In addition to habeas corpus and due process, Hamdi argued that he should also be granted prisoner of war status under Article 4(1) of the Third Geneva Convention. Hamdi reasoned that Taliban members were afforded prisoner of war status as members of the armed forces of Afghanistan. As Al-Qaeda was fighting with the Taliban against the American invasion, he could be designated a member of a "voluntary corp" fighting against an occupying power, and thus he too should be granted prisoner of war status. Though the Supreme Court argued similarly to Rasul that the U.S. Constitution protected Hamdi, it chose not to address whether he would also be granted prisoner of war status under the Third Geneva Convention.

In response to this decision, the Bush Administration decided to create the Combatant Status Review Tribunals (CSRTs). These closed-door tribunals were to be held in the detention center at Guantánamo Bay by the Department of Defense, and they were meant to be a one-time proceeding conducted for all detainees to provide the writ of habeas corpus by determining the status of a detainee as either a prisoner of war or an "unlawful combatant."

In these tribunals, neither detainees nor a representative of a detainee could view any evidence against them that was deemed classified. Instead, they were given unclassified summaries of the charges against them. Moreover, even with the unclassified version of the evidence, neither the detainee nor their personal representative was allowed to advocate for the detainee. Finally, information gathered through "enhanced interrogation" (i.e., torture) was admissible.

The next two cases, *Hamdan v. Rumsfeld* (2006)[18] and *Boumediene v. Bush* (2008),[19] challenged the nature of the Combatant Status Review Tribunals. In each case, the plaintiffs argued that the Combatant Status Review Tribunals failed to meet the Constitutional standards of habeas corpus and due process. The Supreme Court agreed. In *Boumediene v. Bush* (2008), the Supreme Court ruled that all detainees at Guantánamo were entitled to submit habeas corpus petitions directly to U.S. federal judges to determine whether the U.S. government had enough evidence to justify their continued detainment. The writ to habeas corpus could at no point be denied without first a federal judicial court's review.

In 2009, President Obama declared his intention to shut the Guantánamo detention facility down within a year (i.e., Executive Order 13492). This plan involved relocating the detention facilities and transferring some of the remaining detainees into the U.S. mainland. Doing so would presumably have positive consequences for the rights of detainees under the U.S. constitution.

The Obama administration failed to meet its original deadline, in part due to strong resistance by Congress. In 2010, Congress enacted funding restrictions that effectively prohibit the transfer of any Guantánamo detainees into U.S. territory. President Obama again called on Congress to close Guantánamo in 2013, but no action was taken then either. Instead of ending the practice of these tribunals, however, President Obama bolstered the protections afforded to the detainees within them by outlawing "enhanced interrogations" (i.e., torture) as a method for gathering evidence and excluded all information garnered during torture as potential evidence for these hearings.

In September 2014, a Senate report confirming the CIA's use of torture. In response, then-President Obama criticized the techniques described in the Senate report, arguing, "These techniques did significant damage to America's standing in the world and made it harder to pursue our interests with allies and partners." As of 2021, thirty-nine detainees are believed to be at Guantánamo. Of these, only nine have been tried and convicted of war crimes.

Uthman Abdul Rahim Mohammed Uthman

Uthman Abdul Rahim Mohammed Uthman is a citizen of Yemen. He has been held at Guantánamo since 2002. During his Combatant Status Review

Tribunals in 2010, he was determined to be an "unlawful combatant" as he was deemed both a high risk to the United States and of significant intelligence value.

These determinations were based on the claims that the "detainee's brother is an assessed al-Qaeda member" and that Uthman attended a school in Yemen "known for promoting Islamic fundamentalism."[20] The U.S. case is based on three witnesses. The earliest claim that Uthman was a member of bin Laden's security detail was Hakim Abd Al Karim Amin Bukhari, a Saudi who spent five years in Guantánamo. To complicate issues, while in U.S. custody, Bukhari had "become psychotic" and attempted suicide as a result of his detention and interrogations. One military psychologist said Bukhari's mental state rendered his reports about other detainees "unreliable." Another psychiatrist, whose evaluation was offered by the government, described an "unstable personality style" and "malingering psychiatric symptoms" that made Bukhari more dishonest than an average member of society but no more likely to lie than other prisoners with multiple personality disorders. Bukhari was returned to Saudi Arabia in 2007.

The other two witnesses—Sharqawi Abdul Ali al-Hajj and Sanad Yislam al Kazimi—are both currently held in Guantánamo. Each has identified Uthman to have been close to Osama bin Laden. Kennedy said their statements were the government's "most important pieces of evidence" and were "quite damning on their face."[21] Hajj claims that Uthman became a bodyguard for bin Laden a few months before the September 11th attacks and that he saw Uthman with the al-Qaeda leader at a meeting shortly after the attacks. In contrast, Kazimi claims that he knew Uthman from Kabul in early 2001, though Uthman was confirmed to not have arrived in Afghanistan until at least April.

Most problematically, both Hajj and Kazimi each spent at least two years at CIA "black site" facilities before being transferred to Guantánamo in September 2004. Hajj was captured in a raid in Karachi, Pakistan, in early 2002, and then transferred to Jordan, where he was held in two different facilities for nineteen months. Human Rights Watch has his claims of torture while in custody there. He was then transferred to the same CIA prison that housed Kazimi outside Kabul, moved later to Bagram Air Base, and eventually to Guantánamo.

Kazimi was captured in the United Arab Emirates in January 2003. He spent time in five prisons in three countries. In Dubai, he was held secretly for eight months, where he has claimed that he was beaten, shackled naked, exposed to extreme temperatures and simulated drowning, threatened with rape, and sexually assaulted. He was transferred to CIA custody in August 2003 and moved to a facility outside Kabul for nine months. There, his lawyers contend, he was subjected to physical and psychological torture, suspended with his arms above his head for long periods, beaten with electrical cables, given injections, and subjected to continuous loud music. He attempted suicide three times, according to his attorneys. Both claims made against Uthman were not made while Hajj and Kazimi were being tortured but during extensive FBI questioning while each was held as detainees at Guantánamo.

In contrast to these claims, Uthman insists that he traveled from Yemen to Afghanistan in 2001 to teach the Quran (through a local interpreter) to Afghan children. In December of 2001, Uthman was captured by Pakistani forces near the Afghanistan-Pakistan border with thirty other Arabs. The U.S. alleges this group was all Al-Qaeda fighters, some of whom were closely associated with Osama bin Laden as bodyguards or other members of his security detail.

As Uthman's status has been reviewed, the writ of habeas corpus has been granted. That said, he was deemed an "unlawful combatant,"—a designation that falls outside of the Geneva Conventions protections of lawful combatants under the Third Convention and civilians under the Fourth Convention. As the Supreme Court has not ruled on the status of detainees as "unlawful combatants," Uthman is being detained indefinitely.

THE MOOT COURT: *THE REPUBLIC OF CUBA VS. THE UNITED STATES*

Though Uthman Abdul Rahim Mohammed Uthman is a real individual labeled an "unlawful combatant" and currently detained at Guantánamo by the U.S. government, the case between Cuba and the United States is fictional yet plausible. Though Cuba would undoubtedly wish to see the Guantánamo detention center closed and end U.S. presence on the island, the legal question presented before the court challenges the legal grey area of "unlawful combatant" within international humanitarian law. As such, for this moot court, the legal question posed is: *Is the United States in violation of its obligations under international humanitarian law in its detainment of Uthman and others as "unlawful combatants"?*

NOTES

1. Though the four conventions have been signed and ratified by every state, the Common Article and Additional Protocols have not. This chapter will discuss each of these in detail.

2. The Geneva Conventions of 1948 are really the evolution of early treaties on the laws of war, including the Geneva Convention of 1864, the Hague Conventions of 1899 and 1907, and the Second Geneva Convention of 1920.

3. International Committee of the Red Cross, "Convention (IV) Relative to the Treatment of Prisoners of War," August 12, 1949. Available at: https://ihl-databases .icrc.org/ihl/full/GCIII-commentary.

4. International Committee of the Red Cross, "Convention (IV) Relative to the Treatment of Prisoners of War," August 12, 1949. Available at: https://ihl-databases .icrc.org/ihl/full/GCIII-commentary.

5. International Committee of the Red Cross, "Convention (IV) Relative to the Treatment of Prisoners of War," August 12, 1949. Available at: https://ihl-databases .icrc.org/ihl/full/GCIII-commentary.

6. International Committee of the Red Cross, "Convention (IV) Relative to the Protection of Civilian Persons in Time of War," August 12, 1949. Available at: https://ihl-databases.icrc.org/ihl/COM/380-600054.

7. International Committee of the Red Cross, "Convention (IV) Relative to the Protection of Civilian Persons in Time of War," August 12, 1949. Available at: https://ihl-databases.icrc.org/ihl/COM/380-600054.

8. International Committee of the Red Cross, "Convention (IV) Relative to the Protection of Civilian Persons in Time of War," August 12, 1949. Available at: https://ihl-databases.icrc.org/ihl/COM/380-600054.

9. International Committee of the Red Cross, "Protocol Additional to the Geneva Conventions of 12 August 1949, and relating to the Protection of Victims of International Armed Conflicts (Protocol I)," June 8, 1977. Available at: https://ihl -databases.icrc.org/applic/ihl/ihl.nsf/Treaty.xsp?documentId=D9E6B6264D7723C 3C12563CD002D6CE4&action=openDocument.

10. Linzer, Dafna, "DOJ's Troubled Case Against Uthman," *ProPublica*, October 8, 2010. Available at: https://www.propublica.org/article/dojs-troubled-case-against -uthman.

11. Linzer, Dafna, "DOJ's Troubled Case Against Uthman," *ProPublica*, October 8, 2010. Available at: https://www.propublica.org/article/dojs-troubled-case-against -uthman.

12. Ex parte Quirin, 317 U.S. 1 (1942).

13. The Avalon Project, "Agreement Between the United States and Cuba for the Lease of Lands for Coaling and Naval stations; February 23, 1903," Yale Law School. Available at: https://avalon.law.yale.edu/20th_century/dip_cuba002.asp.

14. Linzer, Dafna, "DOJ's Troubled Case Against Uthman," *ProPublica*, October 8, 2010. Available at: https://www.propublica.org/article/dojs-troubled-case-against -uthman.

15. Rasul v. Bush, 542 U.S. 466 (2004).

16. Johnson v. Eisentrager, 339 U.S. 763 (1950).

17. Hamdi v. Rumsfeld, 542 U.S. 507 (2004).

18. Hamdan v. Rumsfeld, 05 U.S. 184 (2006).

19. Boumediene v. Bush, 06 U.S. 1196 (2008).

20. The Guantánamo Docket, "Uthman Abd Al Rahim Muhammad Uthman," *The New York Times*. Available at: https://www.nytimes.com/interactive/projects/ Guantánamo/detainees/27-uthman-abdul-rahim-mohammed-uthman

21. Linzer, Dafna, "DOJ's Troubled Case Against Uthman," *ProPublica*, October 8, 2010. Available at: https://www.propublica.org/article/dojs-troubled-case-against -uthma.

Chapter 12

International Criminal Law

The international community agrees that certain international humanitarian and human rights violations must not be tolerated. However, as noted in the chapter on the use of force, the question is when and how other states address humanitarian and human rights violations outside of their territorial integrity.

Within international law, there is a growing norm called universal jurisdiction. Universal jurisdiction allows for any state to prosecute criminal acts considered most severe by the international community even when these criminal acts occurred outside of a state's territory, did not include any of a state's nationals, and had no indirect impact on the security of the state.[1]

In an article advocating for universal jurisdiction in Foreign Affairs, Kenneth Roth, a former executive director of Human Rights Watch, argued for universal jurisdiction, writing: "Impunity may still be the norm in many domestic courts, but international justice is an increasingly viable option, promising a measure of solace to victims and their families and raising the possibility that would-be tyrants will begin to think twice before embarking on a barbarous path."[2]

In response, former National Security Adviser under President Nixon, Henry Kissinger, responded to Roth with an argument against universal jurisdiction. He notes, "The danger lies in pushing the effort to extremes that risk substituting the tyranny of judges for that of governments; historically, the dictatorship of the virtuous has often led to inquisitions and even witch hunts."[3]

This chapter will first examine the different types of jurisdictional norms within international law. Next, this chapter will explore the atrocities committed by Chile's former dictator, Augusto Pinochet, including torture, forced disappearances, and mass executions from 1973 to 1990. Finally, this chapter will examine Spain's attempt to try Pinochet within the Spanish court system for the crimes he committed within Chile when he was in power.

UNIVERSAL JURISDICTION

Jurisdiction is a complex term. In its simplest form, it is the authority of a judicial organ to preside over the process of hearing and determining the outcome of a case. Within this broad definition are two component parts: to which judicial organ is this authority granted and under what conditions?

In the most straightforward cases, a state's judicial organs would be responsible for hearing all cases within that state's territory. Thus, most often, territoriality principles apply. In some cases, however, a state may claim jurisdiction over its nationals even when they are outside of the territory of the state.[4] As just one example, if an American citizen is jailed for selling or transporting drugs abroad, the United States may claim national jurisdiction to protect the American citizen from being tried in a foreign court. Though territorial claims tend to be paramount, there is no law codifying whether the territorial or national claim will prevail in a given case (though most often the more powerful state prevails in jurisdictional negotiations).

There are other scenarios in which the state may claim jurisdiction as well. Known as the passive personality, a state claims that the actions invoked in a crime were indirectly intended against the state. In the Lotus case,[5] a drunk French captain steered his ship into a Turkish one on the high seas, killing eight Turkish nationals. Though the actions were by no means political in nature and both French and Turkish nationals were involved, the Turkish government insisted it had jurisdiction over the case based on the passive personality principle. This principle argued that Turkey was indirectly affected by the attack. This claim, however, was ineffectively applied, and the French won jurisdiction over the case.

A more effective form of indirect jurisdiction is the protective principle. In such a case where more than one state can claim territorial or national jurisdiction, a state may have success in arguing for jurisdiction if they can convince the other state that the act directly undermined the security of the claimant state. In practice, the protective principle is most often used for lower-level international criminal acts (i.e., not of an egregious nature as determined by international human rights or humanitarian law), such as counterfeiting currency or passports.

A fifth—and final—principle is universal jurisdiction. This principle allows a state to extend its national authority to investigate and prosecute acts—anywhere in the world, conducted by a national of any state, against nationals of any state—if the action is considered to be a grave breach of international law. What is most notable about this jurisdiction is that the focus is on the seriousness of the acts, rather than the actors and the location in which the acts took place. To understand this form of jurisdiction, however, one must examine: to which judicial organs can this right extend and what acts meet the criteria of grave breaches. This section will take both of these topics in turn.

Universal jurisdiction applies to both international courts (e.g., the International Criminal Tribunal for Yugoslavia, the International Criminal Tribunal for Rwanda, and the International Criminal Court) and national courts (as well as hybrids of the two).

Created by UNSC Resolution 827 in 1993, the UN Security Council ordered the establishment of the court due to "grave alarm at continuing reports of widespread and flagrant violations of international humanitarian law occurring within the territory of the former Yugoslavia," and applied to "grave breaches of the Geneva Conventions and other violations of international humanitarian law."[6]

Grave breaches of international law are those acts considered to meet the standard of jus cogens, or fundamental principles of international law for which there is near-universal agreement that breaches should not occur and not go unpunished if they do occur.

Though a debate exists as to what is included in this category, the International Criminal Tribunal of Yugoslavia's statute[7] enumerated eight acts that were determined to be grave breaches of the Geneva Conventions: (1) willful killing, (2) torture or inhuman treatment, including biological experiments, (3) willfully causing great suffering or serious injury to body or health, (4) extensive destruction and appropriation of property, not justified by military necessity and carried out unlawfully and wantonly, (5) compelling a prisoner of war or a civilian to serve in the forces of a hostile power, (6) willfully depriving a prisoner of war or a civilian of the rights of fair and regular trial, (7) unlawful deportation or transfer or unlawful confinement of a civilian, and (8) taking civilians as hostages.

When the UNSC passed Resolution 955 in 1994, it allowed for the creation of the International Criminal Tribunal on Rwanda (ICTR). The Statute of the ICTR expanded the description of the crimes that were considered to be "grave breaches" from those included in the ICTY's Statute. As an example, whereas the Geneva Convention and the ICTY statute both mention "willful killing," it was the ICTR that expanded to specifically mention genocidal acts. Doing so, allowed the ICTR to distinguish kills that were meant to force groups out of territories (e.g., the practice of ethnic cleansing of an area used in the Serbian military) from those acts meant to systematically extinguish another group.[8]

The Rwandan Tribunal went further to resuscitate the term "crimes against humanity," a term used during the Nuremberg Trials following WWII.[9] The ICTR recast these acts as being greater than just threatening the peace (i.e., war crimes) but also may not reach the intent of directly exterminating a group. Instead, the acts classified under crimes against humanity are meant to demoralize and psychologically wound a group so thoroughly so they will not have a will to fight any longer. That is, the acts are intended to dehumanize.

In practice, certain acts may fit the definition of genocide and crimes against humanity. As one example, systematic rape can be seen as a crime against humanity if meant to physical and psychological harm a group or as a genocidal act if, by forcing those within an ethnic group to reproduce outside their group, the act of rape serves as "physical destruction of the group as a whole."[10] It was the ICTR prosecutors' that began to distinguish the motivation for each act to determine which crimes the individuals will be charged with committing.

Another area in which Rwanda's statute expanded upon the previous statute for Yugoslavia was the area in which the acts could occur. While the ICTY was mandated only to hear cases for acts that occurred within the former Yugoslav territory, the Tribunal for Rwanda was able to try cases in which acts occurred both in the "territory of Rwanda . . . as well as to the territory of neighboring States" so long as the acts were "committed by Rwandan citizens."[11] Thus you see the tribunals' jurisdiction moving from beyond the limited application of a territorial principle.

As noted in chapter 4, with the relative success of the Tribunals with limited jurisdiction (i.e., both were meant to handle cases from a specific conflict during a specific time), the International Law Commission sent the UN General Assembly the draft of the Rome Statute. The Rome Statute both expands the jurisdiction over grave breaches from the previous courts and creates the permanent court of the International Criminal Court to apply to all criminal acts committed after July 1st, 2001. What happens, however, to egregious criminal acts that occurred before July of 2001?

Many argue that the principle of universal jurisdiction allows any national court system to adjudicate these criminal acts based on the serious nature of the acts. The principle of universal jurisdiction in national courts is codified in article 146 of the Fourth Geneva Convention, which obliges all states party to the Convention (i.e., all states) to search for "persons alleged to have committed, or to have ordered to be committed, such grave breaches" and to "bring such persons, regardless of their nationality, before its courts" (see Text Box 12.1).[12]

TEXT BOX 12.1   CONVENTION RELATIVE TO THE PROTECTION OF CIVILIAN PERSONS DURING TIMES OF WAR FOURTH GENEVA CONVENTION (1948) [ARTICLE 146]

Article 146

The High Contracting Parties undertake to enact any legislation necessary to provide effective penal sanctions for persons committing, or ordering to be committed, any of the grave breaches of the present Convention defined in the following Article. Each High Contracting Party shall be under the obligation to search for persons alleged to have committed, or to have ordered to be committed, such grave breaches, and shall bring such persons, regardless of their nationality, before its own courts. It may also, if it prefers, and in accordance with the provisions of its own legislation, hand such persons over for trial to another High Contracting Party concerned, provided such High Contracting Party has made out a prima facie case.

Further, Article IV of the Convention Against Torture[13] requires each state that is a party to the treaty to ensure that "all acts of, attempted acts of, complicity in, or participation in torture are all offenses under that state's criminal law and that perpetrators face harsh sentencing if found guilty." Article V of the Convention on Torture noted that each state "shall take such measures as may be necessary to establish its jurisdiction over the offenses referred in article 4 in cases where the alleged offender is present in any territory under its jurisdiction."

TEXT BOX 12.2   CONVENTION AGAINST TORTURE AND OTHER CRUEL, INHUMAN OR DEGRADING TREATMENT OR PUNISHMENT (1984) [ARTICLES 4 AND 5]

Article 4

1. Each State Party shall ensure that all acts of torture are offenses under its criminal law. The same shall apply to an attempt to commit torture and to an act by any person which constitutes complicity or participation in torture.
2. Each State Party shall make these offenses punishable by appropriate penalties which take into account their grave nature.

Article 5

1. Each State Party shall take such measures as may be necessary to establish its jurisdiction over the offenses referred to in Article 4 in the following cases:
   a. When the offenses are committed in any territory under its jurisdiction or onboard a ship or aircraft registered in that State;
   b. When the alleged offender is a national of that State;
   c. When the victim is a national of that State if that State considers it appropriate.
2. Each State Party shall likewise take such measures as may be necessary to establish its jurisdiction over such offenses in cases where the alleged offender is present in any territory under its jurisdiction and it does not extradite him pursuant to article 8 to any of the States mentioned in paragraph I of this article.
3. This Convention does not exclude any criminal jurisdiction exercised in accordance with internal law.

THE CHILEAN GOVERNMENT UNDER PINOCHET

Chile was one of the earliest and proudest states to reject Spanish colonialism in Central and South America. First declaring independence in 1810, the Chilean government became an independent republic successfully in 1818. In the first century of the Chilean republic, the oligarchy—elites who made their fortunes on export products such as copper, silver, nitrate, and wheat—vied for power with the strong military heroes who successfully led the revolution.

When the Great Depression hit, Chile's economy crashed. This was in part because it had come to rely on one single export—nitrate, which was used in commercial agriculture worldwide. As the demand for exports stopped, so too stopped the ability to pay for imported goods. In response, the Chilean economy did what many other Latin American countries did in the interwar period. It began to develop its infant industrial sector to provide finished goods for its population (i.e., to keep the supply and demand cycle at home). With this came the rise of an urban middle class and a strong middle-class oriented party, called the Radicals.

In 1970, the left-leaning political parties that had emerged by this time formed a coalition called the Popular Unity. To head their presidential ticket, they chose a Marxist physician, Salvador Allende. When the election became a three-way race, Allende won the presidential elections with just 38 percent of the popular vote. Though Allende was not the ideal candidate for the

United States, the new Nixon Administration did not become involved in this election as they had in 1964. In part, as Henry Kissinger (Nixon's National Security Adviser at the time) admitted, he did not take the concerns of Chile as seriously as he should have—until after the election.

Perhaps as a dramatic redirection, Kissinger began to make Chilean politics a top priority after Allende's victory. He reasoned that—not only were billions of U.S. dollars at stake if Allende implemented his campaign promise of nationalizing sectors now owned by U.S. companies, but Kissinger also warned that Allende's victory could lead to "the insidious model effect" in which other countries attempted more socialist leanings, rather than liberal ones. Using back-channel negotiations soon after the election, Kissinger offered military officials weaponry and funds to instigate a coup against Allende. The CIA, however, backed out just four days before the plotted coup when internal assessments suggested there was little support in the military to ensure its success.

The move to remove Allende was further fueled by his economic decisions to nationalize the mining and telecommunications companies in Chile in 1971—both of which had U.S. companies as part or total shareholders—and the Chilean government gave little to no compensation for acquiring control of these companies. He went on to implement several other socialist policies, including raising the minimum wage, expanding education, housing, and food assistance programs, setting price controls on certain commodities, launching campaigns against illiteracy and for women's rights, and the federal funding of the arts.

Though much of his early efforts to improve the lives of the working class made him popular, Allende supported these policies with several poor choices. First, when he nationalized much of the companies once belonging to U.S. shareholders without providing them compensation. Second, to offset the lack of available foreign investment, he began overprinting Chilean pesos, which led to the price of goods increasing (as more money in the economy leads to a higher demand for goods and higher prices for the goods available).

As prices began to rise quickly, Allende made his third miscalculation. He chose to freeze the prices for goods. This may have been doable if the government could have efficiently taken over the means of production quickly and expertly without any lag. In practice, however, this led to the government's inability to produce huge quantities of goods for the people—but they were the only ones producing. Further, because prices were artificially low, some people bought the goods they needed, and then everyone went without. By 1972, women took to the streets in a mass protest movement, called the March of the Empty Pots, to protest the lack of supply in essential commodities.

As one source put it, by 1972, "Chile was suffering from stagnant production, decreased exports and private-sector investment, exhausted financial reserves, widespread strikes, rising inflation, food shortages, and domestic unrest. International lines of credit from the United States and western Europe had completely dried up."[14]

Leading up to the successful coup that instated Pinochet in power were several key events that undermined Allende's political rule even further. First, with the direct support of CIA funding, two more right-leaning political parties in the parliament joined forces to oppose Allende's more left-leaning agenda. Second, whereas in many other Latin American countries, the military had roles both in government and as military officials, the Chilean government purposefully chose to keep these two realms separate. That separation, however, meant that Chilean military officers were paid significantly less than most of their counterparts throughout Latin America. This led to public protests concerning wages during the previous administration. The military, however, was largely ignored as Allende focused on increasing workers' salaries. Thus, as inflation skyrocketed and goods became scarce, the low-paid military officers and their families began turning against the government.

At this time, General Carlos Prats was the Commander-in-Chief of the Army and was loyal to Allende. There are two pretty embarrassing stories worth mentioning about him here. First, in March of 1973, he challenged a couple who was mocking him from the next car to get out of their car and fight. The scene ended with the General shooting their back fender and yelling obscenities, which undermined his public reputation as a serious and respectable leader. Second, in August of 1973, his generals' wives—angered by the low wages of their husbands, rising prices, and scarcity of goods—protested in front of his home. Perceived to have lost both the support of his military and the larger public, he chose to resign on August 22nd, 1973. Ironically, Prats was considered to be a loyalist who, though frustrated with Allende's policies, would never have considered a coup.

Augusto Pinochet was born Augusto Pinochet Ugarte in 1915 in Chile. After graduating from the military academy in 1936, Pinochet rose through the military ranks. As a fifty-eight-year-old seasoned officer, he was second-in-command of the army. Once Prats announced his resignation on August 22nd, 1973, Allende—assuming him to be loyal to his administration—announced he would be the Commander-in-Chief. He would launch a coup against Allende just eighteen days later.

On August 21st, 1973, one day before Prat stepped down as Commander-in-Chief, members of Nixon's National Security Council approved a one-million dollar budget to increase support for political parties opposing Allende. The next day (i.e., the same day that Prat stepped down), a coalition of right-wing parties in the Chilean Congress passed a resolution calling for the military to take control of the government.

On September 11th, 1973, the navy captured Valparaíso. Upon hearing of the act, Allende returned to the presidential palace. When he attempted to communicate with the army and air force, they failed to respond. Even after the military took full control of all of Chile but Santiago, Allende refused to surrender or negotiate. In response, the General of the Air Force (under Pinochet's command) ordered the bombing of the presidential palace and Pinochet ordered the infantry to the palace. During the bombardment, Allende chose to take his own life.[15] For the CIA's part, its official statement was that it was "aware of coup-plotting" by the military, though it "did not instigate the coup."[16]

In the days following the coup, Pinochet announced that Congress was to be in recess and that the military junta would assume control of the government. As a declassified CIA document suggested, though Pinochet was not highly partisan, he was extremely critical of Marxism and interested in seeing the leftist agenda, as perpetuated under Allende, ended. In 1973, Pinochet initially banned any political parties with Marxist rhetoric and later any political parties. In 1974, he declared himself to be President. He appointed loyal military officers and mayors of towns and cities, deans of public universities, as well as to serve on his council of advisers. The press was censored.

Beyond attempting to deny the political participation of socialists, Pinochet was alleged to have committed human rights abuses against tens of thousands of people. His abuses tended to fall into four categories: forcible detainment, disappearance, murder, and torture.[17] One estimate suggests that more than 40,000 people became victims to one or more of these crimes by Pinochet's military regime between September 1973 and March 1990, and others suggest that is an extremely conservative number.[18]

Pinochet's strategy for control included the detainment of political adversaries. As early as September 20th, the United States received reports that the Chilean government was detaining thousands of left-leaning political dissidents and their families in the National Stadium as well as at least several other locations. This imprisonment continued for years. The latest report estimates that upwards of 7,000 people were detained during Pinochet's reign. At least one report confirms that at least 3,200 people were killed in political violence during General Pinochet's rule.[19] Further, the official number of those killed or forcibly disappeared is estimated to be around 3,000. And of those killed or disappeared, it is estimated 1,200 (or twenty percent) occurred during the first year of Pinochet's rule. Of these 3,000, around 600 are believed to be Spanish nationals.[20] Finally, at least one estimate published by the New York Times recorded nearly 28,000 people were tortured under the regime.

There were many attempts by the United States to ride the "Southern Cone" (i.e., the countries of Argentina, Chile, and Uruguay) of any threats to turning toward communism. As a result, the United States chose to support right-wing dictators in the region throughout the 1970s and 1980s, including in their acts to rid their territories of left-leaning oppositional forces.

In the days following the coup, Kissinger sent secret instructions to his ambassador to convey to Pinochet "our strongest desires to cooperate closely and establish a firm basis for a cordial and most constructive relationship."[21] When his Assistant Secretary of State for Inter-American Affairs asked him what to tell Congress about the reports of hundreds of people being killed in the days following the coup, he issued these instructions: "I think we should understand our policy-that however unpleasant they act, this government is better for us than Allende was."[22]

It became clear soon after Pinochet obtained power that he planned to reverse many of the more socialist policies promulgated under Allende. Under the advisement of a group of economists known as the "Chicago Boys" (i.e., students and recent graduates from the University of Chicago who studied under Milton Friedman), Pinochet enacted a neo-liberal economic plan in which companies would become privatized and attempt to attract international (i.e., U.S.) investment. The plan worked. By 1980, Chile was experiencing high levels of economic growth (as exports were restarting again) and low inflation (as salaries were more closely aligned with the price of goods). Chile was considered to be an "economic miracle."

Pinochet likely overstepped his boundaries, however, when he ordered the assassination of an anti-Pinochet Chilean in Washington D.C. Orlando Letelier, an economist-turned-diplomat under Allende, accepted appointments as a fellow at the Institute for Policy Studies. Soon after obtaining this position, he began criticizing Pinochet's regime choice to adopt policies of economic liberalization. After Letelier and an American colleague were assassinated in the streets of D.C. in 1976 after a car bomb detonated, the distancing between the United States and Chile began.[23] Though the larger attack on dissidents was covertly encouraged by the United States, the attack on a dissident on U.S. soil proved dangerous political territory. By 1978, a popular test-vote (i.e., a plebiscite) showed that Pinochet benefitted from a 75 percent approval rating. With this vote of confidence, Pinochet determined to draft a new constitution and to begin reenacting certain reforms, including term limits for his presidency.

This Constitution of 1981 reinstated a bicameral legislature—a lower chamber of representatives and an upper Senate chamber. Though both were intended to be occupied through direct elections, both were in recess until 1989. As for the executive's role, the new Constitution determined that after eight years in office (or in 1989), the Chilean people would vote in a referendum to determine if Pinochet would be granted another eight years as Chile's president.

When Chile fell into a recession in the mid-1980s, opposition to the regime mounted. In 1988, Pinochet arranged another plebiscite, asking the people whether he should rule for another eight years. The gambit backfired on him, and the proposition was defeated. Pinochet then negotiated a deal where he remained head of the armed forces until at least 1998, after which he would become "senator for life."

As part of the negotiations with Pinochet, Congressional parties pushed him to remove his ban on left-leaning parties. At his acquiescence, a coalition of the left-leaning parties from Allende's reign reemerged (e.g., the Social Democratic Radical Party and the Communist Party of Chile). Though the regime continued to have economic successes, Pinochet failed to garner the votes needed in a referendum in 1989, with a "no" vote of 55 percent compared to a "yes" vote of 43 percent, in part because of a coalition of center and left parties (named the Coalition of Parties for Democracy) formed against him. After being replaced by a Christian Democrat, Patricio Aylwin, Pinochet assumed the role of "Senator for Life"—a role expressly given to former presidents under the Chilean Constitution of 1981.

UNIVERSAL JURISDICTION EXTENDED TO PINOCHET

During a trip to London for medical treatment in 1998, Pinochet was arrested by the London Metropolitan Police authorities. The arrest came after a Spanish magistrate issued an international warrant, which included an authority to arrest and the extradition of Pinochet to Spain in connection with allegations of torture of Spanish citizens in Chile during his rule as well as genocide. Following the arrest, Pinochet put forth the claim of state immunity as a former head of state. After much debate within the House of Lords, a panel of Lords decided that diplomatic immunity extended to ratione materiae, or acts committed in the formal role of the head of state and did not extend to acts beyond the job description, including the torturing of one's political opponents.

After the British allowed the extradition, the Chilean government appealed—on Pinochet's behalf—to have a review of his ability to stand trial based on medical grounds. Belgium, who had filed a complimentary arrest warrant for Pinochet's arrest if the United Kingdom chose not to extradite him to Spain, pushed to have Pinochet's medical results made public, but the British government rejected this. In February of 2000, Pinochet was released on the ground of being in poor health, though multiple reports suggest that Pinochet immediately returned to Chile, "apparently in good health."[24]

In 2000, the Chilean Supreme Court decided to lift Senator Pinochet's parliamentary immunity and allow prosecution after 119 bodies of Chilean political dissidents were found in Argentina. In 2002, when the proceedings began, Pinochet's defense team successfully convinced the Supreme Court that his senile dementia made him unable to defend himself at trial.

In November 2004 and June 2005, the National Commission on Political Imprisonment and Torture, established by President Lagos, released its report, known as the Valech report. This Commission's report officially documented 30,000 cases of torture and human rights abuses by Pinochet. In November 2005, Pinochet was indicted on tax evasion charges and placed under house arrest for allegedly having held $27 million in U.S. financial institutions. In November 2006, a house arrest was again issued against Pinochet for the kidnapping and murder in 1973 of two bodyguards of former President Allende. Pinochet died of a heart attack a month later, without ever facing trial.

Though Pinochet is almost universally vilified outside of Chile, within Chile, his legacy is far more nuanced. When he died in 2006, nearly 60,000 people filed past his coffin to pay their respects. One poll published forty years after his successful coup showed that almost one in ten Chileans viewed Pinochet's rule favorably, determining he will be remembered as one of Chile's greatest leaders.[25] Though most view the time under Pinochet as having been bad for Chile, a small right-leaning group of supporters who regard him fondly believed that without his control over the government in 1973, Chile would have fallen into a Communist regime similar to Cuba.

Moreover, there are many in Chile who viewed the history of Chile as being "written by the left" and missing the good points: economic success, safety and security, and so on, that many feel they do not have today. Most interestingly, more than one-third of Chileans regard the years under Pinochet either with mixed feelings or had no opinion at all. Another poll suggested that Chileans are evenly divided when it comes to whether victims of human rights abuses have been properly compensated: with one-third saying yes, another third saying no, and yet another third undecided. If Chile is unwilling to hear cases of human rights violations by Pinochet, do other states, including Spain, have a right to extend its jurisdictional reach try Pinochet in their national courts?

THE MOOT COURT: *THE REPUBLIC OF CHILE VS. THE KINGDOM OF SPAIN*

In this fictional scenario, Chile decided to take Spain to the International Court of Justice for Spain's attempt to try Pinochet, arguing that the right to universal jurisdiction robs Chile of the right to sovereignty. For this moot court, the legal question posed is: *Is Spain in violation of its obligations under international humanitarian law in its attempts to try Pinochet within its national courts for crimes committed in Chile?*

NOTES

1. Randall, Kenneth C. "Universal Jurisdiction under International Law," *Tex. L. Rev.* 66 (1987): 785.

2. Ibid.

3. Kissinger, Henry A., "Pitfalls of Universal Jurisdiction, The," *Foreign Aff.* 80 (2001): 86.

4. Murphy, Sean. *Murphy's Principles of International Law, 2d (Concise Hornbook Series)*. West Academic, 2012.

5. *League of Nations, Permanent Court of Justice, France v. Turkey, 1927, Ser. A, No. 10*.

6. United Nations Security Council Resolution 827, 1993.

7. UN Security Council, *Statute of the International Criminal Tribunal for the Former Yugoslavia*, May 25, 1993. Available at: https://www.icty.org/x/file/Legal%20Library/Statute/statute_sept09_en.pdf.

8. UN Security Council, *Statute of the International Criminal Rwanda*, November 8, 1994. Available at: https://legal.un.org/avl/pdf/ha/ictr_EF.pdf.

9. Ibid.

10. Ibid.

11. Ibid.

12. International Committee of the Red Cross, "Convention (IV) Relative to the Protection of Civilian Persons in Time of War," August 12, 1949. Available at: https://ihl-databases.icrc.org/ihl/COM/380-600054.

13. UN General Assembly, *Convention Against Torture and Other Cruel, Inhuman or Degrading Treatment or Punishment*, December 10, 1984, United Nations, Treaty Series, vol. 1465, p. 85. Available at: https://www.refworld.org/docid/3ae6b3a94.html.

14. Encyclopedia Britannica, "Salvador Allende," Available at: https://www.britannica.com/biography/Salvador-Allende.

15. Associated Press, "Chilean President Salvador Allende Committed Suicide, Autopsy Confirms," *The Guardian*, July 20, 2011. Available at: http://www.theguardian.com/world/2011/jul/20/salvador-allende-committed-suicide-autopsy.

16. Central Intelligence Agency, "CIA Activities in Chile." Available at: https://www.cia.gov/library/reports/general-reports-1/chile/#5.

17. Ibid.

18. *BBC News*, "Chile Ups Pinochet Victim Numbers," August 18, 2011. Available at: https://www.bbc.com/news/world-latin-america-14584095.

19. Weiner, Tim, "U.S. Will Release Files on Crimes Under Pinochet," *The New York Time*s, December 2, 1998. Available at: https://www.nytimes.com/1998/12/02/world/us-will-release-files-on-crimes-under-pinochet.html.

20. "'This Was Not an Accident. This Was a Bomb'." n.d. *Washington Post*, February 5, 2020. Available at: http://www.washingtonpost.com/sf/national/2016/09/20/this-was-not-an-accident-this-was-a-bomb/.

21. "'This Was Not an Accident. This Was a Bomb'," n.d. *Washington Post*, February 5, 2020. Available at: http://www.washingtonpost.com/sf/national/2016/09/20/this-was-not-an-accident-this-was-a-bomb/.

22. "'This Was Not an Accident. This Was a Bomb'," n.d. *Washington Post*, February 5, 2020. http://www.washingtonpost.com/sf/national/2016/09/20/this-was-not-an-accident-this-was-a-bomb/.

23. Gattini, Andrea, "Pinochet Cases," June 2007, *Oxford Public International Law*. Available at: https://doi.org/10.1093/law:epil/9780199231690/e859.

24. Long, Gideon, "Chile Still Split Over Gen Augusto Pinochet Legacy," *BBC News*, September 9, 2013. Available at: https://www.bbc.com/news/world-latin-america-24014501.

25. BBC News, "Chile Still Split Over Gen Augusto Pinochet Legacy," September 09, 2013. Available at: https://www.bbc.com/news/world-latin-america-24014501.

Chapter 13

International Human Rights Law

International human rights are rights granted to every individual based on their humanity. As a result, whereas other international laws have conditions (e.g., times of conflict or most egregious acts), international human rights laws are considered to be nearly unconditional.

The right of the refugee rests within the more extensive regime of international human rights. This right affords protection to individuals in another state if there is reason to believe that they would be persecuted in their home state. In meeting this right, other states must provide asylum to those who meet these criteria.

Kenya has been offering asylum to Somali refugees fleeing violence, a failed state, increasing climate disasters, terrorism, and disease since the 1990s. As its refugee camps face overcrowding and terrorists have used the camps as breeding grounds, the Kenyan government questions whether its obligation has been met.

This chapter will first examine the Convention on the right of the Refugee (1951)[1] and its Protocol (1967)[2] to understand better the rights and obligations of both states and refugees in the asylum-seeking process and the conditions under which those rights and obligations must be met. Next, this chapter will review Somalia's turbulent history to better understand the circumstances driving this refugee crisis. Finally, this chapter will examine the steps Kenya initially took to welcome refugees and the growing political frustrations with its continued obligation in the face of increasing need and potential violence.

INTERNATIONAL HUMAN RIGHTS LAW (IHRL)

As noted in the previous Module, there are dozens of treaties on human rights. The three main ones are the UN Declaration of Human Rights, the International Covenant on Civil and Political Rights, and the International Covenant on Economic, Social, and Cultural Rights. Two other treaties focus on specific rights afforded to particular persons (e.g., the Convention on the Elimination of All Forms of Racial Discrimination, the Convention on the Rights of the Child, the Declaration on the Elimination of Violence against Women, and the Convention on the Rights of Persons with Disabilities).

There exists a principle in international customary law of *non-refoulement*, which asserts that a refugee should not be returned to a country where they face serious threats to their life or freedom. This principle has been codified in a human rights treaty called the UN Convention Relating to the Status of Refugees (1951), which codified this principle for all refugees seeking asylum due to events before 1951. Its Protocol Relating to the Status of Refugees (1967) extended this right to all persons at all times.

Section A of the first article of the Refugee Convention of 1951 applies the term refugee to any person who either has a "well-founded fear of being persecuted for reasons of race, religion, nationality, membership of a particular social group or political opinion" and is, for whatever reason, unable or unwilling "owing to such fear" to be granted the protection of the state of which they are a national.[3] Also, the term refugee may apply to people without a nationality.

Section C of the same article then explains when a person can no longer be considered a refugee. The cases in which a person is given the status, but then it no longer applies, include when a person voluntarily returns to the state in which they fled, when a person regains nationality from this state, or when a person acquires a new nationality in a different state.

Article 31 of the Refugee Convention prohibits the imposition of a penalty on a person who illegally crosses a border to seek asylum if this person is deemed to have come "directly from a territory where their life or freedom was threatened," they "provided they present themselves without delay to the authorities," and they "show good cause for their illegal entry or presence."[4]

Article 32 allows refugees to be expelled from states. They seek only cases where the state can claim that this expulsion was based on "grounds of national security or public order" after these persons were afforded due process. Even in cases where removal occurs, Article 33 ensures that no person shall be expelled to the country they initially fled. Finally, Article 35 obligates all states that are party to this Convention to work with the United Nations to ensure these provisions are enacted (Text Box 13.1).

TEXT BOX 13.1   UNITED NATIONS CONVENTION RELATING TO THE STATUS OF REFUGEES, "REFUGEE CONVENTION" (1951) [ARTICLES 1, 31-33, AND 35]

Article 1: Definition of the Term "Refugee"

A. For the purposes of the present Convention, the term "refugee" shall apply to any person who:

1. Has been considered a refugee under previous agreements.
2. As a result of events occurring before 1 January 1951 and owing to well-founded fear of being persecuted for reasons of race, religion, nationality, membership of a particular social group or political opinion, is outside the country of his nationality and is unable or, owing to such fear, is unwilling to avail himself of the protection of that country; or who, not having a nationality and being outside the country of his former habitual residence as a result of such events, is unable or, owing to such fear, is unwilling to return to it.

   In the case of a person who has more than one nationality, the term "the country of his nationality" shall mean each of the countries of which he is a national, and a person shall not be deemed to be lacking the protection of the country of his nationality if, without any valid reason based on well-founded fear, he has not availed himself of the protection of one of the countries of which he is a national.

C. This Convention shall cease to apply to any person falling under the terms of section A if:

1. He has voluntarily re-availed himself of the protection of the country of his nationality; or
2. Having lost his nationality, he has voluntarily reacquired it; or
3. He has acquired a new nationality, and enjoys the protection of the country of his new nationality; or.
4. He has voluntarily re-established himself in the country which he left or outside which he remained owing to fear of persecution; or.
5. He can no longer, because the circumstances in connection with which he has been recognized as a refugee have ceased to exist, continue to refuse to avail himself of the protection of the country of his nationality.

Article 31: Refugees Unlawfully in the Country of Refuge

1. The Contracting States shall not impose penalties, on account of their illegal entry or presence, on refugees who, coming directly

from a territory where their life or freedom was threatened in the sense of article 1, enter or are present in their territory without authorization, provided they present themselves without delay to the authorities and show good cause for their illegal entry or presence.

2. The Contracting States shall not apply to the movements of such refugees restrictions other than those which are necessary and such restrictions shall only be applied until their status in the country is regularized or they obtain admission into another country. The Contracting States shall allow such refugees a reasonable period and all the necessary facilities to obtain admission into another country.

Article 32: Expulsion

1. The Contracting States shall not expel a refugee lawfully in their territory save on grounds of national security or public order.

2. The expulsion of such a refugee shall be only in pursuance of a decision reached in accordance with due process of law. Except where compelling reasons of national security otherwise require, the refugee shall be allowed to submit evidence to clear himself, and to appeal to and be represented for the purpose before competent authority or a person or persons specially designated by the competent authority.

3. The Contracting States shall allow such a refugee a reasonable period within which to seek legal admission into another country. The Contracting States reserve the right to apply during that period such internal measures as they may deem necessary.

Article 33: Prohibition of Expulsion or Return ("Refoulement")

1. No Contracting State shall expel or return ("refouler") a refugee in any manner whatsoever to the frontiers of territories where his life or freedom would be threatened on account of his race, religion, nationality, membership of a particular social group or political opinion.

2. The benefit of the present provision may not, however, be claimed by a refugee whom there are reasonable grounds for regarding as a danger to the security of the country in which he is, or who, having been convicted by a final judgement of a particularly serious crime, constitutes a danger to the community of that country.

Article 35: Co-operation of the National Authorities with the United Nations

1. The Contracting States undertake to co-operate with the Office of the United Nations High Commissioner for Refugees, or any other agency of the United Nations which may succeed it, in the exercise of its functions, and shall in particular facilitate its duty of supervising the application of the provisions of this Convention.

The original Convention explicitly mentions all refugees as a result of events occurring before 1951. As a result, a Protocol was passed in 1967 that allowed for the same protections to extend to all refugees, irrespective of timing. Kenya signed this Protocol in 1981 (Text Box 13.2).

TEXT BOX 13.2   PROTOCOL RELATING TO THE STATUS OF REFUGEES (1967)

The States Parties to the present Protocol,

Considering that the Convention relating to the Status of Refugees done at Geneva on 28 July 1951 (hereinafter referred to as the Convention) covers only those persons who have become refugees as a result of events occurring before I January 1951,

Considering that new refugee situations have arisen since the Convention was adopted and that the refugees concerned may therefore not fall within the scope of the Convention,

Considering that it is desirable that equal status should be enjoyed by all refugees covered by the definition in the Convention irrespective of the dateline January 1, 1951.

Though the Convention mentions that states are obligated to determine whether an asylum seeker meets the requirements for refugee status and asylum in their country, it does not specify a legal process each state must take to determine whether a person is a refugee. As a result, the pace and procedure for determining asylum status are left to each state.

SOMALIA

Somalia is situated at the eastern edge of the African continent, often referred to as the Horn of Africa, and shares borders with Djibouti to the north-west, Ethiopia to the west, and Kenya to the southwest. It also has a long coast that abuts the Indian Ocean to the east and the Gulf of Aden to the north.

History of Somalia

As a coastal state located next to the Middle East, along the Gulf of Aden and the Indian Ocean, present-day Somalia's area became a stop for both Arab and Persian traders beginning in the tenth century. While Arab and Persian traders occupied the coastal areas, further inland lived various ethnic groups. Throughout most of the territory, a clan-based group is estimated to comprise around 85 percent of the population in the areas collectively known as the Somali.

This larger ethnic group can be divided into five noble clans—Darod, Dir, Hawiye, Isaaq, and Rahanweyn—all believed to be ethnically identified as Somali. The entire Somali population is said to have descended from a Yemeni Muslim settler to the region in the ninth century, named Samaale. The first two clans—Dir & Hawiye—have descended from Samaale's son, Irir. The third clan, Rahanweyn, descends from Samaale's brother, Saab, while the Darod and Ishaak were both created when male settlers from the Arabian Peninsula traveled to the region, married daughters of the leaders of the Dir clan, and created clans of their own. Both the Darod and Isaaq clans are considered "minor" Somali clans as their affiliation with Somali people is through the maternal, rather than paternal, line.[5] These minor clans are referred to as "sab" or minor clans to distinguish them from those paternally linked to Samaale or Saab. Each of these clans is further divided into sub-clans. The only sub-clan to maintain a large swath of territory is the Digil (which is part of the Rahanweyn).[6]

Those clans to the north—the Dir, Darod, and Isaaq—were more focused on nomadic herding through this region, mostly filled with hot and dry semi-deserts or savannahs. As these three clans began to expand in the thirteenth century, they pushed further south along the coast. In contrast, the Rahanweyn (and the Digil) were more permanent, subsistence farmers in the southern areas, which has flowing rivers.

Following the Industrial Revolution in Europe, the great powers of Europe accelerated their desire for colonial expansion into Africa in a quest for natural resources. In 1839, Britain became interested in the Somali coast for coaling stations to fuel trade routes to and from the Middle East and India and serve as a check on the Ottoman Empire's claims to the region. France, the lesser power, secured a second coaling station in Djibouti in 1862. Finally, in 1869, Italy opened its station even further north in Eritrea.

To secure its possessions in the region from France, who was pushing south, the British offered the three northern clans—the Dir, Darod, and Isaaq—protection from the French to be part of a British protectorate in the 1880s. In 1888, the French and British signed an agreement disseminating the boundaries between Djibouti and Somalia, thus avoiding war.

As the British and French were focused on the boundary between Djibouti and Somalia, the Italians pushed inland from their coastal post in Eritrea toward Ethiopia. In 1889 Ethiopia signed a treaty with Italy, which the Italians viewed as establishing an Italian protectorate and then pushed east toward the coast, claiming Somali territory. After Ethiopia successfully fought for its independence in 1896 in the Battle of Adwa, Italy was left only with Italian Somaliland in its possession.

In the north, the British attempted to convert the Somali Muslim clans to Christianity, with no success. In 1899, a sub-clan of the Darod fought back against the British in the eastern part of the protectorate. After successful battles against the British, the Darod leaders used solidarity among Somalis along clan and religious lines to encourage a sizable Somali rebellion against colonial powers. Using guerilla tactics and arms and ammunition from their Muslim allies in the Middle East, the Somalis successfully fought against the British, the Italians, and even the independent Ethiopians in four different military campaigns between 1900 and 1904.

For the next decade or so, the British retreated to the coastal ports of British Somaliland. Following the conclusion of WWI, they were able to reinforce their troop presence and, using combined air, sea, and land tactics, regained the entire protectorate. The Somalis in the South never fought as ardently against their Italian rulers as those in the north had done. In part because the more agricultural southern Somalis were interested in the production and trade infrastructure (and a foreign market) encouraged by the Italians, especially around the two main rivers: the Juba and Shabelle. Plantations were developed throughout the region to produce maize, rice, sugarcane, sesame, and fruits and vegetables for the local market.

During World War II, the British successfully captured the Italian Somaliland, bringing it directly under British administration and thus unifying all of Somaliland (excepting French Somalia). After World War II, any territories occupied by the Allies in World War II or as colonies were transferred to the UN General Assembly and became trusteeships to be managed by the UN Trusteeship Council in general and specific states would administer the day to day dealings of the government. As noted previously, trusteeships would remain under UN administrative control to "promote the political, economic, social, and educational advancement of the inhabitants" until they were deemed ready for "self-government or independence."[7] Once again, Britain was given trusteeship control over the north, and Italy had a trusteeship over the south.

The Somali trusteeships became independent in 1960 (the British northern Somali trusteeship on June 26th and the southern Italian one on July 1st). Once separated, the two regions joined together, forming the Somali Republic. The government was to be a parliamentary system. Soon after the government was formed, coalitions were created based on regional affiliation. In the north, the Somali National League (SNL) was formed, while in the south, the Somali Youth League (SYL).

Somali groups within Kenya and Ethiopia saw the unification efforts and wished to succeed from their governments to join the new Somali Republic. Guerrilla wars broke out between Somalis within Kenya and Ethiopia against both governments in 1963. These efforts, however, were thwarted by the Western states who supported the governments of Ethiopia and Kenya (in part as they were Christian). In response to this, the Somali government began to court the Soviet Union for military aid.

In the first two election cycles of the Somali Republic—1964 and 1969—the southern Somali Youth League won a majority of seats in the National Assembly and the Prime Minister and Presidential elections. The concentration of power among the southern Somali clans angered the clans to the north. In response, each clan (and even sub-clan) began forming political opposition parties against each other. In the first election, there were eleven political parties other than the Somali Youth League. By the 1969 elections, sixty-four political parties put forth nearly 1,000 candidates for the 123 National Assembly seats alone. During such a chaotic election, the southern Somali Youth League gained an even more significant number of seats. When accusations of election fraud were made, the SYL responded by ignoring the claim. This led to even greater resentment, which ultimately culminated in a military coup.

During the tense political climate following the 1969 elections, the military launched a coup against the SYL government. The leader of the coup was Major General Mohamed Siad Barre. He was a member of the northern Darod clan and a Soviet sympathizer. Upon successfully gaining control of the government (i.e., by arranging for the then-President Shermarke to be killed by his bodyguard and then staging the coup during his funeral), Barre instituted a Socialist republic, renaming the country the Somalia Democratic Republic. Most interestingly, though fully endorsing the Soviet influence, Barre went to great pains to ensure his Muslim clan's people that the Somali version of socialism was deeply compatible (and not at odds with) their Islam practice.

Barre maintained control through a network of vigilantes loyal to his regime, known as the Victory Pioneers. He also created the National Security Service (headed by his son-in-law) and a court system, called the

National Security Courts, that was not transparent and allegiant to him. One of the more radical methods he used to maintain control was to outlaw clan-ship formally. Instead, former chiefs of each clan would serve on regional committees with a loyal official of the government at these committees' head.

In 1974, Ethiopia's democratically elected regime was overthrown by a Marxist-Leninist coup. In the aftermath of this coup, Somali separatists in Ethiopia began to call for liberation from the Ethiopian government. Forming the Western Somali Liberation Front, they called on Barre to assist them from breaking away from Ethiopia and joining Somalia. The Soviets, for their part, were interested in seeing the new Marxist government of Ethiopia, retain its territory and disapproved of the ethnically based separation movement of the Western Somali Liberation Front. The Soviets were mostly disapproving of Barre when he agreed to assist this movement mainly due to clan affiliation with the group (the Western Somali Liberation Front and Barre were both from the Darod clan and the Ogaden sub-clan).

With Barre's assistance, the Western Somali Liberation Front captured the Ogaden region of Ethiopia in 1977. In a switch of allegiances, the Soviets (and Cubans) began reinforcing the Ethiopian army, and by 1978 the Ethiopians had successfully regained the region. This loss led to a third of the Somali Army being killed, half of its air force destroyed, and the Somali population deeply embarrassed and angered at the defeat.

Amid the defeat, three opposition groups formed against the Barre govern-ment. The Somali Salvation Democratic Front (SSDF) formed from a sepa-rate sub-clan within the Darod clan—the Majeerteens. Unlike the Ogaden that lived in the central interior (closer to Ethiopia), the Majeerteens lived along the central coast. A second group—the Somali National Movement (SNM) formed in London by a group of dissidents from the Isaaq clan of the northern region. The Ogaden War most embittered the Isaaqs as it has occurred close to their borders. Further, after the war concluded, many Ogaden Somalis from Ethiopia began pouring into the northern region. Already an arid and economically weakened area, the influx of Ogaden further embittered the Isaaq clans people.

In 1988, small groups of Isaaqs began attacking Ogaden refugee camps and government facilities in the north. In response, the President encouraged the creation of Ogaden paramilitary groups and, in May of 1988, "gave instruc-tions to exterminate all members of the Isaaq tribe."[8] The government then supported these paramilitary groups with aerial bombardments of three cities: Hargeisa, Berbera, and Bur'o. Various estimates give the number killed in less than one year at between 100,000 and 400,000 Isaaq. During this conflict, more than half a million Isaaq fled to Ethiopia, and some half a million more became internally displaced persons in the northern region.

A third group, a Hawiye-based United Somali Congress (USC), led a popular uprising against a much-weakened Barre in January of 1991. Barre, who had been beaten back to only have control over the capital city, Mogadishu, finally fled to the southwestern Juba province area, where the Ogaden sub-clan of the Darod's still maintained control. Barre formed the Somali National Front (SNF) and attempted twice to take Mogadishu in the spring of 1991. Still, he was unsuccessful and ultimately fled to Nigeria for the remainder of his life.

The third group mentioned above, the Hawiye-based United Somali Congress (USC), reached the capital and successfully ousted Barre. Upon doing so, the leader of the USC (Ali Mahdi Muhammed) declared himself President. This angered people within his clan and led to a USC splintering into two groups. The other group—led by Mohammed Aidid—formed the USC/Somali Salvation Alliance. The two Hawiye groups began fighting each other in the streets of Mogadishu for control of the government of Somalia.

Somalia as a Failed State

As the two Hawiye forces battled for control of Mogadishu, outside of the capital, the Somali Salvation Democratic Front (SSDF) (formed out of the Darod sub-clan, the Majeerteens) began consolidating their control over the northeastern region of the country. It would later determine this region to be the autonomous region of Puntland.

In the north, the second group—the Somali National Movement (SNM), consisting of those from the Isaaq clan, secured control over the territory once under the control of the British, declared the Somali Republic's territorial binding of the former British and Italian Somalilands in 1960 null and void, and then proceeded to name the new administration over this territory the Republic of Somaliland.

Meanwhile, divisions of the Hawiye fought against one another for control of Mogadishu. These conflicts were further fueled by the availability of weapons from the two superpowers (vying for control of Somalia and Ethiopia).

Humanitarian Crisis

Since the collapse of the Somali state in 1991, there have been widespread severe abuses against civilians and, as noted in the UN Secretary-General's report of March 14, 2008, "the lack of accountability, for past and current crimes, reinforces a sense of impunity and further fuels conflict."[9]

In 1991, as Barre attempted to launch attacks to retake Mogadishu from the Juba province, Barre's Ogaden Somali Patriotic Front destroyed water sources, burned crops, and killed livestock of other clans within the southern agricultural region. With food sources destroyed and conflict erupting throughout the semi-arid territory, 300,000 Somalis died of starvation in 1991 alone, while another 1.5 million needed immediate relief.

In March of 1991, the United Nations began UNISOM, its first humanitarian action in Somalia. The issue was that the warring clans would siphon off aid to those fighting and their kin but not allow food to reach many of the most vulnerable.

U.S. Intervention

In December of 1992, the United States led a multinational force in Somalia with 35,000 troops in Operation Restore Hope, the purpose of which was to restore order to Somalia to stop the humanitarian disaster that was unfolding. After Clinton took office in January of 1993, there was a brief try at a peace conference among the now fifteen warring clans (or sub-clans) throughout Somalia, but to no avail, in part as Aidid, the second of the two Hawiye leaders battling for control of Mogadishu declares himself president and encourages all within his clan to take up arms against the other clans and international forces.

When a UN peacekeeping force was ambushed in Mogadishu by Aidid clan members (killing twenty-four Pakistani peacekeepers), the UN Security Council passed Resolution 837 in June of 1993, calling for an increase in troops from member-states and the change in objective to the capture of Mohammed Aidid, the leader of the main Hawiye faction believed to have allowed the attacks to occur. This only accelerated the attacks on the multinational forces. In August that same year, Aidid's group detonated a remote-controlled bomb, damaging a U.S. envoy and killing four soldiers. In response, President Clinton authorized Operation Gothic Serpent—a special task force of around 500 highly trained military officers to search for Aidid.

In October of 1993, two Black Hawk helicopters were shot down in Mogadishu by rocket-propelled grenades, killing eighteen Army Rangers. Hawiye militiamen surrounded those that survived the crash. Upon rescue, it was estimated that around 1,000 militiamen were killed and another 3,000 wounded. As news of the helicopter crashes and deaths of soldiers reach the American public, there is a strong call for the United States to withdraw from Somalia. In March of 1994, President Clinton called for a full withdrawal of U.S. forces. Unable to protect their peacekeepers, the United Nations withdrew as well later that year.

Throughout the rest of the 1990s, there were attempts at peace agreements among the different clans, but to no avail. Within Mogadishu, the two Hawiye groups continue fighting for power. Aidid died in 1996. His son replaces him as the pronounced president of Somalia. One peace conference—held in 2000—offered each of the clans a representation in a new government, an idea which came to fruition after the second conference in 2004. For the president, the newly installed parliament elected a Majeerteen man, Abdullahi Yusuf Ahmed, from Puntland. This government, however, was established in Kenya, as Mogadishu was considered to be too hostile of an environment for a new government to flourish.

Somali Pirates

After the state no longer functioned in Somalia, the Somali Navy disbanded. As a result, its 2,000-mile coastline and multimillion-dollar fishing industry became "an international 'free for all'." The UN estimated that each year, nearly $300 million worth of seafood was stolen from Somalia's unprotected waters by fishing companies in South Korea, Japan, and Spain, among others. There was also a UNEP report in 2005 of radioactive uranium being dumped off its coast by foreign parties (the report cites "Europe" as the culprit), leading to a "rash of respiratory ailments and skin diseases breaking out in villages along the Somali coast."[10] The UN's World Food Program reports that it will suspend food shipments to Somalia as they are continually hijacked.

Initially, the first Somali pirates were fishermen who banded together to protect against illegal fishing. Over time, however, after a tsunami devastated the fishing stocks and infrastructure of Somalia in 2004, these fishermen turned toward more extensive and more complex piracy operations. Whereas before confiscation of a ship usually led to the crew paying the pirates a bribe to be released, now the pirates (many of whom came to the industry more recently from the interior) hold entire ships and sailors hostages for longer periods, extorting their companies for much larger sums of money.

Al-Shabaab

While most of Mogadishu was embattled among warring clans, there were pockets in the south in which Islamic proxy governments were emerging. In a lawless nation, there were local courts (paid for by participants) that arbitrated based on sharia law. These courts began to become more and more powerful, offering police protection services. Finally, in 2006, four of these courts formed a coalition called the Islamic Courts Union to challenge the clans that held Mogadishu directly. In June of 2006, with the backing of local populations and funding and training by Al-Qaeda, the ICU successfully claimed Mogadishu. The newly emboldened ICU joined forces with an ideologically driven group of young Islamists, Al-Shabaab (Arabic for "the youth"). These two organizations worked to establish an Islamic caliphate across Somalia based on their very extreme form of Wahhabi interpretation of Sharia law. To appease these hardliners, the still weakened Somali government agreed to adopt Sharia law to be used throughout the country.

In 2007, Ethiopian troops entered the Somali capital to challenge both Islamist hardliners (Ethiopia is a predominantly Christian country) and the Hawiye clans. After the Ethiopian government successfully regains control of the city from the clans, the U.S. orders airstrikes that target Al-Shabaab operatives. With both of these efforts, the Somali "government" (led by President Abdullahi Yusuf) enters Mogadishu.

Through the rest of the decade, Al-Shabaab remains a presence in the larger Horn of Africa, launching attacks in Kenya, including a shopping center and a university. The United States under Obama and Trump ordered more than forty-five drone strikes from 2016 to 2017 against al-Shabaab strongholds in or around Mogadishu.

Fragile New Government

In 2017, the government of Somalia successfully held elections for president and the parliament within the country proper. Moreover, they did so with a fully operationalized constitution. For the election of President, Mohamed Abdullahi Mohamed was elected out of twenty candidates for president. Holding both U.S. and Somali citizenship, he gained popularity within several diplomatic and bureaucratic roles (he was formerly the prime minister). Further, his plans for Somalia focus on defeating Islamist terrorist presence, providing essential services for the Somali population, and assisting the Somali diaspora with repatriation. For the election of parliament, elders from clans nominate potential candidates to the two houses, requiring 30 percent of all representatives to be women. Though technically successful, the process was alleged to have included voter intimidation, violence, and corruption at every step of the process. Further, though the United States recognizes the Somali government's authority over the territory in name, our embassy representation is based in Nairobi.

SOMALI REFUGEES IN KENYA

Kenya is one state that has signed both the Refugee Convention of 1951 and its protocol. In addition, it has passed national legislation that addresses what process it will take to determine refugee status. Kenya's National Refugee Act established the Kenyan Department of Refugee Affairs to oversee the asylum-seeking process. Part II of the Act focuses on the obligations of refugees to appear in person within thirty days of entry into Kenya. As for the obligations of the Kenyan government, it will have appointed officers responsible for pointing the asylum seeker and their documents to a refugee status determination center. The act states that the burden of proof to establish refugee status on the asylum seeker (Text Box 13.3).

TEXT BOX 13.3   KENYA'S NATIONAL REFUGEE ACT (2006)

Subsidiary Section Part I, Section 6 (2): Establishment of Department:

The Department of Refugee Affairs shall be responsible for all administrative matters concerning refugees in Kenya, and shall, in that capacity, co-ordinate activities and programs relating to refugees.

Subsidiary Section Part II, Section 6: Registration Interview

1. An asylum seeker and members of his family shall appear in person for a registration interview.
2. An appointed officer shall refer an asylum seeker and members of his family already within Kenya to the nearest refugee registration officer for reception and registration interviews.
3. An appointed officer in charge of a registration center shall forward the applications of all the asylum seekers registered in that center to the refugees status determination center.

Article 11: Recognition of Refugees:

1. Any person who has entered Kenya, whether lawfully or otherwise and wishes to remain within Kenya as a refugee in terms of this Act shall make his intentions known by appearing in person before the [Refugee] Commissioner [at the refugees status determination center] immediately upon his entry or, in any case, within thirty days after his entry into Kenya.
2. In the case of a person who is lawfully in Kenya and is subsequently unable to return to his country of origin for any of the reasons specified in section 3(1), he shall, prior to the expiration of his lawful stay, present himself before an appointed officer and apply for recognition as a refugee in accordance with the provisions of this Act.

Subsidiary Section Part II, Part III, Section 22: Burden of Proof and Evidence

1. The asylum seeker bears the burden of proof to establish that he is a refugee as defined in section 3 of the Act.
2. In the absence of documentary evidence, the credible testimony of an asylum seeker in consideration of conditions in the country of origin may suffice to establish eligibility for refugee status.

As noted above, most of the Somali refugees that left Somalia did so following the end of the Barre regime. In 1991, Ethiopia received more than 600,000 Somali refugees, Djibouti received 90,000 (a big influx considering it only had around 1.5 million people at the time), Kenya received around 280,000, and Yemen received around 60,000 people. In 1993, Human Rights Watch documented high incidences of rape, physical attack, and theft in these camps. The perpetrators included local populations who were "as indigent as the refugee population but . . . not receiving relief assistance," as well as fellow refugees and well-armed bandits from inside Somalia.[11]

After 1992, the rains returned to the drought-stricken country and more than 170,000 people repatriated during this period. Some found return unsustainable and found their way back to other countries, while others remain encamped in settlements around the major towns of Somaliland and Puntland to avoid the more intense clan clashes in the south.

These numbers increased again in 2011 when a second severe drought led to mass famine and migration. In 2015, Somalia had the seventh-largest population of internally displaced people, at 1.1 million citizens. Three years later, that number is close to 3 million, with approximately 81 percent of those people being women and children.

With a second serious drought, 113,500 new arrivals were registered in the Dadaab camps between January and August 2011. The Dadaab camp houses "more than 463,000 Somali refugees" in a camp in Kenya "originally intended for 90,000."[12]

Kenya Discusses Closing Dadaab and Failing to Register Refugees (2016)

Beginning in 2011, a presence of Al-Shabaab militants as well as other armed bandits and a periodic outbreak of clan feuding in the camp led to a concern for camp organizers as to the safety of the civilian population within the camp as well as the workers themselves. In September of 2011, a driver for CARE was kidnapped.[13] In October of 2011, two Spanish aid workers from Doctors Without Borders were kidnapped in broad daylight, and their driver was shot. They each were held captive until 2013, and reports suggest they were sold to pirates for $100,000, so they could offer an even larger ransom for them to Spain. When Kenya launched an attack into Somalia against Al-Shabaab operatives, the organization responded with bomb attacks on police and humanitarian convoys in the camp in December.

These efforts have led the United Nations High Commissioner for Refugees (UNHCR) to scale back its operational efforts in the camp. In response, the Kenyan government has been responsible for policing the camps. There are

reports of mass arrests and beatings by these officials during sweeps looking
for Al-Shabaab fighters.

After the Garissa University attack by Al-Shabaab (an attack less than 60
miles away from the camp), Kenya has been discussing two key shifts in
its refugee policy. First, it has stopped accepting any new refugees through
its Refugee Affairs Secretariat. By refusing to register people, these people
are unable to have access to the camp's food and shelter. Second, Kenya
has announced its plans to close Dadaab within one year. Deputy President
William Ruto told the United Nations High Commission for Refugees that it
must either close the Dadaab refugee camp and return the residents to Somalia
or Kenya would "relocate them ourselves."[14] Second, it has stated that the
Kenyan government has fulfilled its legal obligations and will close Dadaab.

THE MOOT COURT: *THE UNITED NATIONS HIGH COMMISSIONER FOR HUMAN RIGHTS VS. THE REPUBLIC OF KENYA*

In this fictional case, the Office of the UN High Commissioner for Human
Rights (OHCHR) encourages the General Assembly to request an advisory
opinion from the International Court of Justice on the decisions of Kenya to
close the Dadaab refugee camp and to no longer register new refugees from
Somalia. This opinion will need to address each of these actions individually
and how the two-steps together may affect the rights of the refugees seeking
asylum within Kenya. For this moot court, the legal question posed before the
International Court of Justice are:

1. *Is Kenya in violation of the Convention on the Rights of Refugees of 1951
   and its Protocol were it to close the Dadaab refugee camp?*
2. *Is Kenya in violation of the Convention on the Rights of Refugees of
   1951 and its Protocol were it to no longer register new refugees from
   Somalia?*
3. *Is Kenya in violation of the Convention on the Rights of Refugees of 1951
   and its Protocol in its decisions to close the Dadaab refugee camp and
   no longer register refugees from Somalia?*

NOTES

1. UN General Assembly, *Convention Relating to the Status of Refugees*, July
28, 1951, United Nations, Treaty Series, vol. 189, p. 137. Available at: https://www
.unhcr.org/en-us/1951-refugee-convention.html.

2. UN General Assembly, *Convention Relating to the Status of Refugees*, July 28, 1951, United Nations, Treaty Series, vol. 189, p. 137. Available at: https://www .unhcr.org/en-us/1951-refugee-convention.html.

3. UN General Assembly, *Convention Relating to the Status of Refugees*, July 28, 1951, United Nations, Treaty Series, vol. 189, p. 137. Available at: https://www .unhcr.org/en-us/1951-refugee-convention.html.

4. UN General Assembly, *Convention Relating to the Status of Refugees*, July 28, 1951, United Nations, Treaty Series, vol. 189, p. 137. Available at: https://www .unhcr.org/en-us/1951-refugee-convention.html.

5. UN General Assembly, *Convention Relating to the Status of Refugees*, July 28, 1951, United Nations, Treaty Series, vol. 189, p. 137. Available at: https://www .unhcr.org/en-us/1951-refugee-convention.html.

6. UN General Assembly, *Convention Relating to the Status of Refugees*, July 28, 1951, United Nations, Treaty Series, vol. 189, p. 137. Available at: https://www .unhcr.org/en-us/1951-refugee-convention.html.

7. United Nations, "Charter of the United Nations," October 24, 1945. Available at: https://unispal.un.org/DPA/DPR/unispal.nsf/0/7F0AF2BD897689B785256C3 30061D253.

8. Crummey, Donald. 1988. "Diplomatic Documents on Ethiopia—Acta Æthiopica, Vol. 1. Correspondence and Treaties, 1800–1854. Edited by Sven Rubenson, with Getatchew Haile and John Hunwick. Evanston and Addis Ababa: Northwestern University Press and Addis Ababa University Press, 1987. Pp Xxxi 263. No Price Stated," *The Journal of African History*. https://doi.org/10.1017/ s002185370002380x.

9. "The Human Rights Crisis in Somalia," *Human Rights Watch*, March 30, 2008. Available at: https://www.hrw.org/news/2008/03/30/human-rights-crisis-somalia.

10. Tharoor, Ishaan, "How Somalia's Fishermen Became Pirates," *Time Magazine*, April 18, 2009. Available at: http://content.time.com/time/world/article/0,8599, 1892376,00.html.

11. Hammond, Laura. "History, Overview, Trends and Issues in Major Somali Refugee Displacements in the Near Region (Djibouti, Ethiopia, Kenya, Uganda and Yemen)," *Bildhaan: An International Journal of Somali Studies* 13 (2013): 55–79.

12. United Nations High Commissioner for Refugees, "Dadaab—World's Biggest Refugee Camp 20 Years Old," February 21, 2012. Available at: https://www.unhcr .org/news/makingdifference/2012/2/4f439dbb9/dadaab-worlds-biggest-refugee -camp-20-years-old.html.

13. Yussuf, Daud. 2011. "Gunmen Kidnap Two Spanish Aid Workers from Kenyan Camp." *U.S. Reuters*. October 13, 2011. Available at: https://www.reuters .com/article/us-kenya-kidnap-idUSTRE79C2T420111013.

14. Botelho, Greg, and C. N. N. Lillian Leposo. 2015. "Kenya: Relocate World's Largest Refugee Camp or We Will - CNN." *CNN*, April 11, 2015. Available at: https://www.cnn.com/2015/04/11/africa/kenya-dadaab-refugee-camp/index.htmln.

Conclusion

Possible Careers in International Law

A COMBINED FRAMEWORK: REVISITED

The first chapter of this text posited that the distinct fields of international law and international studies could learn much about what motivates actors to comply with or violate international law through an interdisciplinary approach. The combined framework offered in this text highlights that actors are continually choosing among a variety of options. To do so, these actors either consciously or subconsciously calculate which options will be benefit-maximizing, the possibility that is expected to bring the most benefit relative to the costs. This is then the actor's state preference.

The framework notes that individuals interacting with one another must negotiate whose preference will be realized and whose will not. This text determines that the power distribution between (or among) actors is based on the previous outcomes of previous negotiations. If an actor has benefited from an earlier negotiation, then it will begin these negotiations with more benefits relative to the other actor(s). As a result, the more powerful actor will be more able to use previous benefits as contemporary costs to ensure its preferences are realized in the current negotiations.

As actors do not exist within a vacuum, their preferences and power are socially formed and socially circumscribed. It is thus essential to understand that these negotiations will shape the individual calculus of certain actors (i.e., the expected outcomes will be gained through wisdom acquired from previous negotiations).

Though this perspective can be applied in all political interactions, legal agreements are shaped differently. As a result, the rights and obligations of actors under the law are codified in political negotiations. Rights are benefits for actors, and obligations are the costs. Laws are written negotiated

209

outcomes. And the power distribution among the actors and the social contexts significantly shape the nature of these outcomes.

Within domestic law, the power distribution can be seen as relatively more zero-sum, with the state having a distinct advantage in negotiations over its citizens. In contrast, the power distribution in the international system varies. In some cases, international law can be more zero-sum in nature if a powerful state can and willing to share benefits impose costs to enforce an outcome on others. And in other cases, the power distribution may not be as acute, *or* a powerful state may grow tired of imposing zero-sum costs. In such cases, the nature of international law may become more positive-sum. This text argues that, even for the most powerful states, it is cost-effective to seek to create social norms that deem the benefits of an outcome suitable for all and therefore lessen the costs of enforcing this outcome against reluctant participants.

If, after reading this text, learning the concepts of international law, studying the cases in which these laws apply, and practicing legal arguments through moot court simulations, you find the notion of international public law compelling, consider exploring a future career in the field. In doing so, however, make sure not to get siloed into assuming that international law works like domestic law, or to the opposite extreme, thinking it does not matter at all. Instead, view domestic and international law along a legal-social continuum, in which politics and the law are always interacting and evolving in tandem.

POSSIBLE CAREERS IN INTERNATIONAL LAW

So often, we focus on teaching students the content of a subject matter and even the skills necessary for a given career in the field with which we are studying. That said, sometimes we do not fully explain the potential careers in which this content and these skills may be applied. This chapter is meant to provide a broad overview of some of the jobs in international public law, specifically for those students approaching it from an international studies perspective.

International Private Law

Before focusing on international public law, it should be noted that there is an entire approach to international law that focuses on private contracts between individuals and corporations. Usually, people would work for a multinational law firm where their services are contracted out by different individuals or legal individuals (corporations). In other cases, you serve as in-house counsel to a corporation. For this area of study, a business focus would be natural.

If you wish to provide a more governmental focus in international private law, one might have a career in which you specialize in consulting with private firms about various government regulations (e.g., labor standards, environmental standards, intellectual property) or perhaps trade or foreign direct investment agreements between states.

International Public Law

A career in international public law focuses, as this book does, on the agreements made between or among states, international organizations, and so on. The role of states is a central part of this area of law. As a result, careers in this area focus on four different pathways.

Advising a State

First, a person may choose a career within a federal government. For the United States, there are positions for attorneys that focus on international law in the Office of the President, the Department of State, the Department of Defense, and even more domestically oriented departments (e.g., Homeland Security and Energy) whose work has international implications. That said, once a person specializes in a specific issue area in international law, there are even more possibilities. As one example, an international environmental lawyer might work for the Environmental Protection Agency (EPA).

International Organizations

As the Justices throughout the semester represent, there are many prestigious careers in international public law. A person serves as a Justice or legal scholar within an international organization. The most noted in this book are the Justices that serve on the International Court of Justice and those scholars who are members of the International Law Commission. That said, most international organizations that have a judicial organ or arbitration panel will be ideal places for a trained attorney to work.

International Non-Governmental Organizations

Suppose you are incredibly passionate about serving as an advocate for a particular issue in international law. In that case, there are many opportunities to use your legal expertise to advocate before the judicial organs of states and international organizations as a representative of an international non-governmental organization. Though you would not likely represent an Applicant or Respondent before a judicial organ, you would most likely provide specialized legal information via an amicus brief. These are widely seen as important documents that help to provide context and clarity in a court and are often impactful on the outcome of a case.

Private Law Firms

Finally, there are private law firms that take cases representing individuals within the judicial organ of an international organization. Consider the defense of those appearing before the International Criminal Court as one example, as well as those witnesses called upon to testify for the prosecution.

Choosing the Right Career for You

Before I conclude, I wish to explain my perspective on choosing the right career. I cannot emphasize enough that there is no one path for every student reading this book. One of you may find an opportunity exhilarating, while another may find the same position exhausting. From my limited experience, I have found a great career path should include an (almost equal) balance of these three components. First, you must be able to use your strengths. Strengths are, most fundamentally, the things you can look back at your entire life and see that you possessed. Likely the earliest compliment you got was about these qualities of yourself. That said, strengths can also be skills you are willing to work on tirelessly as you love the topic area. For example, I was not born a great cook, but I like to work at it to the point that I feel it is a strength.

The second component of a fulfilling career is that it allows you to work on your weaknesses. I have been in jobs that suited my strengths so well that they did not challenge me. I found myself wondering why I was irritable and uninspired in a position so well-suited for me. Then I realized that it did not challenge me. I needed to grow, expand, and challenge my current understanding. A necessary component of a job that you will love is to always be in awe of its vastness and to work to broaden your impact within that realm over time.

And finally, a job must align with your core values. I often refer to this as the "last day on earth" criteria. If you knew you had one more day to live, and that day had to be spent working, what work would you feel like was meaningful and impactful? Though a job may align with your strengths or challenge you, I would argue that if you do not feel that it aligns with a greater purpose for you, it will not be a job to which you will give your all and from which you will gain a lot.

Bibliography

"A Week of Terror in Drenica." 1999. *Human Rights Watch*. Available at: https://www.hrw.org/reports/1999/kosovo/.

Associated Press. "Chilean President Salvador Allende Committed Suicide, Autopsy Confirms." July 20, 2011. *The Guardian*. Available at: http://www.theguardian.com/world/2011/jul/20/salvador-allende-committed-suicide-autopsy.

Associated Press. "Clinton's Words: "The Right Action."" January 1, 2001. *New York Times*. Available at: https://www.nytimes.com/2001/01/01/world/clinton-s-words-the-right-action.html.

BBC News. 2011. "Chile Ups Pinochet Victim Numbers." August 18, 2011. Available at: https://www.bbc.com/news/world-latin-america-14584095.

Belgian Criminal Code. Available at: https://www.legislationline.org/documents/section/criminal-codes.

Bellinger, John. B. "The United States and the International Criminal Court: Where We've Been and Where We're Going." April 25, 2008. *Remarks to the DePaul University College of Law*. Available at: https://2001-2009.state.gov/s/l/rls/104053.htm.

Bolton, John. "Unsign That Treaty." January 4, 2001. *The Washington Post*. Available at: https://www.washingtonpost.com/archive/opinions/2001/01/04/unsign-that-treaty/36e310be-072d-44df-9aa4-6cff7ef098ce/.

Botelho, Greg, and C. N. N. Lillian Leposo. "Kenya: Relocate World's Largest Refugee Camp or We Will." April 11, 2015. *CNN*. Available at: https://www.cnn.com/2015/04/11/africa/kenya-dadaab-refugee-camp/index.html.

Boumediene v. Bush. "06 U.S. 1196." 2008.

Britannica Encyclopedia. "Kiribati." Available at: https://www.britannica.com/place/Kiribati/History.

"Burning Secrets of the Corfu Channel Incident." September 9, 2014. *Wilson Center*. Available at: https://www.wilsoncenter.org/publication/burning-secrets-the-corfu-channel-incident.

Caramel, Laurence. "Besieged by the Rising Tides of Climate Change, Kiribati Buys Land in Fiji." June 20, 2014. *The Guardian.* Available at: https://www.theguardian.com/environment/2014/jul/01/kiribati-climate-change-fiji-vanua-levu.

Central Intelligence Agency. "CIA Activities in Chile." Available at: https://www.cia.gov/library/reports/general-reports-1/chile/#5.

Central Intelligence Agency. "Oceania: Kiribati." 2020. *The World Factbook.* Available at: https://www.cia.gov/library/publications/the-world-factbook/geos/kr.html.

Citizens United v. Federal Elections Commission. "558 U.S. 310." 2010. Available at: https://www.supremecourt.gov/opinions/09pdf/08-205.pdf.

Climate Change Knowledge Portal. "Kiribati." *World Bank Group.* Available at: https://climateknowledgeportal.worldbank.org/country/kiribati#:~:text=Kiribati%20is%20amongst%20the%20most,variability%20and%20sea%2Dlevel%20rise.

Clinton, William. "State of the Union Address." January 25, 1994. Available at: https://clinton.presidentiallibraries.us/items/show/16126.

Committee for Development Policy 20th Plenary Session. "Ex-Ante Impact Assessment of Likely Consequences of Graduation of Kiribati from the Least Developed Country Category." *United Nations.* Available at: https://www.un.org/development/desa/dpad/wp-content/uploads/sites/45/CDP-PL-2018-5b.pdf.

"Convention on International Civil Aviation—Doc 7300." n.d. Available at: https://www.icao.int/publications/pages/doc7300.aspx.

Crummey, Donald. 1988. "Diplomatic Documents on Ethiopia—Acta Ethiopica, Vol. 1. Correspondence and Treaties, 1800–1854." Edited by Sven Rubenson, Getatchew Haile, and John Hunwick. Evanston and Addis Ababa: Northwestern University Press and Addis Ababa University Press, 198Pp Xxxi 26No Price Stated." *The Journal of African History.* https://doi.org/10.1017/s002185370002380x.

Dalton, Matthew. "How a Floating Island Could Save Pacific Nation From Rising Seas." December 8, 2015. *Wall Street Journal.* Available at: https://www.wsj.com/articles/how-a-floating-island-could-save-pacific-nation-from-rising-seas-1449589251.

Dan, Blumenthal, Michael Auslin, and Michael Mazza. "A South China Sea Strategy." *American Enterprise Institute.* Available at: https://www.aei.org/a-south-china-sea-strategy/.

Danish Criminal Code. Available at: https://www.oecd.org/daf/anti-bribery/anti-briberyconvention/37472519.pdf.

de Vattel, Emer. *The Law of Nations or the Principles of Natural Law Applied to the Conduct and to the Affairs of Nations ADN of Sovereigns.* Oceana Publications, 1964.

Dutch Criminal Code. Available at: https://www.legislationline.org/documents/section/criminal-code.

Encyclopedia Britannica. "Salvador Allende." Available at: https://www.britannica.com/biography/Salvador-Allende.

European Economic Communities European Commission. "Commission Decision of 6 July 1979 on an investigation pursuant to Article 14 (3) of Regulation No 17 into AM & S Europe Ltd, Bristol (Dossier IV/AF 379)." July 7, 1979. *9/670/*

EEC. Available at: https://eur-lex.europa.eu/legal-content/EN/ALL/?uri=CELEX %3A31979D0670.

European Union. "Treaty Establishing the European Community." March 25, 1957. *Treaty of Rome*. Available at: https://www.europarl.europa.eu/about-parliament/en/ in-the-past/the-parliament-and-the-treaties/treaty-of-rome.

Ex parte Quirin. "317 U.S. 1." 1942.

Federation of American Scientists. "The Covenant of Hamas: Main Points." Available at: https://fas.org/irp/world/para/docs/880818a.htm.

French Criminal Code. Available at: https://www.legal-tools.org/doc/418004/pdf/.

Gattini, Andrea. "Pinochet Cases." June 2007. *Oxford Public International Law*. Available at: https://doi.org/10.1093/law:epil/9780199231690/e859.

General Assembly Resolution 63/308, The Responsibility to Protect, A/RES/67/97. September 14, 2009. Available at: https://www.un.org/en/ga/63/resolutions.shtml.

German Criminal Code. Available at: https://www.gesetze-im-internet.de/englisch _stgb/englisch_stgb.html.

Greek Criminal Code. Available at: https://www.iadclaw.org/assets/1/7/17.13_ Greece_2011.pdf.

Hamdan v. Rumsfeld. "05 U.S. 184." 2006.

Hamdi v. Rumsfeld. "542 U.S. 507." 2004.

Hammond, Laura. "History, Overview, Trends and Issues in Major Somali Refugee Displacements in the Near Region (Djibouti, Ethiopia, Kenya, Uganda and Yemen)." *Bildhaan: An International Journal of Somali Studies* 13 (2013): 55–79.

Hayton, Bill. "Calm and Storm: The South China Sea After the Second World War."August 13, 2015. *Asia Maritime Transparency Initiative, Center for Strategic and International Studies*. Available at: https://amti.csis.org/calm-and -storm-the-south-china-sea-after-the-second-world-war/.

Human Rights Watch. "The Human Rights Crisis in Somalia." March 30, 2008. Available at: https://www.hrw.org/news/2008/03/30/human-rights-crisis-somalia.

Human Right Watch. "Two Authorities, One Way, Zero Dissent." October 23, 2018. Available at: https://www.hrw.org/report/2018/10/23/two-authorities-one-way -zero-dissent/arbitrary-arrest-and-torture-under.

Human Rights Watch. "U.S.: 'Hague Invasion Act' Becomes Law." August 3, 2002. Available at: https://www.hrw.org/news/2002/08/03/us-hague-invasion-act -becomes-law.

"Humanitarian Law Violations in Kosovo." October 1, 1998. *Human Rights Watch*. Available at: https: //www.hrw.org/report/1998/10/01/humanitarian-law-violations -kosovo.

Hurtes, Sarah. "What Happens to a People When Their Land Sinks Into the Ocean?" September 5, 2019. *Vice*. Available at: https://www.vice.com/en/article/gyzxd7/ what-happens-to-a-people-when-their-land-sinks-into-the-ocean-v26n3.

International Center for Settlement of Investment Disputes. "Mediation & Conciliation." *World Bank Group*. Available at: https://icsid.worldbank.org/ser- vices/mediation-conciliation/conciliation/overview.

International Committee of the Red Cross. "Convention (IV) Relative to the Protection of Civilian Persons in Time of War." August 12, 1949. Available at: https://ihl-databases.icrc.org/ihl/COM/380-600054.

International Committee of the Red Cross. "Convention (IV) Relative to the Treatment of Prisoners of War." August 12, 1949. Available at: https://ihl-databases.icrc.org/ihl/full/GCIII-commentary.

International Committee of the Red Cross. "Protocol Additional to the Geneva Conventions of 12 August 1949, and Relating to the Protection of Victims of International Armed Conflicts (Protocol I)." June 8, 1977. Available at: https://ihl-databases.icrc.org/applic/ihl/ihl.nsf/Treaty.xsp?documentId=D9E6B6264D7723C3C12563CD002D6CE4&action=openDocument.

Irish Common Law. Available at: https://www.sgrlaw.com/ttl-articles/916/.

Israel Ministry of Foreign Affairs. "Declaration of Establishment of State of Israel." December 14, 1948. Available at: https://mfa.gov.il/mfa/foreignpolicy/peace/guide/pages/declaration%20of%20establishment%20of%20state%20of%20israel.aspx.

Italian Common Law. Available at: https://www.altalex.com/documents/news/2014/10/28/dei-delitti-contro-la-persona.

John Charles Dent. *The Story of the Upper Canadian Rebellion: Largely Derived from Original Sources and Documents*, Vol. CB Robinson, 1885.

Johnson v. Eisentrager. "339 U.S. 763." 1950.

"Kiribati Minister of Labour and Human Resource Development, Kiribati National Labour Migration Policy, United Nations Economic and Social Commission for the Asian Paciific." Available at: https://www.unescap.org/sites/default/files/Kiribati%20National%20Labour%20Migration%20Policy.pdf.

Kissinger, Henry A. " The Pitfalls of Universal Jurisdiction." *Foreign Affairs* 80 (2001): 86.

Lachenmann, Frauke, and Rüdiger Wolfrum, eds. *The Law of Armed Conflict and the Use of Force: The Max Planck Encyclopedia of Public International Law*. Oxford: Oxford University Press, 2016.

League of Nations, Permanent Court of Justice, France v. Turkey, 1927, Ser. A, No. 10.

Linzer, Dafna. "DOJ's Troubled Case Against Uthman." October 8, 2010, *ProPublica*. Available at: https://www.propublica.org/article/dojs-troubled-case-against-uthman.

Livanios, Dimitris. "The 'Sick Man' Paradox: History, Rhetoric and the 'European Character'of Turkey." *Journal of Southern Europe and the Balkans* 8, no. 3 (2006): 299–311.

Long, Gideon. "Chile Still Split Over Gen Augusto Pinochet Legacy." September 9, 2013. *BBC News*. Available at: https://www.bbc.com/news/world-latin-america-24014501.

Luxembourg Criminal Code. Available at: https://www.legislationline.org/documents/section/criminal-codes.

McLaurin, Luke A. "Can the President "Unsign" a Treaty? A Constitutional Inquiry." *Washington University Law Review* 84 (2006): 1941. Available at: https://heinonline.org/HOL/LandingPage?handle=hein.journals/walq84&div=73&id=&page=.

Minority Rights Group International. *World Directory of Minorities and Indigenous Peoples*. Banabans: Fiji Islands, 2008. Available at: https://www.refworld.org/docid/49749d251e.html.

Munro, Hector A. "The Case of the Corfu Minefield." *Modern Law Review* 10 (1947): 363.

Murphy, Sean. *Murphy's Principles of International Law, 2d (Concise Hornbook Series)*. West Academic, 2012.

National Geographic Society Newsroom. "Our Heart Is on Banaba: Stories from 'The Forgotten People of the Pacific.'" October 14, 2017. *National Geographic*. Available at: https://blog.nationalgeographic.org/2015/10/14/our-heart-is-on-banaba-stories-from-the-forgotten-people-of-the-pacific/.

North Atlantic Treaty Organization. "North Atlantic Treaty." April 4, 1949. Available at: https://www.nato.int/cps/en/natolive/official_texts_17120.htm.

Oxford Encyclopedic Dictionary of International Law. *Quasi-State*. Oxford University Press. Available at: https://www.oxfordreference.com/view/10.1093/acref/9780195389777.001.0001/acref-9780195389777.

Pike, Richard S. "The English Law of Legal Professional Privilege: A Guide for American Attorneys." *The Loyola University Chicago International Law Review* 4 (2006): 51.

Posts By This Contributor. n.d. "Sputnik's Impact on America." November 6, 2007. Available at: https://www.pbs.org/wgbh/nova/article/sputnik-impact-on-america/.

Randall, Kenneth C. "Universal Jurisdiction Under International Law." *Texas Law Review* 66 (1987): 785.

Rasul v. Bush. "542 U.S. 466." 2004.

Teaiwa, Katerina Martina. *Consuming Ocean Island: Stories of People and Phosphate from Banaba*. Bloomington: Indiana University Press, 2014.

Tharoor, Ishaan. "How Somalia's Fishermen Became Pirates." April 18, 2009. *Time Magazine*. Available at: http://content.time.com/time/world/article/0,8599,1892376,00.html.

The American Presidency Project. "Message to the Senate Transmitting the Vienna Convention on the Law of Treaties." November 22, 1971. Available at: https://www.presidency.ucsb.edu/documents/message-the-senate-transmitting-the-vienna-convention-the-law-treaties.

The Avalon Project. "Agreement Between the United States and Cuba for the Lease of Lands for Coaling and Naval Stations." February 23, 1903. *Yale Law School*. Available at: https://avalon.law.yale.edu/20th_century/dip_cuba002.asp.

The Avalon Project. "British-American Diplomacy." *Yale Law School*. Available at: https://avalon.law.yale.edu/subject_menus/brtreaty.asp.

The Avalon Project. "British White Paper of 1939." *Yale Law School*. Available at: https://avalon.law.yale.edu/20th_century/brwh1939.asp.

The Avalon Project. "Covenant of the League of Nations." *Yale Law School*. Available at: https://avalon.law.yale.edu/20th_century/leagcov.asp.

"The Fall of Srebrenica and the Failure of UN Peacekeeping|Bosnia and Herzegovina." October 15, 1995. *Human Rights Watch*. Available at: https://www.hrw.org/report/1995/10/15/fall-srebrenica-and-failure-un-peacekeeping/bosnia-and-herzegovina.

The Guantánamo Docket. "Uthman Abd Al Rahim Muhammad Uthman." *The New York Times*. Available at: https://www.nytimes.com/interactive/projects/Guantánamo/detainees/27-uthman-abdul-rahim-mohammed-uthman.

The Seventh International Conference of American States. "Convention on Rights and Duties of States." December 23, 1933. Available at: https://treaties.un.org/pages/showdetails.aspx?objid=0800000280166aef.

"This Was Not an Accident. This Was a Bomb." September 21, 2016. *Washington Post*. Available at: http://www.washingtonpost.com/sf/national/2016/09/20/this-was-not-an-accident-this-was-a-bomb/.

Trump, Donald J. "Remarks by President Trump at a Meeting with the National Space Council and Signing of Space Policy Directive-3." June 11, 2018. *The White House, The United States Government*. Available at: https://www.whitehouse.gov/briefings-statements/remarks-president-trump-meeting-national-space-council-signing-space-policy-directive-3/.

UN General Assembly. "Convention Against Torture and Other Cruel, Inhuman or Degrading Treatment or Punishment." December 10, 1984. *United Nations, Treaty Series*, Vol. 1465, p. 85. Available at: https://www.refworld.org/docid/3ae6b3a94.html.

UN General Assembly. "Convention on the Law of the Sea." December 10, 1982. Available at: https://www.un.org/depts/los/convention_agreements/texts/unclos/unclos_e.pdf.

UN General Assembly. "Convention Relating to the Status of Refugees." July 28, 1951. *United Nations, Treaty Series*, Vol. 189, p. 137. Available at: https://www.unhcr.org/en-us/1951-refugee-convention.html.

UN Security Council. "Statute of the International Criminal Rwanda." November 8, 1994. Available at: https://legal.un.org/avl/pdf/ha/ictr_EF.pdf.

UN Security Council. "Statute of the International Criminal Tribunal for the Former Yugoslavia." May 25, 1993. Available at: https://www.icty.org/x/file/Legal%20Library/Statute/statute_sept09_en.pdf.

United Nations. "About Permanent Observers." Available at: https://www.un.org/en/sections/member-states/about-permanent-observers/index.html.

United Nations. "Antarctic Treaty, Treaty No. 5778." June 23, 1961. Available at: https://treaties.un.org/pages/showDetails.aspx?objid=0800000280136dbc.

United Nations. "Charter of the United Nations." October 24, 1945. Available at: https://unispal.un.org/DPA/DPR/unispal.nsf/0/7F0AF2BD897689B785256C330061D253.

United Nations. "Charter of the United Nations." October 24, 1945. Available at: https://www.un.org/en/charter-united-nations/.

United Nations. "Statute of the International Court of Justice." April 18, 1945. Available at: https://www.icj-cij.org/en/statute.

United Nations. "Vienna Convention on the Law of Treaties." May 23, 1969. Available at: https://treaties.un.org/doc/publication/unts/volume%201155/volume-1155-i-18232-english.pdf.

United Nations. "Vienna Convention on the Law of Treaties." May 23, 1969. Available at: https://legal.un.org/ilc/texts/instruments/english/conventions/1_1_1969.pdf.

United Nations Dag Hammarskjold Library. "What is the difference Between Signing, Ratification and Accession of UN Treaties?" Available at: https://ask.un .org/faq/14594.

United Nations General Assembly. "Future Government of Palestine." November 29, 1947. *A/Res/181(II)*. Available at: https://unispal.un.org/DPA/DPR/unispal.nsf/0 /7F0AF2BD897689B785256C330061D253.

United Nations General Assembly. "Rome Statute of the International Criminal Court." June 17, 1998. Available at: https://www.icc-cpi.int/resource-library/documents/rs-eng.pdf.

United Nations High Commissioner for Refugees. "Dadaab: World's Biggest Refugee Camp 20 Years Old." February 21, 2012. Available at: https://www.unhcr .org/news/makingdifference/2012/2/4f439dbb9/dadaab-worlds-biggest-refugee -camp-20-years-old.html.

United Nations International Criminal Tribunal for the Former Yugoslavia. "Slobodan Milošević Trial—The Prosecution's Case." Available at: https://www.icty.org/en/ content/slobodan-milo%C5%A1evi%C4%87-trial-prosecutions-case.

United Nations International Law Commission. "Draft Articles on Responsibility of States for Internationally Wrongful Acts." 2001. Available at: https://legal.un.org/ ilc/texts/instruments/english/commentaries/9_6_2001.pdf.

United Nations International Residual Mechanism for Criminal Tribunals. "International Criminal Tribunal for Rwanda." Available at: https://unictr.irmct .org/.

United Nations International Residual Mechanism for Criminal Tribunals. "International Criminal Tribunal for the Former Yugoslavia." Available at: https:// www.icty.org/.

United Nations Security Council. "Middle East." November 22, 1967. *S/Res/242*. Available at: https://www.un.org/securitycouncil/content/resolutions-adopted -security-council-1967.

United Nations Security Council. "Resolutions." Available at: https://www.un.org/ securitycouncil/content/resolutions-0.

United States Congress. *Proceedings and Debates of the 85th Congress: First Session 1957*. Bloomington: Indiana University Press, 2013.

United States of America. "Constitution [United States of America]." September 17, 1789. Available at: https://www.archives.gov/founding-docs/constitution -transcript.

United States Space Force. "About the Space Force." Available at: https://www .spaceforce.mil/About-Us/About-Space-Force/.

U.S. State Department Archives. "Vienna Convention." Available at: https://2009 -2017.state.gov/s/l/treaty/faqs/70139.htm.

Weiner, Tim. "U.S. Will Release Files on Crimes Under Pinochet." December 2, 1998. *The New York Times*. Available at: https://www.nytimes.com/1998/12/02/ world/us-will-release-files-on-crimes-under-pinochet.html.

Wickramatunga, Robert. "General Assembly Resolution 1721 (XVI)." Accessed February 2, 2020a. https://www.unoosa.org/oosa/en/ourwork/spacelaw/treaties/ resolutions/res_16_1721.html.

Wilson, Woodrow. "Wilson's Fourteen Points." *Woodrow Wilson Presidential Library Retrieved* 12, no. 5 (1918): 2007.

Yussuf, Daud. 2011. "Gunmen Kidnap Two Spanish Aid Workers from Kenyan Camp." October 13, 2011. *U.S. Reuters.* Available at: https://www.reuters.com/article/us-kenya-kidnap-idUSTRE79C2T420111013.

Index

About the Author

Dr. Leah L. Carmichael is a lecturer in the department of international affairs at the University of Georgia.

www.ingramcontent.com/pod-product-compliance
Lightning Source LLC
Chambersburg PA
CBHW050642280326
41932CB00015B/2745